SINGLE MARKET TO SOCIAL EUROPE

Insights on Contemporary Issues Series is an important collection of books which concentrate on a wide range of social geography and policy-related issues of direct concern to students, lecturers, policy-makers and opinion formers.

All the books have been written by experts from the social science disciplines. They will bring together theoretical viewpoints and empirical data, in ways that allow the reader to evaluate contemporary issues, and to assist in the forecasting of future trends and developments.

Already published:
Johnston R J, Pattie C J & Allsopp J G: A Nation Dividing?
Blacksell M, Economides K & Watkins C: Justice outside the City

Forthcoming:
Smith S J: Gender and Housing
Smith C J: Urban Crisis

Single Market to Social Europe:

THE EUROPEAN COMMUNITY IN THE 1990s

MARK WISE

AND

RICHARD GIBB

Longman
Scientific &
Technical

Copublished in the United States with
John Wiley & Sons, Inc., New York

Longman Scientific & Technical,
Longman Group UK Ltd,
Longman House, Burnt Mill, Harlow,
Essex CM20 2JE, England
and Associated Companies throughout the world.

Copublished in the United States with
John Wiley & Sons, Inc., 605 Third Avenue, New York, NY 10158

© Longman Group UK Limited 1993

First published 1993

ISBN 0-582-06088-5

British Library Cataloguing in Publication Data

A catalogue record for this book is available from the British Library

Library of Congress Cataloging-in-Publication Data

A catalogue record for this book is available from the Library of Congress

Set by 131 in 10/12pt Palatino
Printed in Malaysia by VP

Dedications

Richard: To my Mum and Dad for their encouragement and support

Mark: To Martine, Luc, Sophie and Louis for their long-suffering patience and days missed on the moors!

Contents

Preface

This book has been the product of an equal effort by the two authors. Normally, the privilege endowed by alphabetical order would have meant that Richard Gibb's name took precedence over that of Mark Wise on the book cover. But in a typically generous gesture, Richard Gibb conceded pride of place to his older colleague in recognition of a long-held commitment to study of the European Community. Nothing more than this should be read into our reversal of the usual 'A to Z' convention.

Although there was a general collaboration on all parts of the book, Mark Wise assumed primary responsibility for the Introduction and the chapters dealing with 'Social Europe', whereas Richard Gibb dealt mainly with those analyzing the 'Single Market' project. Both worked on the concluding chapter with Richard Gibb relating the study to recent changes in Eastern and Central Europe while Mark Wise, reflecting the extraordinary rate of change in Europe in recent years, wrote a 'postscript' examining the implications of the Maastricht agreement on the economic and social issues discussed in this book.

With an interest in the European Community stretching back more than two decades, Mark Wise was able to bring a certain experience to the project and place '1992 and all that' in historical perspective. His younger colleague, Richard Gibb, was able to cast a fresh pair of eyes on the Community scene, as well as the dynamic enthusiasm of someone more recently attracted to the idea of European unity. Thus, there has been a complementarity about their different but equal contributions. Hopefully, this fusion of their different characters, experience and expertise has produced a book of some use to its readers. Furthermore, both authors hope that this volume is not seen as yet another book on '1992'! First of all, it has cast a critical eye on the optimistic economic expectations associated with this almost over-quoted deadline. Secondly, the book places the Single Market project alongside the parallel efforts, often ignored in Britain, to produce a more meaningful 'social dimension' to the Community's activities, thus making it more than a simple free-trading area. Whether we have succeeded, only the reader can decide.

Mark Wise and Richard Gibb
Plymouth March 1992

List of Figures

List of Tables

Acknowledgements

Many people help in some way with the preparation of a book, but we would especially like to express our thanks to Brian Rogers and Tim Absalom for their excellent cartographical contribution, to Adrian Holmes for his patience and skill in directing us through the thickets of the word-processing world and to Julie Sugden for coping with the intricacies of reference lists both lost and found! We would also like to express our gratitude to the staff at Longman Group UK Ltd. Their encouragement, calmness and understanding in dealing with authors under pressure has been greatly appreciated.

We are grateful to the following for permission to reproduce copyright figures and tables:

The Economist Newspaper Limited for fig 8.4 (Economist, 1988a); Europe 2000 for figs 8.2 & 8.5 (Europe 2000, 1989); Gower Publishing Company Limited for table 3.2 & figs 4.2 & 4.3 (Cecchini, 1988); Pinter Publishers Ltd, London for table 8.1 (Wijkman, 1990) All rights reserved; Office for Official Publications of the European Communities for figs 2.3, 5.1, 6.2, 8.1 & 8.3 (Eurostat, 1975-90), figs 2.1, 2.2 & tables 6.1, 6.2, 6.3, 6.4 & 6.5 (Eurostat, 1989) table 7.1 & fig 7.1 (Eurostat, 1990a), figs 2.4, 3.1, 4.1, 4.4 & tables 2.1, 3.1, 3.4, 3.6, 3.7, 3.8, 4.3 (Commission of the EC, 1988a), fig, 7.3 (Commission of the EC, 1988i), table 3.3 (Ernst & Whinney, 1988), table 3.5 (*European Economy*, 1988)

Whilst every effort has been made to trace the owners of copyright material, in a few cases this has proved impossible and we take this opportunity to offer our apologies to any copyright holders whose rights we may have unwittingly infringed.

1. The nature of the European Community

After years of relative stagnation characterized more by acrimony than by harmony, the ideal of economic and political union amongst the Member States of the European Community (EC) was given fresh impetus in the latter part of the 1980s. The project to create a Single European Market (SEM) by the end of 1992 caught the imagination of politicians and public alike in an extraordinary way. This renewed drive to create a genuine 'common market', first demanded in the 1957 Treaty of Rome, appeared to be yet another example of EC political leaders giving priority to the economic integration of Western Europe rather than unity in wider social and political fields. Thus, old fears arose that a 'Businessman's Europe' was being reinforced with scant regard for the interests of ordinary 'workers'. However, the Single European Act (SEA) of 1986 which laid down the legal foundations for a single market was also concerned to develop social and other common policies within the Community as an essential complement to the moves towards economic integration. The formulation in 1989 of the so-called 'Social Charter' on the 'fundamental rights of workers' was indeed a direct consequence of provisions in the SEA calling for measures to enhance both 'economic and social cohesion' within the EC.

Whereas all Member States accepted the principle of the single market, Britain alone rejected the notion of a 'Social Charter' despite the insistence of its partners that it was an unavoidable corollary of the SEM. This rejection highlights the major theme running through this book which examines the balance of economic and social objectives in the development of the European Community. Numerous questions arise in this context which are likely to be prominent in the political deliberations of the EC during the 1990s. Does the removal of economic barriers in a SEM conform more to the demands of big multinational corporations rather than the needs of employees, many of whom could lose their jobs or see their living standards decline in large open markets where social protection could be eroded in the struggle to compete both within and beyond the Community's geographical limits? Is a meaningful European 'social dimension' being developed to counterbalance the creation of a genuine common market within which goods, services, labour and capital will freely move across abandoned national barriers? To use the geographical terminology common to EC policy-makers, to what extent is a European 'social space' being built to parallel the 'economic space' associated with the much-trumpeted '1992' deadline?

The aim of this book is therefore threefold: to examine the economic rationale and implications of the effort to create a single internal common market amongst the Member States of the European Community; to chart the nature and evolution of the EC's developing social policy which has been given fresh impetus by the potential for increased social costs arising from the ambitious SEM programme; and to explore the relationship that exists between the economic and social policies of the Community. The complex and often conflicting relationship between the economic and social aspirations of the Community is an area of concern likely to dominate policy negotiations increasingly in the Community. The objective of creating a genuine common market some 45 years after the Rome Treaty is largely projected to the general public in terms of the gains to be had in economic efficiency and productivity. A 'Europe without frontiers' will, according to the tenets of liberal economic theory, create an enormous 'domestic' market free of national restrictions within which economies of scale can develop, investment will flow unhampered to the most productive localities, and products will be sold to some 320 million consumers unfettered by national barriers. In other words, all the costs inherent in the EC's politically fragmented market will be eliminated, thus releasing the productive energies of western Europe and allowing it to compete more effectively with the USA, Japan and the NICs of the Pacific Rim and elsewhere. But it would be naive to assume that there are no social costs associated with the SEM programme. The Community itself recognizes this reality in its commitment within the SEA to strengthening its 'social policy'. In fact the agreement to increase the amount of EC resources destined for the social and regional programmes was part of the price exacted by the poorer countries for agreeing to the single market objective. A major debate is now taking place within the Community about what sort of 'Europe' should emerge in the 1990s. On the one hand there are those who desire a rather limited 'economic' Community with a limited loss of national sovereignty and minimum government intervention, particularly at the EC level. On the other hand, there are those who are moving towards some form of European Union encompassing all forms of political endeavour, 'social' as well as 'economic'. A central theme of the present text is this debate on the merits of adopting an economic minimalist approach as opposed to a wider social version of European unity and the geographical implications of these divergent approaches. This volume is therefore an account of two competing visions of Europe.

A EUROPEAN COMMUNITY OR A EUROPEAN ECONOMIC COMMUNITY?

The general perception of the EC has always been of a rather narrow economic character, especially in the UK. For much of the last thirty years, the unofficial term of 'Common Market' has enjoyed widespread currency, as has the abbreviation 'EEC' (European Economic Community) which, in confusing fact, is but one of three interrelated European Communities. However, the use of 'EEC' was not too inappropriate in that the other two Communities, namely the European Coal and Steel Community (ECSC) and the European Atomic Energy Community (Euratom), were essentially economic in character. This economic terminology also reflected the tenor of public debate about the EC over many years. One aspect of the original EC arrangements amongst the 'Six' founder Member States was a series of economic trade-offs whereby the Germans would get access to a large common market for their industrial products, the French would obtain the agricultural arrangements they required, the Dutch were attracted by the prospect of a single transport policy transcending national boundaries, and so on. Later, the prolonged and tortured discussions that preceded Britain's entry into the Community in 1973 were centred on rival estimations of the material costs and benefits of membership.

Once inside the Common Market this 'balance-sheet' approach continued to dominate Britain's relationship with its partners. In the first decade of UK membership, this relationship was particularly soured by the question of Britain's 'contribution' to the Community budget; Mrs Thatcher's demands to 'get our money back' strengthened the view of the EC as essentially a commercial arrangement. Those who found the complex budgetary arrangements of the Community too much to handle found the high price of Common Market butter a simpler target at which to aim their material discontent. Similarly, a series of inter-state trade conflicts, journalistically exaggerated as 'wars', over such humdrum commodities as Golden Delicious apples, beer, wine, and even the humble little lamb, did nothing to change the predominant perception of the EC as some sort of gigantic multinational market-place composed of rather fractious national stall-keepers of dubious probity. Partly in order to eliminate some of the causes of these frictions and partly in response to a desire to match the economic power of Japan and the USA, the project to attain a Single European Market by 1993 was launched, reinforcing once again the view of the EC as an essentially economic trading bloc.

That such a view should predominate is not surprising. Economic matters certainly have predominated in the history of the EC. The first Community was concerned (at least overtly) with the production of coal and steel, vital foundations of the West European economy in the 1950s. Similarly, the Euratom of 1957 was aimed at mastery of what was then seen as the new source of energy to fuel increasing production. Obviously, the EEC was designed to foster even wider economic cooperation and competition. Furthermore, the tenets of liberal economic ideology were very apparent in the strategies adopted to construct European unity with their anticipation of the productive benefits that would flow from the free movement of goods, people and capital within a competitive common market.

But there has always been more to the Community than a concern to produce ever more efficiently in an ever more common market. The present efforts to put legislative flesh on the bare bones of the so-called 'Social Charter' flow out of a long history of initiatives to develop common social policies for the Community (Chapter 5). Similarly, the contemporary debates about forging greater political union, including one that deals with the sensitive area of defence, can trace their roots back to the Second World War and beyond. In truth, although an economic theme has drowned out others in the often discordant orchestration of European integration, social and other political variations have always been present, if only faintly heard. In the 1980s, a fuller conception of European unity gradually emerged from intellectual and political backrooms to colour the public debate about the future of an organization which clearly was concerning itself with more than trade and commerce. In this book we shall be focusing first on how the '1992' project is trying to forge a genuine 'European economic area' and then the argument that this needs to be complemented by development of a 'European social area'. This analysis will take us beyond those narrow economic conceptions of the Community that have dominated in the past. But the reader must remember that this will still be a partial view of the great aim to create a full economic and political union amongst its Member States; for example, it is likely that the 1990s will also see further steps towards a common foreign policy as well as a more common security system. The full significance of the semantic shift from reference to a limited European Economic Community to a more comprehensive European Community openly concerning itself with all aspects of political life, including social policy, will, it is suggested, become increasingly apparent.

THE SCOPE OF THE STUDY

As already stated, a primary aim of this book is to examine the balance between the efforts to create an integrated single EC 'economic space' and an accompanying European 'social space'. Thus, throughout this study there is a focus on the economic logic propelling the twelve Member States to cooperate further and the political responses to a perceived need to develop a 'social dimension' to cope with the consequences of a Single European Market. This aim raises a question that will continue to loom large during the next decade: to what extent should the Community's 'single market' be a 'social market' as well? Or, put another way, to what extent does the EC need a stronger set of common social policies to counterbalance the economic policies which have dominated in the development of the Community hitherto?

The remaining section of this introductory chapter provides a theoretical model to be used as a tool of analysis when examining the various stages of European integration. In particular, it is designed to help the reader see the inextricable links between things 'economic', 'social' and 'political' in a Community framework. It also highlights the difficulty, indeed impossibility, of trying to view the Community in some limited economic 'common market' light which ignores its inevitable social and political dimensions. Some of the wider and more theoretical issues involved in European Union are then examined in order to place our analysis in its broader setting and remind the reader that there are political dimensions to the Community that go beyond the economic and social dimensions addressed in this book.

Following this introductory chapter, the book is divided into three broad sections. The opening chapters deal directly with the economic dimension of the single market programme. The second section evaluates the social role and legislation being developed by the Community whilst the third section illustrates the relationship between the economic and social dimensions with the use of case-studies. In the light of the evidence presented, the final chapter then returns to some of the more theoretical issues originally examined in Chapter 1. The concluding chapter also looks to the future, examining the influence of east-central Europe on Community integration, the EC's agenda for the 1990s and moves towards a United States of Europe.

Chapter 2 examines the economic logic behind the single market programme and its objective to remove all internal Community barriers to the free movement of goods, people, capital and services. The desire to create a truly integrated European economy is linked to the under-performance of that economy within the world economic system. At one level therefore, the primary aim of the '1992' programme is remarkably simple: to enable

Europe to compete on more equal terms with the USA and Japan. However, the goal of creating an internal market duplicates that objective first set out by the Treaty of Rome in 1957. This chapter therefore evaluates why and how the Community economy remained fragmented some 35 years after the signing of the Rome Treaty.

In Chapter 3, the precise mechanisms by which the Commission plans to remove all the physical, technical and fiscal barriers to an integrated EC economy are reviewed. In particular, attention is focused upon the philosophy behind the way in which the so-called non-tariff barriers are being eliminated. The primary objective of the '1992' legislation is to remove all barriers impeding the free movement of trade. Taken at face value, much of the legislation appears extremely detailed and technical whilst at the same time being relatively straightforward in character. However, the underlying principles supporting the legislation are critical to an understanding of the '1992' process and its associated economic benefits. Policies are being devised to strengthen the competitive environment in order to allow different regulatory systems and companies to confront and compete with one another. The economic benefits likely to arise from this enhanced competition are the focus of discussion in Chapter 4. Here, a detailed and critical evaluation of Paulo Cecchini's (1988) Report into the 'Cost of non-Europe' is presented. Many of the predictions and associated expectations of the single market programme are thrown into question as the present study exposes some fundamental inconsistencies in the economic evaluations undertaken by both Cecchini and the Commission.

Chapter 5 examines the extent to which a 'social Europe' has been evolving to accompany the 'economic Europe' which has been the focus of the previous three chapters. Whilst many commentators perceive the idea of creating a European social space to be a relatively new phenomenon, this chapter shows that there has always been a strand of Community thought maintaining that some degree of common social policy is required to prevent charges of social inequity, unfair competition and so on in the developing Common Market. The long history of social policies in the EC is thus reviewed and an understanding built up of why the concept of a European social space is inextricably interlinked to the economic space being reinforced by the '1992' programme.

The role of the Single European Act in fostering a 'social Europe' is then discussed in Chapter 6, which highlights contemporary developments such as those associated with the so-called Social Charter. Strong arguments for and against the creation of European social policies will continue into the 1990s and this chapter brings this ongoing debate up-to-date with a critical evaluation of opposing positions. For example, can the 'free enterprise' economic elements of the '1992' programme form an adequate basis upon which to build European unity, or do anxieties about the dangers of so-called 'social dumping' have to be taken seriously?

Chapters 7 and 8 take the debate deeper by a detailed examination of such issues in particularly relevant case-studies which highlight the interplay of things economic and social in Community affairs. Chapter 7 looks inwards by examining the Community's regional policy. It argues that the policies designed to promote regional development are intrinsically social in nature, evolving as they have in response to fears that increased economic integration may be increasing the enormous geographic inequalities which have always existed in the Common Market. Chapter 8, on the other hand, looks outwards and examines why the development of a vigorous social policy has a number of profound implications for the global economy as a whole and the EC's established trading partners. Clearly protectionism has an important social dimension and to most non-EC countries the SEM represents a threat to world trade. The regional policy and external trade case studies have been chosen to highlight the complex relationship that exists between the economic and social dimensions of the EC.

However, this relationship is by no means confined to these two areas of Community policy. Almost every single sphere of Community activity, in the environment, in energy, in agriculture, in transport, in fishing and even in foreign policy, has important social as well as economic ramifications. Indeed, similar problems arise from this interplay of economic and social forces right across the broad range of Community policies. This can be briefly illustrated by reference to the the Common Fisheries Policy (Wise 1984). Introduced in 1971, this policy has had a stormy political history with conflict occurring as the attempt to apply liberal common market principles has clashed with socially-inspired efforts to protect certain fishermen, certain regions and, of course, the fish stocks on which they depend. In keeping with the common-market provisions of the Rome Treaty (free movement of goods, people, capital and services), the CFP has always had a commitment to the principle that access of EC fishermen to fishing grounds under Member State jurisdiction should be free of national discrimination. Apart from the legal imperative behind this approach (Article 7 of the Rome Treaty prohibits such national discriminations), economic justification for it was found by arguing that access to fish markets free of national discrimination had to be counterbalanced by a similar equality of access to fishing grounds. It would, according to liberal economic tenets, be inequitable to open up national fish markets to Common Market competition and then allow a few geographically privileged maritime Member States to block the entry of their fishing competitors to vast areas of 'national' sea, thus monopolizing fish supplies. In the words of one French commentator, 'a Common Market means a common sea' (Regnier 1977: 5).

Whilst not denying that such liberal common market principles have indeed moulded several aspects of the CFP, social factors have also played an important role. In reality, the policy has evolved as politicians have sought to reconcile competing free-market and protectionist principles in a pluralistic political system. For a start, the principle of access to fishing grounds free of national discrimination has never been translated into policy provisions requiring a competitive 'free-for-all' amongst fishermen at sea. In fact, the national non-discrimination principle, which, more or less respected, is found in all EC policies, does not mean, as some tend to assume, that ruthless, deregulated competition must take place in the common market. For example, in the case of the CFP, controls on fishing involving non-national forms of discrimination have always been permissible. Indeed, as the problems of overfishing (stemming from an anarchic open seas situation not intrinsic to the EC) worsened, the Community has increasingly intervened to regulate the industry rather than encourage 'laissez-faire' on the high seas. Similar forms of EC interventionism to regulate free-market forces can be found in all areas of Community activity, hence EC regional policy to reduce spatial disparities, EC agricultural policy to support farm prices and incomes, EC health, safety and product standards to protect workers and consumers from unbridled common market capitalism, EC environmental measures to ensure that unchecked single market competition does not destroy the quality of life, and so on.

As in other areas of EC policy, a explicit concern with social and regional issues has also played a prominent part in formulating CFP provisions which have never permitted fishermen to fish what, where, when and how they like in some anarchistic liberal 'free-market' fashion. The objective of protecting geographically peripheral communities 'particularly dependent' on fishing has long been embedded in Community fishery policy-making leading to numerous provisions which do not conform to simple models of open competition. Thus, protective 12-mile national fishing limits, along with even more extensive zones reserved for particular regions, still exist around Member States. The CFP's use of national quotas (again commonly found in other EC policies, despite the fact that the Rome Treaty forbids national discriminations!) is also justified as a means of protecting resources and fishing communities. Each year, in classic interventionist style, the Community decides how much of what fish each Member State can catch in what fishing zones. In making these decisions, the Community must seek to ensure that every year each Member State receives approximately the same share of the overall EC catch. It is difficult to imagine a more direct challenge to the principles of open international competition than this 'status quo' arrangement!

These complex 'single market versus social protectionism' disputes rarely have a 'final' resolution in a world where forces for change and stability will always compete in all EC policy areas. A whole raft of unresolved issues remains for CFP policy-makers to tackle which merge into more general discussions about the balance between the Community's economic and social dimensions. For example, elements of the 'social dumping' debate (Chapters 5 and 6) thrust their way into the fisheries sphere. Contradictions of this nature abound in all areas of EC activity as people brought up to think in national terms struggle to cope with the economic and social demands of policy-making in a Community framework. Like other EC policies, the CFP is full of compromises between competitive free-market and social protectionist approaches. The balances struck between these various currents reflect the political strength of the various protagonists at any given time. However, the ideological divide between the groups involved is not always what might be expected; the avid supporter of 'free' competition in a general sense can become a firm protector of social and regional interests threatened by 'foreign' challengers.

The balance and tension that exist between things economic and social is as evident in external matters and foreign affairs as within domestic Community issues. Many non-EC states, both developed and developing, have expressed anxiety about the emergence of a more protectionist Community arising from the SEM reforms. The Community will be under pressure to adopt restrictive common external barriers to shelter those areas of the economy adversely affected by the adjustment processes inherent within the internal market programme. In other words, the Community may be tempted to shift parts of the burden from internal adjustment to third countries (Langhammer, 1990). The impact of the SEM on the world economy in general, and developing countries in particular, has received very little attention. Indeed Cecchini's 1988 report into the 'Cost of Non-Europe' notably ignored the external dimension.

The EC is keen to stress the positive results arising from extra imports stimulated by the assumed Community income-growth generated by the internal market. The scope for increased EC imports from developing countries, via the stimulative effect of '1992' on economic growth, has been estimated at US$ 5 billion for primary exports alone. Economic growth of such a magnitude would be a most effective barrier against the emergence of a protectionist lobby in the EC. However, the greater competition, specialization, innovation and economies of scale will enable the Community producers to lower costs and prices, allowing EC suppliers to replace outside suppliers. The replacement of such imports would lead to a welfare loss that is the principal concern to suppliers outside the EC. For developing countries, perhaps the greatest concern lies in the propensity of Member States to protect domestic industries adversely affected by the adjustment process. A legitimate concern over the social consequences associated with greater competition may well result in greater pressure for a more vigorous and protectionist external trade policy. In addition, the threat of protectionism may be enhanced by

Community 'social harmonization', particularly if the discrepancy between labour costs in the 'core' and 'periphery' are reduced. If social harmonization does take place and the peripheral areas of the EC lose their competitive advantage, then production could be shifted to areas outside the Community. Under such a scenario, the EC would come under intense pressure to protect labour intensive and low-technology industries, exactly those industries upon which developing countries depend most.

Many elements of the Community's existing external policy are incompatible with the aims of the internal market. The Member States' tradition of discriminating in trading agreements is deeply rooted. The Lome Agreement, the Generalized System of Preferences and the Mediterranean Preferences enable Member States to manipulate a resource transfer to developing countries. This is made possible by Article 115 of the Treaty of Rome, which enables national quotas to be imposed on imports from third countries being directed through other Member States. Because Article 115 limits the free movement of goods within the Community, and is dependent on physical border controls, it will eventually be replaced by a Community-wide common policy. There is a genuine fear amongst non-EC states that when the Community replaces national quotas there will be a tendency to adopt relatively high levels of protection. The task of producing a collective customs union for the textile industry, clothing, steel products, some agricultural products, the entire service sector and the car industry has proved to be extremely difficult. Those Member States, such as France, which have a high level of protection in goods markets are tempted to transfer at least some of the adjustment burden stemming from internal liberalization to non-EC countries. However this can only take place if the more open Member States, such as Germany, agree. Again the issue focuses on the internal social costs of adjustment versus the economic benefits arising from free trade, both within the EC and externally. Langhammer states:

> the most relevant test case of whether remnants of national sovereignty in trade policies can be abandoned…is the car industry and the common treatment of Japanese car exports to the Community. (Langhammer 1990: 142)

It is for this reason that Chapter 8 examines the external economic impact of 1992, paying particular attention to Japanese foreign direct investment (FDI) and the car industry. Many of the themes identified in this chapter, such as 'fortress Europe', reciprocity, Article 115, the protectionist reaction to the internal adjustment problems and the pressure to pass on the burden of adjustment, highlight the tension that exists between the economic and social objectives of the EC. As far as the Community's external trading relations are concerned, similar issues arise in varying degrees with almost every third country or trading group – the USA, Lome countries, members of the European Free Trade Area and the African, Caribbean and Pacific (ACP) states. It is therefore neither possible nor desirable to deal with such a wide range of case-studies in one volume. By concentrating on the Community's relationship with Japan, and in particular Japanese FDI in the Community economy, the issues and tension that exist between the economic and social objectives of the EC's external policies can be examined in greater detail. Chapter 8 does, however, examine one further aspect of the economic and social policy debate: the causes and consequences of the desire to join the Community by some of the states belonging to the European Free Trade Area (EFTA). One of the most important factors influencing the decision of the Twelve on whether to enlarge is the economic and social opportunities and costs associated with expanded Community membership. The internal market programme put the EFTA states under enormous pressure to re-evaluate their relationship with the EC. With 65 per cent of their non-mutual exports destined for the EC, EFTA countries fear trade diversion created by the momentum of the internal market programme. '1992' has therefore persuaded many EFTA countries to either apply for Community membership or to negotiate an EC-EFTA 'European Economic Space' (EES).

The case-studies selected are appropriate in highlighting the fact that although the economic dimension of '1992' has taken priority over all others, there are important social implications to be considered which have always been present in the desire to integrate Europe further. The structure of this book and the case-studies chosen reflect this primary concern with things economic and social.

In a Britain, where a simplistic 'free-trade' view of the Community has often prevailed, there is still great ignorance of the wide-ranging motives driving the process of European integration as well as much conceptual confusion debasing discussion of the Community. For example, many politicians, let alone the publics they represent, talk loosely about 'free trade areas' and 'common markets' as though they are the same thing, whereas crucial differences separate them. When the debate turns towards issues of economic, social and political union, semantic muddle sometimes makes communication of ideas almost impossible; for example, the word 'federal' in centralized unitary Britain often generates a very different set of visions (and fears) than in Germany where people are much more familiar with decentralized federalism as an everyday reality. To cope with such confusion, some clarification of concepts and vocabulary is essential. Furthermore, the workings of the EC's unique and poorly understood political system will be described. It is impossible to understand the attempts to create economic, social and other forms of integration in the Community without reference to it. For example, a tendency to see the EC as a very separate entity, largely divorced from the Member State governments and dominated by powerful 'Eurocrats' in the Commission, needs to be corrected. The mass of political processes linked with moves towards greater unity within the Community are little illuminated by crude thinking which suggests that most things 'European' can be explained by a quick reference to a small all-powerful Commission in Brussels! Furthermore, some consideration of theoretical models of the state can direct us towards questions about which groups or forces are doing most to mould the Community's evolution.

THE INSTITUTIONS OF THE EUROPEAN COMMUNITY

In the following chapters dealing with the economic rationale of the SEM and associated demands for a European 'social space', frequent reference will be made to the unique institutions of the EC (Fig 1.1). This very uniqueness makes their workings difficult to comprehend. A distorted view of EC institutions often prevails, seeing them as detached from national governments and

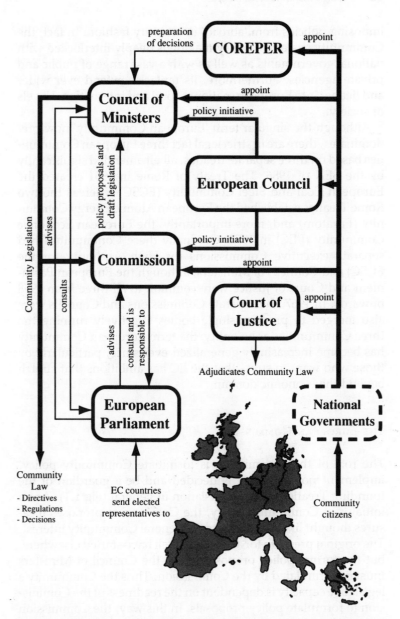

Figure 1.1 European Community institutions and decision processes

imposing policies from 'abroad' in arbitrary fashion. In fact, the Community system of policy-making is deeply interlocked with national governments as well as with a vast range of public and private agencies. Furthermore, its tentacles extend ever wider and deeper into European, national, local and international levels of society.

Although the singular term 'European Community' now pre-dominates, there are in strict legal fact three European Communities based on three separate treaties, albeit amended significantly by the SEA of 1986. The Treaty of Rome in 1951 created the European Coal and Steel Community (ECSC) whereas the two Rome Treaties established the European Atomic Energy Community (Euratom) and, more importantly, the European Economic Community (EEC) in 1957. Originally these Communities had separate executive Commissions (or High Authority for the ECSC) and Councils of Ministers, although the European Parliament and Court of Justice were common to all three from 1958 onwards. In 1967, the separate Commissions and Councils were also merged to produce single bodies effectively running the three Communities as an entity; the term European Community has become increasingly generalized ever since, particularly by those who want to stress that the EC has ambitions that stretch beyond the economic domain.

THE EUROPEAN COMMISSION

The role of the Commission is to initiate Community policy, implement policy once it is decided and be a guardian of the founding Treaties and EC legislation in general (Fig 1.1). As an initiator of Community policy, the Commission proposes measures thought likely to promote the general Community interest. The original pressure for action may well have started elsewhere, but the formal policy proposal put to the Council of Ministers must be formulated by the Commission. Thus the Community's legislative capacity is dependent on the readiness of the Commission to formulate policy proposals. In this way, the Commission is more than a supranational civil service, playing an overt political role in setting goals for the Community. Indeed prominent politicians are influential in the Commission; during the 1980s its

President, Jacques Delors, had a much publicized impact on policy directions taken by the Community, not least the single market and social Europe initiatives at the heart of this book. In formulating its proposals the Commission must pursue the elusive concept of a 'Community interest'. This means that much effort has to be spent seeking acceptable compromises between different national, regional and sectional interests.

At the head of the Commission are 17 Commissioners who, whilst having individual responsibilities for particular policy areas, operate as a collegiate body. Each of the five larger countries provide two Commissioners whereas the smaller states send one each. The crucial role of Member State governments in making these appointments should be noted. In the intricate intermeshing of national and European bodies in the Community system, national governments maintain a firm grip on the main levers of power. However, all Member States must approve the appointment of each Commissioner, thus stressing that they are supposed to be pursuers of wider European interests rather than national representatives. In practice they tend to be a bit of both, although it is striking how their 'solemn undertaking...neither to seek nor to take instructions from any government' is adhered to in practice. One example of the way in which Commissioners maintain a marked degree of independence from their countries of origin relates to a major theme of this book. In the mid-1980s, the British Conservative government successfully nominated Lord Cockfield, a party member, to become the Commissioner responsible for the '1992' single internal market project. However, his vision of what this project entailed became far more comprehensive and 'European' than the then British Prime Minister, Mrs Thatcher, had anticipated. Her more restricted 'free-trade' concept of this market clashed with his belief in the need to move towards a single European currency. Thus, when he sought re-nomination to the office for a second four-year term he found that British governmental support was not forthcoming and he was forced to leave the Commission.

The Commission does not act alone in drawing up proposals for submission to the Council. An extensive network of advisory committees and less formal processes link it to national governments, civil services, employers' organizations, trade unions, scientific advisory bodies, consumer groups and so on. All this firmly interlocks the Commission into national and other bodies which contribute substantially to the process of policy formulation. Once policies have been adopted by the Council, the Commission makes extensive use of Management Committees to help it in the task of implementing them. These Committees are again composed of Member State representatives operating together with the Commission. Although the Commission has substantial powers of political initiative and policy implementation, it is ultimately held in check by Member State governments in the Council of Ministers.

THE COUNCIL OF MINISTERS

The Council of Ministers is the key centre of decision-making in the Community system (Fig 1.1). It is here that EC policy is finally decided. The Council is composed of ministers from the Member State governments, with its precise composition varying according to the issue at stake: agricultural ministers decide farm policy, environment ministers deal with environmental issues and so on. Its decisions can become Community law which is binding throughout EC territory and, in case of conflict, takes precedence over national legislation. As with the Commission, the Council does not sit in splendid European isolation, but forms the centre of a dense network of committees and working groups linking it to national and other Community bodies. In particular, the role of the Committee of Permanent Representatives (COREPER) should be noted. It is made up of high-powered delegates from each Member State who are constantly present in Brussels backed up by a substantial staff. In effect, COREPER tries to reach as much agreement on Commission proposals as possible, leaving only the most difficult issues for the hard-pressed national Ministers in the Council.

The Rome Treaty states that 'save as otherwise provided in this Treaty, the Council shall act by a majority of its members'. More precisely, in areas where applicable, the Council is required to decide on the basis of a qualified majority vote which is carefully designed to afford greater voting power to the more populated countries without crushing the smaller countries under their collective weight. At present, the votes are allocated as follows: 10 each to France, Germany, Italy and the UK; 8 to Spain; 5 each to Belgium, Greece, Portugal and the Netherlands; 3 each to Denmark and Ireland; and 2 to tiny Luxembourg. A qualified majority vote is made up of 54 votes out of the total of 76. In effect this means that the five larger states cannot outvote the smaller seven and that two larger states cannot by themselves constitute a blocking majority.

Although qualified majority voting occurs and has been reinforced in the Single European Act as a means of getting agreement on measures needed to create the single market by the end of 1992, the Council generally tries to reach unanimous agreement. The reasons for this go back to a serious constitutional crisis in 1965 which focused attention on the realities of national governmental power within the Community. As the Community moved towards a stage in its development where majority voting was due to become more widespread in policy-making, the French government under President de Gaulle objected to the full supranational implications of this evolution. Faced with the resistance of the Commission and the other Member States, the French withdrew their representatives from the Community's decision-making institutions during the latter half of 1965, although they continued to apply existing EC regulations. This strategy of the 'empty chair' was an effective demonstration of the limits of supranationalism confronted with effective national authority; there was little or nothing France's partners could do to make the French government accept majority voting against its will. Eventually the so-called 'Luxembourg Compromise' was reached in January 1966. It was a rather uneasy accord reflecting in its ambiguities the inevitably 'grey area' (which still exists) between the ambitions of European supranationalism and the desire of Member State governments not to relinquish essential elements of national sovereignty. In it the principle of majority voting was not abandoned, but

> when issues very important to one or more Member States are at stake, the members of the Council will try, within a reasonable time, to reach solutions which can be adopted by all Members of the Council while respecting their mutual interests, and those of the Community. (Nugent 1989: 103)

The French were rather more emphatic in insisting that in such circumstances 'discussion must be continued until unanimous agreement is reached'. This compromise agreement, which has no constitutional status, was a reflection of the political (rather than strictly legal) realities of power at the time. De facto if not de jure, it conceded a virtual power of national veto to any Member State which cares to define some issue as a vital national interest and then insist on unanimity. If such agreement cannot be reached then the proposal is effectively blocked.

Of course, there is nothing to stop Member States 'calling the bluff' of an obstructing partner by trying to force through agreement on a majority vote. In fact this happened in 1982 when Britain tried unsuccessfully to invoke the Luxembourg Compromise in order to block farm price increases. The UK accepted its defeat because to take drastic action – as the French had done by their 'empty chair' tactic in 1965 – seemed counterproductive to their other Community interests at the time; the Falklands War was being waged, the UK 'contribution' to the EC budget was high, and the British needed the support of its Community partners. Here we touch on the political nub of decision-making reality in the Council. Whatever the wording of Treaties and compromise accords on voting procedures, the process of decision in the Council between twelve often powerful states inevitably involves political bargaining of the most traditional kind. Furthermore, there has been an understanding that a body as diverse as the Community can best develop if a consensual rather than confrontational approach is more common in the resolution of conflicts.

THE EUROPEAN COUNCIL

In 1974 the Community Heads of Member State governments decided to meet regularly on a formal basis at least once every six months in a European Council. These 'Euro-summits' are designed to bring the leaders of national governments together to exchange ideas, give the Community strategic direction and try to break some of the major policy log-jams which inevitably build up in an organization of twelve states. The European Council has become very important in the making of 'big decisions' such as the one to revise the founding Treaties in the Single European Act of 1986. In fact, this Act formally enshrined the European Council as a formal part of the Community system of government. Large projects like the single market and the Social Charter also need the approval of this Council of the Community's most powerful politicians. However, as so often in Community affairs, it is hard to make a definitive statement about what is a dynamic, evolving system. For example, it is the custom that the Council should act on the basis of unanimous accord. Nevertheless, when Britain tried to resist adoption of the Social Charter in 1989, it found that it could do nothing to prevent the other eleven states going ahead without it (Chapter 6).

THE EUROPEAN PARLIAMENT

The Parliament was set up to provide a measure of democratic supervision of the workings of the Community's decision-making system. Its own powers to influence EC policy are growing but remain relatively limited. Unlike national parliaments it does not make laws (EC legislation is based on decisions made by national Ministers in the Council), but it does discuss the Commission's proposals and can make amendments to them. Indeed, at least 50 per cent of final legislation gets altered by the Parliament en route from the Commission proposal to the Council decision. It also has the power to dismiss the Commission by a two-thirds vote of censure, although this has never been done. Such an action would bring the Parliament into direct conflict with the Member States who, it will be recalled, have the greater power of being able to appoint the Commissioners! The Parliament also has significant powers to control the Community budget drawn up by the Commission and the Council, although it cannot prevent the large amounts of 'obligatory expenditure' which are still directed towards agricultural support.

The Single European Act strengthened the role of the Parliament, although not as much as European federalists would have liked, through the so-called 'cooperation procedure'. This involves it more closely in the final decision-making process. Before reaching a final decision, the Council must now transmit its 'common position' to the Parliament which has three months to endorse it, reject it or amend it. If the Parliament rejects the Council's proposed decision, then the Council can only pass it on the basis of a unanimous vote, although amendments proposed by the Parliament can be incorporated by a qualified majority. If the Council fails to reach a decision on the Parliament's response within three months, then the proposal is dropped.

Since 1987, European Members of Parliament (MEPs) have been elected by direct universal suffrage. Elections every five years produce 518 MEPs: 81 each for France, Germany, Italy, and the UK; 60 for Spain; 25 for the Netherlands; 24 each for Belgium, Greece and Portugal; 16 for Denmark; 15 for Ireland; and 6 for Luxembourg which is grossly over-represented given its tiny population. This again reflects a desire to stop combinations of big countries overwhelming the smaller ones in the process of Community policy-making.

THE EUROPEAN COURT OF JUSTICE

This Court is the final arbiter of disputes related to the application of Community law. Such law is routinely applied through national courts, but obviously some conflicts are referred to this higher European Court for a definitive judgement. In fact, the Court has become a very important interpreter of Community law, establishing numerous precedents which become the basis of further judgements, not least in the fields of EC common market and social policy legislation. Conflicts involve Community institutions, Member State governments, private companies and even individuals. For example, the Commission can take a Member State to the Court for allegedly failing to apply Community legislation in an appropriate manner. Similarly, Member States can challenge Commission actions before the Court, and so on. Once a judgement has been made it is binding and takes precedence over national law. In general the judgements of the Court are accepted, but there is growing concern about the Court's ability to cope effectively with implementation disputes thought likely to arise as a mass of single market legislation is put into effect.

SUPRANATIONALISM, INTERNATIONALISM AND INTERGOVERNMENTALISM

We have shown how national governments (if not parliaments) remain at the heart of the Community system. However, it is wrong to think of the EC as just another international organization. Its creators deliberately used the term 'supranational' to distinguish it from other international bodies, and the two terms should not be confused.

International can be employed to describe a whole multitude of dealings between nations (or, more precisely, states). For example, international conferences may bring a number of states together in order to reach a common agreement. Nevertheless, within such conferences the individual governments retain their legal sovereignty and recognize no higher authority whatever the nature of the agreement they reach. However, 'supranationalism' involves the establishment of new authoritative institutions which are literally 'above' those of the state. In effect, the Member States of a supranational institution decide to pool part of their national sovereignty in a distinctive decision-making body which makes laws that have to be applied throughout the territories of all partner countries. Thus, supranational processes take place in permanent institutions which lie above, or alongside, those of a nation-state character. Obviously, they owe much to federal concepts where states can group together under common policy-making and legislative institutions without renouncing all of their sovereign rights to make separate decisions in certain fields of activity. Clearly, the EC's political system has marked supranational characteristics.

However, although there is more than a hint of federalism in EC structures, the dominant role of Member State governments at the decision-making heart of the Community institutions still makes comparisons with most federations unconvincing. Indeed, the persistent power of national governments has led some analysts to use the term 'intergovernmental' in preference to 'supranational' when describing the Community (Wallace, 1983). The 'empty chair' crisis of the mid-1960s, when the French government withdrew from Community affairs until it had asserted its right to a 'de facto' veto on matters of 'very important' national interest, encouraged this shift in terminology. Other institutional changes tilted political power even more towards the Council and the network of bodies binding it to national government. For example, at the very top of the system, Member State power has also been reinforced by the creation of the European Council in 1974 (see above). This body grouping the governmental leaders of Member States has taken over much of the strategic thinking and goal-setting role originally reserved for the Commission, which often finds itself working out detailed proposals to achieve an objective fixed by the European Council. However, none of these shifts justify the wholesale replacement of 'supranational' with 'intergovernmental' interpretations of how the EC works. The unique law-making powers of the Community-level institutions remain, whatever the influence of Member States within them.

FREE TRADE ASSOCIATIONS, COMMON MARKETS AND POLITICAL-ECONOMIC UNIONS.

To help illuminate the linkages that exist between matters economic, social and, of course, political, a series of interrelated models envisaging five levels of ever-increasing integration from a simple Free Trade Association to a fully-fledged Political Union of a federal nature is presented (Figs 1.2 to 1.6). It focuses attention on a basic question related to the book's pivotal theme, namely: to what extent are demands for development of an EC social dimension an unavoidable corollary of its increasingly integrated economic dimension? Does pursuit of the single market programme inevitably trigger off demands for an equivalent social action programme flowing out of the EC's Social Charter?

The model also clarifies concepts such as 'free trade', 'common markets', 'single markets', 'social Europe', 'social dumping' and 'supranationality', not to mention 'political and economic union'. Discussion of European integration is often confused because terms are not defined. The word 'federation', for example, stimulates a range of contradictory visions in different national minds; many in Britain (where federalist traditions are very weak) associate the term with some massive centralized European 'superstate' whereas Germans (already living in their own national federation of powerful Lander) can more easily envisage a form of European unity in which nations and regions retain substantial political powers over economic and social affairs along with central EC institutions.

Of course, Figs 1.2–1.6 only make-up a series of models. Any temptation to see them representing five inevitable linear steps from national independence to federal interdependence must be resisted. Indeed, the present European Community does not fit neatly into any of the integration levels described. Whilst not yet the genuine 'common market' its popular name would imply (Fig 1.4), it nevertheless possesses elements of a real political union (Fig 1.6), despite protestations of national politicians to the contrary! How else can the constant formalized activity of politicians from all Member States within permanent European policy-making institutions making laws on everything from international trade (CETs) to international education (ERASMUS) be described? In truth, the question is not so much whether there should be a political union – there is one of sorts already – but what form it should take in the future. The Community is an extremely complex phenomenon which does not lend itself easily to simple theoretical formulations.

①

Free Trade Area

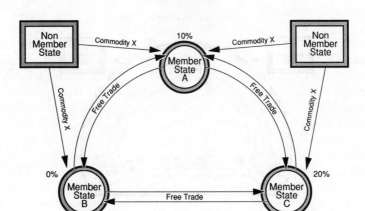

Tariff and quota restrictions removed between Member States

BUT

Each Member State determines its own tariffs and quotas with Non-Member States.

Figure 1.2 Model of a Free Trade Area

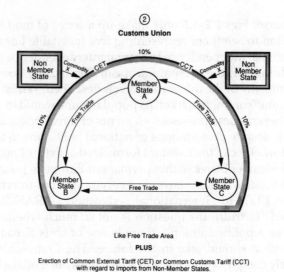

Figure 1.3 **Model of a Customs Union**

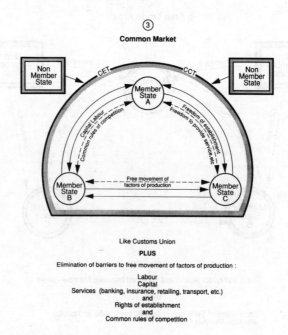

Figure 1.4 **Model of a Common Market**

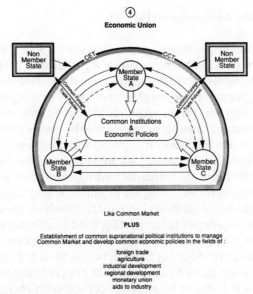

④
Economic Union

CET   CCT

Non Member State

Non Member State

Member State A

Common Foreign Trade Policies

Common Foreign Trade Policies

Common Institutions & Economic Policies

Member State B

Member State C

Like Common Market

PLUS

Establishment of common supranational political institutions to manage
Common Market and develop common economic policies in the fields of :

foreign trade
agriculture
industrial development
regional development
monetary union
aids to industry

Figure 1.5 Model of an Economic Union

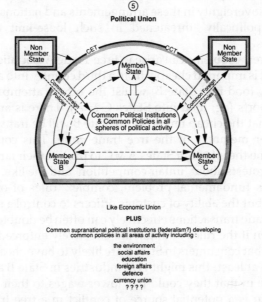

⑤
Political Union

CET   CCT

Non Member State

Non Member State

Member State A

Common Foreign Policies

Common Foreign Policies

Common Political Institutions & Common Policies in all spheres of political activity

Member State B

Member State C

Like Economic Union

PLUS

Common supranational political institutions (federalism?) developing
common policies in all areas of activity including :

the environment
social affairs
education
foreign affairs
defence
currency union
????

Figure 1.6 Model of a Political Union

1. Free Trade Associations (Fig 1.2)

The model envisages three independent states (States A, B and C) which have decided to move closer together into a Free Trade Association, whilst two other states have decided to stay outside any such agreement (the non-Member States or third countries). The degree of integration required in a free trade area is very limited. Member States agree to remove the classic trade barriers of customs tariffs (ie, taxes on imports) and quota restrictions (ie, limits on quantities imported) amongst themselves, but remain free to decide their own particular trading arrangements with the non-member countries. Thus, for example, whilst accepting free trade in agricultural products amongst themselves, they can have separate arrangements for importing food from third countries. For instance, State A could place a 10 per cent tariff on foodstuffs bought from a non-Member State, whereas State C might protect its farmers even more by erecting a 20 per cent barrier. In stark contrast, State B might be more concerned with cheap food for consumers and place no tariff barrier or quota restrictions on agricultural imports. Clearly, there is little impingement on national sovereignty in these arrangements and nationalists rarely feel 'politically' threatened in such loose-knit economic structures.

However, problems can arise in Free Trade Associations when a product is imported cheaply from a third country into a Member State (eg, food into State B) whilst the others attempt to resist such imports (eg, food into States C & A). There is an obvious danger that the cheap imports into State B will be transferred on into other members of the free trade zone. This could easily undermine the efforts of States A & C to protect their farmers and lead to protests about 'unfair competition' and the like. To counteract this fundamental problem, complex 'rules of origin' are devised, but the ability of customs officers to control a multitude of such trade transactions effectively can often be doubted. Moreover, even if the rules of origin are effectively enforced, the fact remains that consumers in State B are likely to have cheaper food. In theory at least, this might give industries in State B a competitive edge in that they could pay lower wages to their workers. This again is a potential source of conflict in a free trade zone where industrialists are likely to be very sensitive to issues of unequal competition. It is problems such as these that can make Customs Unions seem attractive.

2. Customs Unions (Fig 1.3)

The model still assumes that there are the three integrating states of A, B & C which have adopted the essentials of a Free Trade Association. However, to counteract the problems arising from Member States having separate trade deals with third countries, a Common Customs Tariff (CCT) or Common External Tariff (CET) is now adopted. There is no longer any question of States A, B & C importing, for example, food from non-members at different tariff rates; they must all impose an identical trade barrier to be decided in concert amongst themselves. There may be no overt surrender of national sovereignty, but once in such an arrangement there is a compulsion on states to work together to produce common decisions about the duties and quota restrictions they place on imports from third countries. They have freely agreed to relinquish a little more of their political freedom of action, albeit in the restricted, but important, field of trade.

3. Common Markets (Fig 1.4)

A Common Market structure retains all the features of a Customs Union, but moves still further down the road of economic integration. This system is concerned not only with the free trade of goods inside a CET but with the free movement of those things needed to produce those goods. In other words the basic factors of production – capital and labour – can cross national boundaries without impediment. Furthermore, services – banking, insurance, transport – can be sold freely throughout the common market regardless of national frontiers. Moreover, the 'freedom of establishment' is granted to those who wish to set up businesses in a Member State of which they are not a citizen; no discriminatory rules should prevent them from so doing simply because of their nationality. Common rules of competition should be devised by the Member States acting in concert to ensure that producers throughout the Common Market compete on equal terms. Such rules might deal with permissible levels of subsidy to industry or regions in need of development. Likewise, similar health, safety and social security standards might be sought in order to prevent producers in one state obtaining an unfair competitive advantage by adopting lax, low-cost measures in order to attract investment away from partner countries. Clearly, this degree of economic integration tugs the Member States towards ever more cooperative political decision-making procedures. For example, negotiations about acceptable levels of public assistance to poorer regions cannot be seen as 'purely technical' operations of a 'purely economic' character. Whatever they might try to pretend to their national electorates, politicians engaged in deciding common economic rules are indeed involved in politics. Economic integration can thus spill over into political integration, at least in certain areas, and lead into the concept of an Economic Union.

4. Economic Union (Fig 1.5)

Economic Union in our model retains all the features of a Common Market, but common supranational institutions are added to it. It is possible to imagine the policies required to manage a common market being made in numerous intergovernmental meetings without a separate layer of supranational institutions. However, there is a logic in establishing a distinct decision-making body to administer the Market and make policies for it. For example, the apparently simple task of setting up of a Common External Tariff (in reality many different tariffs and quotas for different imports) requires a constant flow of detailed decisions about the multitude of products involved in international trade. The problems of several Member States trying to cope with these matters in ad hoc intergovernmental meetings would be enormous. Also, action in international trade negotiations would be facilitated if the Member States produced common positions and then negotiated as a single body in dealings with third countries. Similarly, sensitive common problems related to acceptable levels of regional assistance, state aids to industry, agriculture and so on are likely to require constant attention, thus producing pressure for common institutions to resolve the inevitable conflicts that will arise. At this degree of economic integration it might be expected that pressures for strict monetary cooperation between different national currencies would grow. It is hard to imagine a smooth functioning of a Common Market without some harmonization of currency fluctuations and macroeconomic policies in general. If one Member State continues to cope with its balance of trade problems by frequent currency devaluations designed to stimulate its exports and stem its imports, partner countries are likely to protest about 'distorted' competition and call for greater stability of exchange rates. Likewise, in a market of free capital movements, disruptions are likely to occur if interest rates are markedly higher in one country than in others, thus attracting capital unimpeded across its borders. In other words, in a single market where goods, people, services, and capital move freely from country to country, a logic for common political institutions to formulate common economic policies inexorably grows and leads towards the concept of Economic Union. However, within such a union, common supranational decision-making would still be restricted to what are conventionally viewed as economic matters. It is only at the next and final stage that a fully-fledged Political Union is envisaged.

5. Political Union (Fig 1.6)

A Political Union includes all the previous stages of integration, but here there is no attempt to restrict policy-making to specific areas. Inhibitions about keeping strictly to 'economic' affairs and preserving national political sovereignty intact are abandoned. That is not to say that the Member States would give up all their authority; indeed it is conceivable that they remain the most powerful individual actors in the system. Nevertheless, they are here moving towards federal concepts such as 'pooling sovereignty' and dividing responsibilities between different governments and legislatures in a complex intermeshing of institutions at national, supranational and, if desired, regional levels. At this state of integration there would be no more semantic splitting of hairs about where 'economic' matters ended and those of a 'political' nature began. A view of an international society evolving in an integrated political economy would be frankly accepted. Thus, Member States would feel free to deal with any matter thought appropriate at a supranational level. Common economic policies could be supplemented by those of a social, educational, environmental, cultural or whatever nature as the perceived need arises.

Moreover, in a Political Union it becomes hard to conceive of separate national currencies competing with each other in potentially disruptive ways. At the very least, multinational businesses dominating the Common Market are likely to demand a common currency to facilitate their activities, reduce uncertainty and eliminate the weighty burden of exchange costs. It might even be expected that the general public, emotionally attached to national monies, would eventually weary of the time-consuming and costly currency swops in an Economic Union where many millions cross the old national frontiers each year for business and pleasure. Furthermore, released from a desire (or electoral need) to put a rigid ring-fence around national sovereignty, the Member States could even envisage moving into that most sensitive of policy areas, military security. When the economic interests, both within and beyond the Common Market, of Member States have become so inextricably interlinked, the sense of having separate common foreign and defence policies is likely to be questioned. For example, it becomes not unreasonable to assume that all the partner countries would share a more-or-less common interest in protecting security of access to vital resources (eg energy imports) and markets. Even more obvious, perhaps, would be a common interest in each other's security from outside threat; at this stage of mutual economic interdependence can one really imagine one Member State being indifferent to the military security of another? National self-interest itself would suggest the logic of a common approach to these basic problems of the state and result in a Political Union within which all the functions of the modern state are dealt with at one level or another.

THEORETICAL PERSPECTIVES ON EUROPEAN INTEGRATION; THE SPILLOVER EFFECT

Our simplified model suggests a process of ever deepening political, economic and social integration. In so doing it highlights the 'spillover' theory which has permeated much academic literature on the processes of European unity (Lindberg 1963 and 1970, Haas 1968, Ionescu 1972, George 1985). This theory states that integration of one area of political-economic activity inevitably builds up pressures to integrate others. Thus, 'one thing leads to another' in cumulative fashion, drawing states inexorably into ever closer political and economic union. For instance, if the theory is valid it could be expected that the removal of trade restrictions in a simple free trade area would lead to situations where producers in one country feel that they are faced with 'unfair competition' from those in another because of differing subsidy levels, environmental standards, social costs to industry, minimum wages or whatever. In turn this would stimulate demands for common social, environmental and other policies designed to eradicate such distortions to the free play of market forces. Furthermore, once the simplest trade blocks have been removed, the realization would grow that a mass of 'non-tariff barriers' continue to impede the establishment of genuinely free trade; for example, tax systems, product quality standards, government purchasing restrictions, protective social legislation and, above all, currencies vary from state to state, thus providing effective barriers to the movement of goods across national borders even in so-called 'free trade' or 'common market' areas. Any attempt to eliminate such barriers would, according to the theory, draw the Member States into an ever more complex process of policy coordination, with pressures building up to create common political institutions capable of producing the mass of common regulations required in a whole range of fields. Thus economic integration would spill over ever more overtly into indisputably social and political fields. This cumulative progress of economic, social and political integration would involve ever larger policy spheres. For example, the economic history of all western states suggests that elimination of trade barriers in a common market is likely to generate more growth in central 'core regions' at the expense of the more remote 'peripheries'. The political history of such countries also tells us that social groups in the disadvantaged regions are likely to demand government policies to redress these spatial imbalances. Thus regional policies are almost certain to be placed on the agenda of the common political institutions at the centre of the integrating states. Similarly, an increasing number are likely to feel that the creation of a common 'economic space' could threaten their welfare in some way unless complemented by the building of a more harmonized 'social space' to protect potential losers in a common market. In other words, the spillover concept suggests that the indivisibility of the economic, social and political dimensions of life will become impossible to deny as integration proceeds with a dynamic of its own. The relevance of this theory to the central 'economic-social' theme of this book is obvious. To what extent are the processes and predictions of the spillover theory of integration borne out in reality? What evidence is there that the single market programme has set in train processes leading to proposals for a social Europe? Can there be a single market which is not in effect a single social market?

The spillover theory could be dismissed as excessively academic. However, practical people concerned with changing the political shape of Europe have subscribed to its tenets, whether knowingly or not. Most notably, Jean Monnet (Monnet 1962, Mayne 1967) and Robert Schuman (Schuman 1950), founders of the first steps towards today's Community, thought in terms akin to those sketched out above. They may have used the French term 'engrenage' (literally an enmeshing of gear wheels) to describe a process where European unity would be built up progressively step by step, with one cog driving another in an increasingly complicated and interlocking system, but the intellectual concept is essentially the same.

FEDERAL AND FUNCTIONAL CONCEPTS OF EUROPEAN INTEGRATION

The spillover theory of integration is closely associated with so-called 'neofunctionalism' (George 1985: 21). This school of thought is a hybrid variant emerging from the 'federalist' and 'functionalist' intellectual traditions concerned with European unity. Federalism has a long intellectual history in Europe. Unbridled nationalism in Europe triggered off two World Wars, stimulating a renewed interest in some form of European cooperation. Consequently, a European Union of Federalists (EUF) was formed in 1946. A basic strategy of its adherents was to establish federal institutions in Europe in order to weaken, perhaps even eliminate, the continent's nation-states. Nation-state sovereignty would be directly challenged by these institutions which would lead the process of integration, thus stimulating a shift of popular loyalties from national to federal European level. Such optimistic ideas were presented to the Hague Congress of 1948 which brought together political leaders and pro-European activists from all West European states. But the idea of ceding national sovereignty to a new federal structure in one mighty constitutional stroke proved impractical. Consequently, the Congress created an intergovernmental organization of very limited scope – the Council of Europe – still adhered to by all West European states but almost totally unknown to their citizens.

'Functionalists' think the direct federalist strategy is politically unrealistic and/or undesirable. They have a more pragmatic idea of how to integrate sovereign states within structures where conflicts can be peacefully resolved. The term 'functionalism' in this context owes its origin to an academic – David Mitrany – who had been writing on the topic since the early 1930s (Mitrany 1933, 1966, 1975). Like federalists, Mitrany was concerned with creating a peaceful international order. But the idea of creating great new federal structures in Europe or elsewhere worried him. In his view they could easily become new superstates which might well reproduce national rivalries on a larger 'regional' scale. He feared that individual liberties might be jeopardized in ever larger, more centralized and bureaucratic societies. Thus, Mitrany envisaged networks of overlapping international agencies, each having a specific 'function' or task. Unlike all-encompassing federal institutions, these agencies would be set up to deal with specific problems or areas of activity where different groups of countries could see a common interest in cooperative action. By willing surrender of more and more areas of authority to such agencies, states would gradually find themselves woven inextricably into a 'spreading web of international activities and agencies' which would imperceptibly erode effective national sovereignty and encourage internationalist behaviour across state boundaries of diminishing importance (Mitrany 1966: 35).

NATIONALISM AND EUROPEAN INTEGRATION

However, these integration theories, with their suggestion of inevitable moves towards greater unity, must be tempered by reference to the more familiar force of nationalism. A concern with the nation and its interests has not withered away within the European Community. Indeed some nationalists have embraced a limited version of European unity as the best way of protecting their national economic interests and security. It could be argued that in reality the 'nationalist-European' is the most common breed of all. In 1987 the French minister for European Affairs gave unequivocal expression to this notion:

> I believe that, today, the more one is nationalist, the more one is European. In tomorrow's world, there is no chance of being a major power ('grand'), free and respected without working through Europe (Bosson, 1987: 59)

The French have always been especially articulate in expressing this concept. Charles de Gaulle – often seen as a perfect symbol of French nationalism – made many references to the need for some form of European unity in order to protect French interests by promoting peace and prosperity across the continent. Although critical of European federalists – whom he found divorced from nationalist realities – he envisaged a loosely-knit 'Europe of States' in which national sovereignty would be preserved. Such a Europe would share common institutions but a national right to say 'no' would always be present. It was the possibility that a democratically-elected French government might be outvoted against its will in the institutions of the European Communities devised by his compatriots Monnet and Schuman in the 1950s that led de Gaulle to oppose these ventures. However, when he became President of France in 1958, he did not reject the EC but strove to mould its institutions to his concept of a confederal 'Europe of States' which left essential national sovereignty intact. De Gaulle successfully resisted the movement towards supranational EC majority decision-making of a more federal character.

The principle of majority voting was retained for many areas of EC activity, but could be effectively resisted by a determined national government evoking its duty to defend the vital interests of a national population which had elected it to power. The argument was about democracy as well as nationalism.

Although the French may be more skilled than most in blending national and European ambition, they are certainly not alone in seeing the unity of Europe as a way of furthering state interests. Indeed, one can see Britain's reluctant application to join the EC in 1961 after years of refusing to join as a prime example of 'national-Europeanism'. Britain's rejection of invitations to join the ECSC in 1950 and the EEC/Euratom in 1957 resulted from a belief that it was still a great power whose interests were best pursued in the geopolitical frameworks of the Empire/Commonwealth and the 'special relationship' with the USA. Secure within these two circles of influence, there was no need to become embroiled in the supranational structures of the developing European Communities with all their federal implications. However, when Britain lost its Empire and sought a new role in a world where it was falling fast from global power status to medium-sized statehood, the EC took on a more attractive allure. Within it, the UK could protect its national economic interests and continue to wield an effective influence on world affairs. Inside the EC, Britain would be able to mould the trading systems of Europe to its advantage. As an outsider, it feared being on the uninfluential receiving end of decisions made by the combined power of the original 'Six'.

The inherent tensions in a nationalist-European perspective were very apparent in the British government of the 1980s as it tried to cope with moves towards a more federal United States of Europe. Fears of some 'Euro-superstate' were intensified when the President of the Commission, Jacques Delors, confident of spillover effects, predicted that:

> in ten years time, 80 per cent of economic, and perhaps social and tax, legislation will be of Community origin. (Delors 1988)

Delors' vision of Europe was in sharp contrast to the views held by British Ministers who stressed that the aim of European unity should be to liberalize markets, widen choice and reduce governmental intervention rather than transfer more powers to the Community centre. They considered the best way to build a successful EC was through the willing cooperation between independent sovereign states unforced by majority votes. This was the sense of Mrs Thatcher's speech to the College of Europe in Bruges when she insisted:

> Europe will be stronger precisely because it has France as France, Spain as Spain, Britain as Britain, each with its own customs, traditions and identity. It would be a folly to try to fit then into some form of identikit European personality. (Thatcher 1988: 4)

In truth, many federalists would not quarrel with these particular words, although they would be far more prepared than the former UK Prime Minister to pool national sovereignty in a larger European entity. But to the nationalist-European, the EC is acceptable as a means of safeguarding national interests so long as it does not encroach upon what is perceived as vital national sovereignty.

This propensity to see the EC as a means of safeguarding basic national interests in a world where even the bigger European states are increasingly dwarfed by American, Soviet and Japanese 'superpowers' of one sort or another has not been confined to France and Britain. The West Germans, for example, saw European unity as a way of working back to national respectability, influence and economic prosperity following the nationalistic catastrophe of the Nazi era. The enormous efforts of German leaders to relate the unification of their country in 1990 to the wider process of European unification (the latter being presented as a prerequisite of the former) is testament to the way in which they interlink national and European interests. In turn, the Italians produce their own special blends of national interest and European commitment; they are exceeded by nobody in the rhetoric of European unity and general public support for it, nor. in their slowness actually to implement EC legislation designed to build it! As for the small Benelux countries, profitably located in the Community's geographical heart, the happy marriage of

national benefit and Community membership is too ob
to be seriously questioned.

Of course, not all those of a nationalist persuasion
pursue national interests under a cloak of Europeanism.
clearly resist any structures thought likely to challenge a
ished national independence. That was why Britain originally
stayed outside of the EC, and countries like Switzerland, Sweden
and Norway have not yet joined (although the chances are that
they soon will). Also, some nationalists within Member States
still dream of leaving the Community (Chapter 8), although their
numbers appear to be dwindling and their leaders ageing. However, some nationalist groups, like the National Front in France,
remain attached to a certain idea of European unity, albeit one
that conforms to their ideology and strengthened by a world-
view which tends to see Europe surrounded by threatening
forces such as Muslim fundamentalism, Japanese economic power and rising populations in poor countries.

In Britain, the Scottish Nationalist Party and the Welsh nationalists of Plaid Cymru are also supporters of European unity. For
them, the notion of 'national independence' conjures up a vision,
not of separation and barriers at state borders, but of 'international interdependence' within the supranational political and economic structures of the European Community. In fact, they are
tapping an old strand of European idealism encapsulated in the
phrase 'a Europe of Regions'. Thinkers in this vein (usually out of
a federal tradition) describe a Europe in which certain powers
would be transferred to central European institutions, whilst
others would be devolved down from existing state governments
to regions, often with a national character, such as Scotland,
Wales, Brittany, Catalonia, Lombardy, Bavaria, Flanders, Fries-
land or whatever. After all, if countries as small as Luxembourg
and Denmark can flourish in the existing EC system, why not
imagine a European Federation of numerous regional states?

THE EUROPEAN COMMUNITY AND THEORIES OF THE STATE

Theoretical analyses of the EC have focused mainly on the integrative processes binding an increasing number of sovereign
states into the 'ever closer union' envisaged by the Rome Treaty.

Less attention has been paid to the political nature of this new entity. The fact that political theory focuses more on 'the state', rather than groups of states coming into some undetermined form of political-economic integration, makes it difficult to formulate convincing theoretical generalizations. There is a tendency to lurch from excessive simplifications (the Community is the product of capitalist forces in need of larger markets) to extremely detailed empirical studies of how a tiny fragment of the Community system works (the implementation of EC policies at local level).

Nevertheless, reference to state theory can help to focus our analysis and highlight some important general issues concerning the EC's developing economic and social dimensions. Here is not the place to review the vast literature on this subject, nor attempt to summarize the plethora of views concerning the role and nature of 'the state'. However, a contrasting of liberal democratic-pluralist concepts with those arising from a Marxist tradition directs us towards a number of critical questions relevant to the central theme of this book.

The Western liberal-democratic tradition sees the state as a kind of neutral arbitrator set up to resolve the inevitable conflicts between competing interests in diverse pluralist societies composed of many different groups, classes, regions and so on (Dahl 1956). This liberal state permits these different groups to organize themselves into political parties, pressure groups or whatever so that they can seek to promote their particular interests within the institutional and legal framework provided by the state. These diverse, often conflicting, groups can seek to defend themselves in a multitude of ways as long as the basic rules of conflict resolution are respected; for example, the submission of governments to periodic elections, majority voting, acceptance of the rule of law, and so on.

The more idealist formulations of this theory suggest that the diversity of competing groups is so great and their ability to articulate their interests so effective that no one entity in this pluralist society can dominate another; they are all competing on equal terms on the 'level playing field' laid down by the state's institutions. However, others maintain that some groups are consistently more powerful than others in these pluralist societies (Galbraith 1967). The broad structure of public policy is seen to be moulded mainly by very large groupings, in particular those associated with capital (big business) and organized labour (trades unions). This belief gives rise to the concept of the 'corporate state' where major decisions are seen to be the outcome of deals struck between the leaders of these 'big battalions' in cooperation with the government of the day. Elected representatives in the state parliament tend to be marginalized by this central dialogue between leaders of large business interests, large unions and the government of the day. This concept can be elaborated in many ways. It can be argued that these big groups not only play a dominating role in influencing government decisions, but that they also have a large measure of control in determining what issues appear on the political agenda in a supposedly open society. In other words, they can use the large financial resources at their command to control or dominate the media through their public relations machines or even by direct purchase of newspapers, radio and television networks.

This train of theoretical thought leads on to conceptions of the state arising out of the Marxist intellectual tradition. These views reject the idea of the state as an arbitrator established to contain and resolve conflicts in a more-or-less neutral manner. The state is not seen to be above the conflicts of a pluralistic society, ready to resolve them in a democratic manner; rather it is viewed as part of these struggles. Marxists view society as being divided into classes with, to put it very crudely, one class (the capitalists) dominating the others (the workers). The state is thus seen as a structure through which the 'ruling class' manipulates society to serve its interests. The state does this in a number of ways (Miliband 1977). First, it maintains law and order by creating regulations (property rights, public order measures, etc.) which facilitate capitalist accumulation. It maintains social harmony by propagating a mass ideology (in educational bodies and the media) which proclaims the benefits of capitalist society and undermines alternative ideas. Furthermore, it ensures, in Marxist eyes, the provision of a compliant and appropriately skilled workforce for capitalist production, as well as providing it with other essential services such as infrastructure (transport, etc.) and financial assistance when necessary. Finally, the state is seen to defend the interests of its capitalist class in the international arena, by facilitating the search for new markets and protecting foreign investments.

From a Marxist perspective, the creation and growth of the European Community can be seen in this latter light. Member States are seen as responding to the interests of their capitalist classes by breaking down national barriers to trade, investment and labour movements in an ever larger common market; one commentator observed:

> ...a similar process of capitalist internationalization has recently gathered force in Western Europe, sometimes in opposition to American penetration, more often in conjunction with it. New and formidable capitalist complexes are thus coming into being in Western Europe, whose transnational character has very large implications not only in economic terms but in political terms as well. The European Economic Community is one institutional expression of this phenomenon and represents an attempt to overcome, within the context of capitalism, one of its major 'contradictions', namely the constantly more marked obsolescence of the nation-state as the basic unit of international life. (Miliband 1973:15)

However, others see today's Community resulting from a number of different forces, some of them contradictory. Without denying the influence of capitalist interests, other factors are added into the mix of ingredients producing the EC. Most notably these include: a desire to preserve peace in Europe, a concern to contain Germany, a fear of communist expansion from the Soviet Union, a search for nation-state security within a larger European framework, and a wish to emulate the economic, cultural and political power of the United States. In a complex world defying tidy theoretical constructs, no single vision of why there should be a Community and what form it should take is found to be totally convincing. Different actors at different times, in diverse countries with differing political interests have advocated different forms of unity and still do; hence the continuing struggle over the form European political-economic union should take.

This rather messier conception of the Community's nature sits more easily in the pluralist framework of liberal-democratic theories of the state outlined above; here the EC is portrayed as:

...a unique supranational polity where pluralism held sway. Indeed, political and economic pluralism has been held to be the sine qua non of European integration: only those states having a West European conception of liberal democracy broadly conceived may become EC members. (Lodge 1989a: 27)

Thus, as a collectivity of parliamentary democracies which have come together for a variety of reasons, the EC can be seen as one enormous pluralistic entity of constantly evolving character. In effect:

The EC has become the central frame of reference for an incalculable number of actors most of whom will hope to influence and/or gain from the eventual outputs of the EC's decision-making process. (Lodge 1989a: 26)

Although attention tends to be focused narrowly on the 'Commission-Council' axis in EC policy-making, the Community system is deeply interlocked with national government. Indeed, the network of political exchanges extending out from the central supranational institutions stretches out into regional and local government as well as incorporating contacts with numerous professional bodies and interest groups. This extension of the Community system into more and more corners of life in all Member States continues to grow; moreover, 'as the effects of 1992 spill down to a local level, the number of actors involved in vertical and horizontal interactions will grow exponentially' (Lodge 1989a: 33).

Various types of group can be discerned amongst this 'vast range of non-governmental interests (which) cluster around Community processes' (Nugent 1989: 194). First, as EC policy penetrates more obviously into all layers of society, regional and local authorities have increasingly sought a direct role in Community policy-making. In so doing, they often enjoy the encouragement of a European Commission keen to ease the grip of national government on Community affairs. Companies and corporations, both public and private, also pursue direct dealings with Community authorities. All the major motor and electronics companies are, for example, organized to make the Commission and MEPs well aware of their views on Community policy. National interest groups, such as environmentalists, have also become increasingly efficient in feeding their wishes into EC policy-making and implementation processes, often appointing people with specialist EC responsibilities who form part of the growing mass of lobbyists in Brussels. In addition, pressure groups organized on a European scale have flourished. There are now some 500 or more 'Euro-groups' including the powerful COPA (representing farmers), the UNICE (employers), ETUC (trade unions), CEEP (public enterprises), EEB (environment), and BEUC (consumers). These groups often play an influential role, with the Commission seeking their views before drawing up policy proposals. Indeed, the UNICE, the ETUC and the CEEP are formally recognized by the Community as 'social partners' with a special role to play in EC affairs (see Chapter 6). This 'social partner' arrangement with European organizations representing employers, employees and public enterprises contains a strong hint of the 'corporate state' ideology identified above. Thus, democratic-pluralist and Marxist models direct us to ask whether some groups have significantly more influence than others in the shaping of the Community's major contours.

Clearly, those of a Marxist persuasion would have no hesitation in identifying a dominant role for capital interests. It has been recently noted, albeit with qualifications, that '...the Treaty of Rome with its emphasis on growth, competition and economies of scale...can be seen as a manifesto for capital' (Williams 1991: 135). A major critique of the EC from this perspective came in Stuart Holland's *Uncommon Market* (Holland 1980). He criticized the assumptions of the liberal economic theory underpinning the Community's 'common market' development strategy . First, the belief that free movement of economic factors across national borders would be to the long-term benefit of all countries, regions and social classes was strongly challenged. Supported by a vast body of research on the development of regional inequalities (Holland 1976), he pointed to the tendency for firms to locate towards the centre of their market area and the losses this implied for the more peripheral parts of the developing Common Market:

> But the market of the Community is essentially a capitalist market, uncommon and unequal in the record of who gains what, where, why and when. Its mechanisms have already

disintegrated major industries and regions in the Community, and threaten to realise an inner and outer Europe of rich and poor countries. And in part, such disintegration is the result of the dominance of liberal capitalist policies which, for many federalists – because they are enshrined in the Treaties – have the status and relevance of the ark of the Community covenant. (Holland 1980:8)

According to Holland, multinational corporations enjoy a preeminent role in moulding patterns of socio-economic welfare in the Community's pluralistic but unequal society. Whether of USA, Japanese or European origin, their importance has been growing steadily in the post-war era along with their ability to influence national and EC policy. Their importance as sources of investment and employment has given them enormous political power which, in Holland's view, they use to strengthen the economic dimension (the common market) of the moves towards European unity at the expense of any would-be social dimension. The democratic-pluralist aspects of Community institutions, notably a weak European Parliament, are seen by Holland as a 'fig-leaf of democracy', hiding a real picture of 'centralization of power in the hands of big business and bureaucracies operating in their interest' (Holland 1980: 7).

In what remains a stimulating critique, Holland does not dispute the international and even social idealism of many promoting the European idea. They had not embraced the liberal common-market philosophy underpinning the Treaty of Rome to pursue narrow capitalist ends. With European political union as their ultimate goal, they accepted economic liberalism as the best means of generating social welfare for the greatest number, an essential part of political pluralism and individual freedom (the right to own property, set up private enterprises, etc), and an effective means of breaking down national barriers and creating transnational European linkages. For example, in line with 'spill-over' theory, a common market would lead to European companies and European unions, as well as European interest groups and associations of many kinds in an open democratic European political union.

Holland, and others on the Left, clearly found this vision too optimistic, particularly as recession halted the economic boom associated with the EEC's first decade and a half of existence. They criticized what they saw as the 'negative' integration theory embedded in the founding Treaties and lamented the lack of more a 'positive' strategy for the Community's development. In other words:

> ...by drawing on the prevailing ideology of liberal capitalism, the Treaties and the Commission are mainly concerned with preventing abuses to competition and the market mechanism rather than with providing a framework for joint intervention to achieve what the market itself cannot do. (Holland 1980: 10)

In this perspective, 'negative' integration involved the knocking down of national barriers to freedom of movement for goods, persons, services and capital, whilst 'positive' integration required governmental intervention at EC level to produce public policies able to tackle the problems of unemployment, regional disparities or whatever that stubbornly persisted in the Common Market. It was a classic 'Right versus Left' argument. In Holland's view, the negative integration approach favoured by the Right was gaining in strength in a bureaucratic Community dominated by the power of private big business. Thus, public power of the sort springing from democratically elected national parliaments was being pushed increasingly to one side as decision-making focused increasingly on restricted interchanges between national governments in the Council of Ministers and an unelected Commission imbued with a liberal capitalist ideology. Holland wanted the Community to develop a more interventionist strategy of integration with positive policies for employment, regional investment and industrial regeneration.

The validity of Holland's thesis could be debated at length. Clearly, the growing power of the multinationals and an undoubted emphasis given to the 'negative' liberal economic aspects of integration cannot be denied. Nevertheless, social objectives have always been present in EC affairs along with some potential for action. Indeed, 'positive' interventionist EC policies have, at times, been pursued by some powerful forces. For example, well organized politically to press their interests at all levels in Community affairs, EC farmers have long proved able to maintain an extremely interventionist Common Agricultural

Policy which still absorbs the bulk of the Community budget and contains a strong element of social policy within it (Chapter 5). It has resisted the demands of those (not least on the British Left!) who wanted to apply more liberal economic principles to agriculture in order to produce cheaper food for consumers. Such demands, emanating from dominantly urban-based interests, were deaf to arguments that small farmers needed a substantial measure of market protection to avoid severe social and environmental disruption of rural areas. In the long run, however, it can be argued that the ability of the declining numbers of small farmers to exert influence in the EC's pluralistic system is fading as the dominating interests of multinationals and the urban masses (freer trade and cheaper food) assert themselves. Also agriculture can be seen as an atypical special case; the fact that it has been absorbing between two-thirds and three-quarters of the EC's budget over the last thirty years underlines the lack of 'positive' interventionist integration in other policy areas. But the case of the CAP, as well as that of the CFP (see above) warns against excessively simple classifications of the EC as a 'capitalist club'. Furthermore, the fact that some opposition to Community policies also comes from business interests on the nationalist Right of the political spectrum – fearful of increased competition as national markets are opened up – encourages further caution in formulating simple theoretical generalizations.

However, whatever reservations Holland's thesis might attract, its theoretical formulations put the spotlight on a question of central relevance to this book, namely: are political efforts to build a single market more effective than those aimed at constructing a more social Europe? Theories emanating from left-wing critics lead us to expect such an outcome. On the other hand, many on the Right, not least in Britain, have claimed to detect a prevailing interventionist consensus in EC affairs, with the Commission under the corporate influence of large socialist parties and organized labour. What evidence is there that such a prevailing ideology has built a social European edifice of ever greater proportions? Or, on the contrary, have demands for social policies to complement a 'Businessman's Europe' floundered in ineffectual parliamentary debate, received mere gestures from those in power, and stagnated in a pluralist mass because there is no coherent electoral, party political or trade union force to give them sufficient weight? If the economic side of the Community's development is being favoured by the '1992' project at the expense of social objectives, is there any indication that potential losers in this process are triggering off 'spillover' reactions which will build a single social market rather than one closer to a purely free-market model? This book does not pretend to answer these questions in definitive fashion, but it does invite the reader to bear them in mind throughout the following chapters and will attempt to draw some conclusions at the end of them.

2. The Economic Rationale of a Single European Market

The under-performance of the EC economy compared to its Japanese and American counterparts was the major stimulus behind the economic reforms embodied in the SEA. The productivity disadvantage arising out of the costs imposed by a fragmented and 'uncommon market', the so-called 'non-Europe', was perceived to be restricting the full potential of the European economy. Only by harnessing the economic advantages inherent within a single internal market could this productivity disadvantage be changed, allowing the EC to compete effectively in the world economy. As Mrs Thatcher argued in her speech of 20 September 1988 to the College of Europe, Bruges:

> By getting rid of barriers, by making it possible for companies to operate on a Europe-wide scale, we can best compete with the United States, Japan and other new economic powers emerging in Asia and elsewhere. (Thatcher 1988: 6)

Undoubtedly, the fragmented nature of the Community market is the major factor making European business less competitive. In terms of overall population size, no individual Member State of the EC can match the size of Japan or the USA (Fig 2.1). Even Germany, with 79 million inhabitants in 1990, is approximately half the size of Japan. Similarly, the EC lags well behind the USA and Japan in respect of Gross Domestic Product (GDP) per head

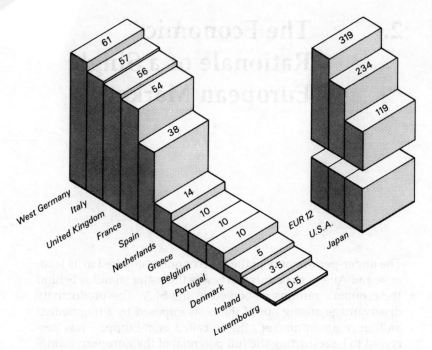

Figure 2.1 The population of EC Member States, Japan and the USA, 1988 (in millions), (*Source:* Eurostat, 1989).

of population. As Fig 2.2 illustrates, the GDP per head of population in the USA and Japan was at least 25 per cent higher than that existing in the Community. Whilst the overall GDP figure for the EC conceals a considerable diversity amongst the 12 separate Community economies, it nonetheless reflects poorly on the economic vitality and levels of integration existing in the EC economy (Commission 1988a). Collectively however, the EC, having 323 million inhabitants in 1987, constitutes the largest market in the industrialized world and has a combined GDP of ECU 3,669 billion, compared with ECU 3,869 billion for the USA and ECU 2,058 billion for Japan. Although each individual Member State is relatively weak compared to the two major trading blocs, the EC as a whole is a great trading bloc in its own right, equal in size to any other. Whilst this aggregation of pop-

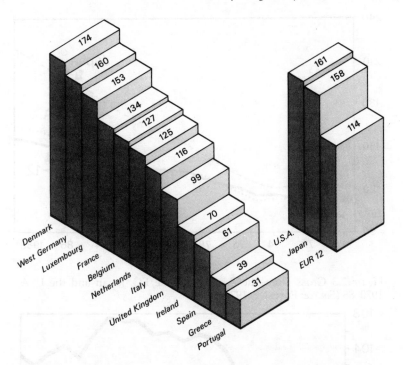

Figure 2.2 Gross Domestic Product per head of population in EC Member States, Japan and the USA, 1987 (ECU 100), (*Source:* Eurostat, 1989).

ulation and GDP data highlights the potential economic power of the Community, it is only meaningful if a genuine internal market exists in a situation where most 'artificial' impediments to the free movement of goods, people and services have been eliminated.

If this rather simple and static representation of relative economic well-being represented the whole picture, then the economic problems facing the EC would appear more manageable and the drive towards a SEM would probably be lessened. Unfortunately, the Community economy has been experiencing a long-term reduction in its strength relative to both Japan and the USA. Although most of the western World experienced a slow pace of growth in the 1970s and early 1980s, with an associated rise in the levels of unemployed and inflation, the European economy fared

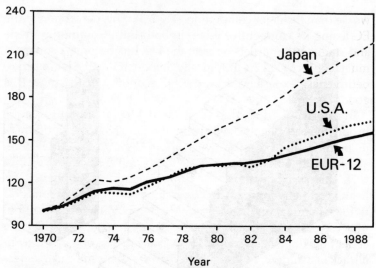

Figure 2.3 Gross Domestic Product for the EC, Japan and the USA, 1970–88 (*Source:* Eurostat, 1975–90).

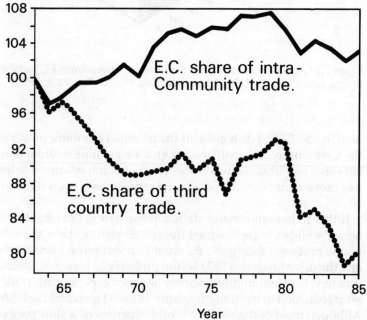

Figure 2.4 Shares of world market of EC exports of industrial goods (*Source:* Commission, 1988a).

worse than its major competitors (Fig 2.3). This perception of the EC losing its competitive edge, in both intra-Community trade and trade with markets outside the EC, has become a source of much concern. Fig 2.4 graphically demonstrates the loss of competitiveness experienced by the EC economy in the industrial goods sector.

In external markets, the EC is rapidly losing ground to more productive suppliers. Collectively, the EC's share of world trade in manufactured goods, which in 1973 stood at 45 per cent, amounted to only 36 per cent in 1985 (Curzon Price 1988). Since 1978 this situation has been compounded by Member States losing competiveness in their own domestic markets. From 1973 to 1985, manufactured goods imported from outside the Community increased by 4.4 percentage points, representing 13.1 per cent of the domestic demand for manufactured goods. This overall lack of competitiveness in both the EC's domestic and overseas markets conceals widely different situations according to industrial sector. When the competitiveness of different industrial sectors is calculated according to the level of value added (revenues received less the cost of brought in raw materials, services and components), the Community has an advantage over the USA in a number of sectors: food products, beverages, leather, clothing, textiles, tobacco, steel products and metalliferous ores (Emerson 1988). However, these are industrial activities experiencing weak or moderate demand with little prospect for enhanced growth. Furthermore, they are also industries adversely affected by downturns in the business cycle. In those industries where demand is greatest, data-processing, office automation, electrical, electronic and precision instruments, the Community lags behind the USA and is at a level comparable with Japan. In Japan, however, high-demand industries are expanding at a rate far greater than that being experienced in the EC. Between 1979 and 1985, the proportion of industries classified as experiencing high demand increased by 3 per cent a year in the Community, compared to 17.1 per cent in Japan. These high-demand industries are dominated by a high technological input together with a dependence on research and development (R&D). As a consequence, the Community's industrial base is concentrated upon economic sectors which have a secularly moderate or weak demand.

The varying levels of performance in different sectors of the Community economy reflect the differences in productivity rates, as measured by an index of 'man-hours' divided by an index of output for a sector. Using the afore-mentioned formula and a system based on the use of purchasing power parities developed by Mathis and Mazier (1979), the Commission developed a method of comparing productivity levels for a number of industrial sectors in different countries. This measure of productivity (Table 2.1) highlights variations in efficiency rates amongst the largest

Table 2.1 Level of productivity in the United Kingdom, France, Germany, the United States and Japan (value-added per employee in specific purchasing power parities) – 1985 (USA = 100)

	UK	F	D	USA	Japan
Strong demand sectors					
Electrical and electronic goods	28	47	43	100	236
Office and data-processing machines	37	43	45	100	94
Chemical and pharmaceutical products	54	79	75	100	119
Moderate demand sectors					
Transport equipment	23	54	60	100	95
Food, beverages, tobacco	56	73	47	100	37
Paper and printing products	43	67	76	100	89
Industrial and agricultural machinery	20	49	46	100	103
Weak demand sectors					
Metal products	38	60	54	100	143
Ferrous and non-ferrous ores and metals (steel)	66	72	92	100	149
Textiles, leather, clothing	59	62	71	100	53
Non-metallic minerals (construction materials)	40	64	71	100	43
Total	42	65	65	100	100

Source: Commission, 1988a.

Community countries, Japan and the USA. These results re-emphasize the Community's lack of competitiveness in the high technology sector and other areas of greatest demand. Variations in productivity levels are an essential basis for trade. The Community's reduced competitiveness in the strong demand areas has not only resulted in a loss in foreign market share generally, it has also caused a substantial increase in the levels of import penetration within the European domestic market. Again, the pattern of import penetration correlates with the differing productivity rates achieved by various sectors of industry. Fig 2.5

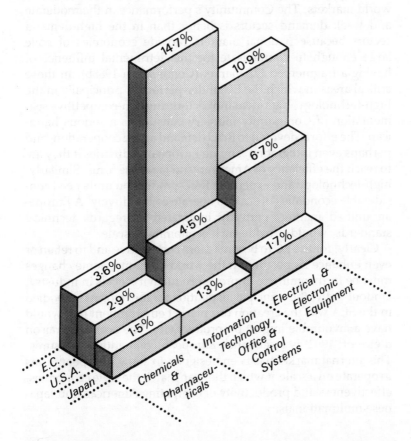

Figure 2.5 Import penetration of EC, Japanese and US markets for selected products (*Source:* Commission, 1988a).

graphically illustrates that for the dynamic and high value-added sectors, the level of import penetration in the Community is far greater than in either the USA or Japan. The high level of import penetration in the information technology and control system sector is particularly striking. Between 1979 and 1983, import penetration in this sector rose by 34 per cent.

If it is an accepted truth that productivity differences are the essential basis for trade, and the law of comparative advantage favours economies with the lowest costs and highest productivity, then the EC economy has to change radically its overall efficiency in the high-demand areas if it is to be competitive in world markets. The Community's performance in the moderate and weak demand sectors is better than in the high-demand sectors because national markets provide economies of scale large enough to compensate for the detrimental influence of having a fragmented EC market (Commission 1988b). In those critical areas in which the EC under-performs, principally in the high-technology, high-demand sectors, the non-competitive segmentation of Community industry constitutes a serious handicap. The efforts devoted to R&D demand active cooperation, and perhaps even integration, among European industries if they are to reach the efficiency of American and Japanese firms. Similarly, high-technology and expensive R&D production units need considerable economies of scale to operate competitively. A European unified market, perfectly integrated as regards technical standards, would provide such economies of scale.

Clearly, for the EC to become more competitive and to retain or even enhance its position in the world economy, some changes must be forthcoming to improve productivity levels in industry. Undoubtedly, the principal inspiration for the reforms embodied in the SEA was the creation of a market environment that would have a favourable impact on productivity. The economic raison d'être of '1992' is to enhance European competitive pressures. The internal market has been designed to allow European firms to operate on a scale at which they can match the scale economies, effectiveness and productivity of competing American and Japanese multinationals.

THE FRAGMENTATION OF THE COMMUNITY ECONOMY

As outlined in Chapter 1, creating an internal common market is not a new idea. The cornerstone of the Treaty of Rome was to establish a European tariff-free customs union. According to the Rome Treaty, the activities of the Community shall include:

> the elimination, as between member states, of customs duties and quantitative restrictions in regard to the import and export of goods, as well as other measures having equivalent effect.

and:

> the abolition, as between member states, of obstacles to freedom of movement for persons, services and capital. (HMSO 1967: 3)

In accordance with the timetable provided by the Treaty of Rome, the original six Member States were given a twelve-year transitional period for the achievement of a full customs union. The first internal tariff cuts took place in 1959 and by 1st July 1968 all tariffs had been abolished between them, and the Common Customs Tariff had been implemented. The creation of the common market, well ahead of schedule, had a dramatic impact upon the levels of intra-Community trade. By 1969, trade between Community countries was approximately 50 per cent greater than if no Community customs union had existed. Furthermore, the competitive pressures released into the market place increased the efficiency of production methods, which in turn led to lower costs. There is no doubt that the customs union created by the Treaty of Rome allowed for a more rational use of resources, leading to welfare gains throughout the whole Community. Between 1957 and 1972, the average yearly growth of Community GNP was 5.7 per cent, and per capita income rose by approximately 4.5 per cent per annum.

Despite the EC's impressive track record up to 1972, the Community's goal of achieving a common internal market based upon Community-wide production, supply and demand has not been achieved. There are many other barriers, apart from tariffs and quotas, that restrict the free flow of goods and result in a fragmented market. The Treaty of Rome required not only the abolition of tariffs and quotas but the elimination of 'all measures having equivalent effect'. However, during the 1970s and early 1980s, the drive to dismantle barriers affecting intra-EC trade slowed down in the face of world-wide recession. Member States tried to protect their own domestic industries by lessening the competitive pressures from elsewhere, whether from the EC, Japan or America. Individual Member States adopted national solutions to solve the problems presented by the international economic recession of the 1970s and early 1980s. These national policies were based upon protectionist measures designed to favour national suppliers. Consequently barriers to the free movement of goods were erected in the form of non-tariff barriers, which often took the form of national regulations and safety standards. The effect of these non-tariff barriers, which were by design incompatible with those of neighbouring EC states, was seriously to inhibit intra-Community trade. Member States were therefore able to exploit the incomplete nature of the EC market. During the 1970s non-tariff barriers, which were originally perceived to be of minor importance compared to tariff and quota restrictions, multiplied and fragmented the Community economy into twelve separate markets. According to Pelkmans and Winters (1988), the Community's failure to complete its common market and ensure the free movement of the factors of production was a result of two competing trends: widening and enlargement. Throughout the 1970s much political attention was focused upon widening the Community's sphere of influence to incorporate issues other than those explicitly mentioned in the Treaty of Rome. The construction and implementation of a regional policy, an environmental policy and many other common policies drew attention away from the structural faults in the Community's internal market. Similarly, the Community's political attention was focused on three enlargements, which over a period of thirteen years saw membership double from the original six to the present twelve (Fig 2.6). The Community's success at enlarging and widening took place at the direct expense of deepening. The process of completing the internal market had become bogged down in the long and slow process of enacting harmonization policies designed to remove impediments to free trade. Over the

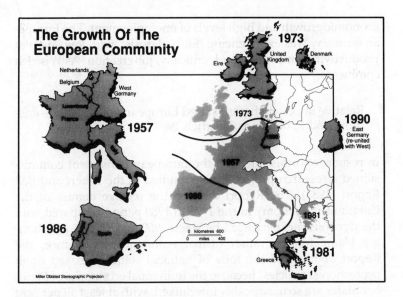

Figure 2.6 The growth of the European Community, 1957–90.

past 30 years the harmonization approach has been the cornerstone of Community action designed to strengthen the internal market. The results were spectacularly disappointing. It took the Council of Ministers six years to agree on the first directive harmonizing the noise level of lawnmowers and in the 18 years to 1985, harmonization had succeeded in producing just 177 Directives.

This unsatisfactory position in the development of the Community market was highlighted when Member States began increasingly to recognize the inadequacy of nationally oriented protectionist policies designed to fight an international economic recession. Indeed, the limited success of any economic policy enacted exclusively at the domestic national level was recognized. Following the election of François Mitterrand to the Presidency of France in 1981, France attempted an expansionary policy that quickly faded in the face of international economic pressure on the franc, a balance of payments crisis and high inflation. Other Community states, determined not to create the inflationary trends experienced in the 1970s, experienced slow economic growth and high levels of unemployment. The European economy was experiencing 'Eurosclerosis', with low levels of productivity, innovation and, critically, job creation. As Wistrich comments:

> Relative impoverishment stared Europe in the face and something had to be done. (Wistrich 1989: 3)

In response to this dilemma the European Parliament commissioned a research project which resulted in the Albert and Ball Report (1983). The Report detailed the relative demise of the Community economy in the 1973 to 1980 period compared with the dynamism experienced between 1960 and 1973. Apportioning blame for the rather dismal economic performance, the Report highlighted the folly of national solutions based upon protectionist policies. Because the individual economies of Member States are so inextricably interlinked, with at least 50 per cent of exports being destined for the EC market, national solutions were a manifestly inadequate solution to an international economic problem. Non-tariff barriers and subsidising loss-making firms, both having the equivalent effect of a tariff, fragmented the market and inhibited intra-Community trade. Furthermore, the uncoordinated nature of the national policies enacted by Member States increased the segmented nature of the Community market. Overall therefore, the Community's raison d'être was falling apart, with a manifestly un-common market and an increasing division between those states prepared to take Europe one stage further and those wishing to keep controls within the realms of national sovereignty. As Curzon Price states:

> Macro-economic demand management policies suddenly failed as inflation and unemployment moved in the same direction – rapidly upwards

and:

> This spelled disaster for economic integration in Europe… The Common Market was in fact dead and had degenerated into a mere preferential trading zone. (Curzon Price 1988: 11)

COMPLETING THE INTERNAL MARKET

The causes of 'Eurosclerosis' were therefore identified as the barriers to the free movement of the factors of production (land, labour, capital and trade). As the recession had caused many Community states to adopt policies based upon free-market principles, principally privatization, deregulation and the cutting of public expenditure, the importance of having a single internal market, to complement the market-oriented national policies, was increasingly acknowledged. In the early 1980s, European Community Governments recognized that if the Community economy was to regain its competitive position in the world economy, all restrictions to trade had to be abolished and, most critically, common policies had to replace the uncoordinated actions of individual countries. At the European Council meeting held at Copenhagen, December 1982, the Heads of Government pledged themselves to reinforcing the internal market. At subsequent Council meetings in Fontainebleau, Dublin and Brussels in 1984/5, the pledge was repeated and the SEM itemized as a priority area.

This gave the newly appointed Commission, under the presidency of Jacques Delors, the impetus to review attempts to introduce a genuine single internal market. The vice-president of the Commission, Lord Cockfield, seized the opportunities presented by the previous Council meetings and produced a White Paper entitled *Completing the internal market* (Commission 1985a). The 1985 White Paper outlined a programme of legislative measures deemed necessary to achieve a single integrated market. It was concerned primarily with the technical difficulties and solutions of integrating the economies of Member States. The White Paper did not attempt to address every possible issue affecting the integration of the economies of Member States. For example, it did not directly address the issues of industrial research or, most crucially, the European Monetary System (EMS). *Completing the internal market* proposed no less than 300 legislative items, together with a strict timetable, needed to ensure the removal of non-tariff barriers. The introduction to Lord Cockfield's White Paper takes the form of an extract taken from the Commission's presentation to the European Parliament on 6 March 1985. This extract clearly defines the Commission's primary goal:

Unifying this market (of 320 million) presupposes that Member States will agree on the abolition of barriers of all kinds, harmonization of rules, approximation of legislation and tax structures, strengthening of monetary cooperation and the necessary flanking measures to encourage firms to work together.... The Commission will be asking the European Council to pledge itself to completion of a fully unified internal market by 1992 and to approve the necessary programme together with a realistic and binding timetable. (Commission 1984: 4)

The White Paper identifies three aspects to the overall economic objective of completing the internal market:

1. The welding together of the twelve individual markets of the Member States into one single market of 320 million;
2. ensuring that this single market is also an expanding market;
3. to this end, ensuring that the market is flexible so that resources, both of people and materials, and of capital and investment, flow into the areas of greatest economic advantage.

Whilst the actual detail of the White Paper is extremely complex and technical, reflecting Lord Cockfield's background as a tax expert, it is at the same time a simple and highly practical stratagem to define and complete the SEM. The tactic adopted by the Commission to gain support from Member States for the White Paper was shrewd. By presenting the 300 proposals as purely technical matters to be executed in order to fulfil the ideas proposed by successive Council meetings, the Commission created a political situation whereby it gained the support of all twelve member states.

THE SINGLE EUROPEAN ACT

Lord Cockfield's White Paper was approved by the Heads of Governments at the Milan EC Council meeting in June 1985. However, the Milan meeting was the scene of a bitter dispute over what the EC should do to enforce the proposals identified by the White Paper. Whilst Member States could agree to unite behind the guiding principles of Lord Cockfield's Paper, there was a considerable diversity of opinion as to what legislation was needed to translate these principles into practice. This diversity of opinion is based upon a conflict of perception as regards the economic rationale of '1992'. Some Member States consider the logic of an integrated market as a step inextricably linked to full European economic and political union whereas others regard it as a step designed to enhance the free-trading conditions of the European economy. The United Kingdom and Denmark saw no reason why the SEA should amend the Treaty of Rome and considered the proposed increase in the use of majority voting in the Council of Ministers with suspicion. Indeed, Mrs Thatcher argued for a 'gentlemen's agreement', similar to the Luxembourg Compromise of 1966, to overcome the defects inherent in the Community decision-making processes (Owen, Dynes 1989). Furthermore, the United Kingdom and Denmark were ideologically committed to 'deepening' the Community with the sole aid of free-market principles. Anything that went beyond enforcing the free movement of goods, people, capital and services was considered to be interfering in the market place or an infringement on national sovereignty. Most other member states wanted the SEA to amend the Treaty of Rome into an Act of European Union, incorporating an expanded secretariat to oversee a new EC foreign policy division. They argued that the internal market and its associated benefits would not materialize if it was considered to be independent and separate from European union. The Milan Council meeting ended as it has started, in division. However the Milan meeting did establish, but only after Mrs Thatcher had been outvoted, an Inter-Governmental Conference (IGC) to examine outstanding issues in more detail. If it thought necessary, the IGC was to recommend amendments to the original treaties (ECSC, Euratom, EEC). By the time the next Council meeting was convened in Luxembourg in December 1985, most of the really contentious issues had been resolved by the IGC. The Heads of Governments agreed that the '1992' programme should emphasize free-market principles, particularly those of competition and deregulation. However, the Luxembourg meeting also agreed to amend the original treaties so as to enable the legislative programme to be more easily implemented and to

widen the activities of the EC. The Luxembourg meeting therefore succeeded in negotiating the terms of the SEA (Commission
1986a) which, after ratification, came into force on 1st July 1987.

The SEA was a far-reaching and reforming Act covering much
more than the specific measures needed to complete the SEM.
The Act dealt with issues relating to the environment, research,
technological development and foreign policy. Although the
Community had been active in these areas throughout the early
1980s, they are not specifically mentioned in the original treaties.
Overall the SEA covered three main areas. The first was concerned with policy objectives necessary to complete the SEM. The
second extended the original Treaties to widen the Community's
responsibilities and the third reformed the decision-making and
legislative process to ease the passage of bills necessary to complete the internal market. The remaining section of the present
chapter briefly outlines the economic justification associated with
the first aim: that of establishing throughout the Community, by
31 December 1992, an area without internal frontiers in which the
free movement of goods, services, persons and capital is
ensured. The issues surrounding the establishment of the internal market are analysed in more detail, and the task of removing
the barriers and the subsequent impact on the European economy are examined in chapters 3 and 4.

THE 'COSTS OF NON-EUROPE'

The 'costs of non-Europe', the term often used to denote the
inefficiencies of a segmented Community economy, are in theory
equal to the benefits of completing the SEM. The Commission of
the EC has spent a considerable amount of time and money in
trying to quantify the benefits of a SEM. The economic analysis
produced, both theoretical and empirical, suggests the Community can expect considerable welfare gains arising out of the '1992'
programme. The largest and most thorough study of the costs of
non-Europe, funded under the stewardship of Paulo Cecchini,
concludes that the SEM could:

> ...propel Europe onto the blustery world stage in the 1990s in a
> position of competitive strength and on an upward trajectory
> of economic growth into the next century. Such additional

growth, following the progressive impact of EC market integration, could, in the space of a few years, put between four and five percentage points on the Community's domestic product. (Cecchini 1988: XVII)

Interestingly, the results of the Cecchini Report were published in 1988, almost 12 months after the signing of the Single European Act and three years after Lord Cockfield's White Paper. Whilst the Report supported the economic rationale behind the drive to create a SEM, it did not provide the initial stimulus for the '1992' programme. The Cecchini Report described its task as an 'unprecedented research programme' to 'provide a solid body of scientifically-assembled evidence as a means of judging the extent of market fragmentation'. However, the objectivity of the Cecchini Report has been questioned, particularly in its assessment of the overall benefits likely to experienced by the EC economy. In many ways the Report is similar to the Club of Rome's 'Limits to Growth' (Meadows 1972), in its selective use of micro-economic data to justify global, or in this case supranational, policies. This issue will be examined in more detail in Chapter 4.

Both the Commission and Cecchini consider the potential benefits of the SEM to be a product of two separate but interrelated economic processes. First, and the starting point of the whole process of economic gain, is the immediate and direct economic benefit derived from the removal of all barriers to the free movement of the factors of production. By dismantling non-tariff barriers to free trade, the costs of production will be reduced. In other words, the removal of non-tariff barriers will reduce the price of traded goods and stimulate demand. Secondly, economic benefits will arise from the indirect effect on production and efficiency levels. The removal of non-tariff barriers will then enhance the competitive pressures within the market place which, according to Cecchini, will produce long-term gains in excess of those experienced in the short term. Essentially, a distinction can be made between the static and dynamic effects of market opening measures. In the short term, removing non-tariff barriers will reduce the price of traded goods and increase demand. The removal of barriers that impose costs on intra-Community trading transactions will therefore have a static one-off effect of reducing costs. This static short term effect is, further-more, relatively easy to quantify. Internal market barriers impose a direct cost on European businesses which can be measured through microeconomic and sectoral studies together with ques-tionnaire surveys. Analytically, the direct benefits of completing the SEM will be the same as the direct costs of non-tariff barriers (Emerson 1988). A large section of the Cecchini Report was con-cerned with detailed and in-depth studies into these immediate costs. However the Cecchini Report and the Commission antici-pate the release of existing non-tariff constraints will precipitate a supply-side shock to the European economy. In the medium to long term, such a supply-side shock is expected to lead to the indirect effects of increased competition, productivity and effi-ciency. As the Cecchini Report states:

> The name of the shock is European market integration. Costs will be down. Prices will follow as business, under the pres-sure of new rivals, on previously protected markets, is forced to develop fresh responses to a novel and permanently chang-ing situation. (Cecchini 1988: XIX)

Based upon the findings of the Cecchini Report, the Commission expects increased competition to precipitate a restructuring proc-ess and a widespread lowering of the costs and prices of total production. Critically, the restructuring process depends on increased competition introducing economies of scale which pro-duce redundancies in those industries at present protected by non-tariff barriers. The economic gains to be derived from enhanced competitive pressures depend upon the excess released resources being effectively redeployed productively in areas of the economy experiencing high demand. The Commis-sion admits that until redundant workers are productively re-employed, which will take time as the economy adjusts to a new competitive environment, there will be unemployment costs to be counted against the benefits. It is anticipated that the benefits arising from the SEM will be progressively larger as the positive feedback, or so-called 'virtuous circle', of competition becomes fully operational. The quantification of the welfare benefits aris-ing out of the enhanced competitive environment produced as a result of removing the non-tariff barriers is the most contentious issue arising from the Cecchini Report, and is examined in detail in Chapter 4. Whilst an exact quantification of the long-term economic gains is perhaps impossible, given the complexity of the market and the impossibility of predicting business reaction, there are widely differing views as to whether the overall result will be positive or negative. There is a fear, expressed vociferously by the left, that whilst the mobility of capital and labour will result in a more efficient allocation of the factors of production, the beneficiaries of such economic gains will be spread unevenly throughout the Community, both spatially and structurally. In order to elaborate on these issues in more detail it is first necessary to go back to the starting point of the SEM programme and examine how non-tariff barriers are going to be removed and what the immediate and direct economic benefit is likely to be.

3.   Removing the Barriers

The removal of non-tariff barriers is the essential starting point for the SEM programme. The successful elimination of all impediments prohibiting the free flow of the factors of production is the critical enabling mechanism needed to stimulate the European economy. This chapter looks at the nature and purpose of the existing non-tariff barriers and examines the mechanisms and policies being adopted by the Community to eliminate them. Non-tariff barriers which segment the Community economy have been categorized by the Commission into three separate types:

1. physical barriers
2. technical barriers
3. fiscal barriers.

Although the present chapter goes on to examine the character and economic impact of removing these barriers, it is important to recognize that the three categories of barriers are by no means distinct and separate. They are interlinked to such an extent that it is in many ways too simplistic to view each category individually. For example, physical barriers have in the past been retained in order to collect the duties levied as a result of differing fiscal policies. A failure to remove the fiscal barrier imposed as a result of differing VAT rates would inevitably make the removal of physical barriers much more difficult. Nonetheless, the three categories of barriers adopted by both the Commission and Paulo Cecchini (1988) are a useful starting point for evaluating the direct economic benefits of achieving an integrated European market.

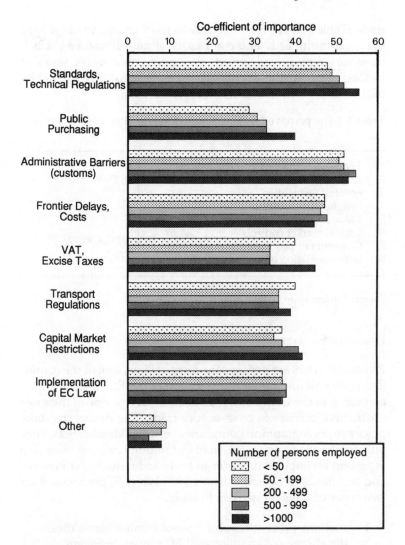

Figure 3.1 The perceived seriousness of different categories of barriers according to size of company (*Source:* Commission, 1988a).

In order to assess the economic significance various non-tariff barriers have on the economic segmentation of the EC economy, the Commission instigated a Community-wide survey of over 20,000 European enterprises. The survey ranked the perceived seriousness of different non-tariff barriers to intra-Community trade (Table 3.1; Fig 3.1). The results from this survey highlight the great multiplicity and complexity of market barriers, which have varying economic effects dependent on a whole series of factors, involving the size of enterprise, its nationality and industrial sector.

Table 3.1 The perceived seriousness of different categories of barriers

1. Technical standards and regulations	⎤
2. Administrative barriers	⎬ approx. equal
3. Frontier formalities	⎦
4. Freight transport regulations	
5. Value added tax differences	⎤
6. Capital market controls	⎬ approx. equal
7. Government procurement restrictions	
8. Implementation of Community law	⎦

Source: Commission, 1988a: 44.

PHYSICAL BARRIERS

Physical barriers are perhaps the most obvious sign of the continued economic and political dislocation of the EC. They are also, according to the Commission's business survey, one of the most obstructive barriers to cross-border trade. The delays that take place at the geographical boundaries between Member States not only inhibit the free movement of Community citizens, they also represent an important barrier to trade and industry, commerce and business. The Commission's 1985 White Paper focused on two types of physical barriers to trade:

1. customs procedures and general frontier formalities
2. the absence of an integrated EC transport system.

Again these two types of physical barriers are interlinked as any administrative delay inevitably increases total transport costs. In 1985 intra-Community trade in goods amounted to approximately ECU 500 billion, equal to around 14 per cent of the Community GDP. The Commission (1988a) estimated that in 1985 administrative delays at frontier posts represented approximately 5 per cent of total transport costs. Simply put, it was costing the Community economy ECU 8 billion per annum. Frontier costs involve not only those directly linked to the burden of satisfying administrative controls, but also the costs of maintaining these controls. For example, in 1985 the EC had 45,000 full-time jobs involved in customs clearing. However, the largest cost burden was associated with administrative delays which, in 1985, totalled ECU 7.5 billion, corresponding to 1.5 per cent of the total value of internal Community trade. Moreover, Cecchini's (1988) survey on the costs of frontier formalities (based in six EC Member States: France, Britain, Belgium, Germany, Italy and the Netherlands) estimates that as a result of administrative formalities, company turnover is between ECU 4.5 to 15 billion less than it should be (Table 3.2). Illustrating the extent and cost penalty of frontier delays, the Commission quotes the now notorious example of two 750-mile truck trips. On one of the trips a truck drives from London to Milan and takes, excluding the time lost in crossing the Channel, 58 hours. The other trip, a comparable journey within the United Kingdom, takes only 36 hours. This suggests that intra-Community delays can amount to increasing overall transport costs by over a half.

Table 3.2 The cost of administrative formalities and border controls

ECU millions	Costs
7,500	administration
415 – 830	delays
4,500 – 15,000	business foregone
500 – 1,000	government spending* on intra-EC customs controls

* On 6-country basis: Belgium, France, Germany, Italy, The Netherlands, UK.

Source: Cecchini, 1988:6.

Whilst the costs imposed as a result of physical barriers are considerable, the importance attached to these costs varies according to company size. According to a Commission survey (Nerb 1988), the cost burden imposed as a result of physical barriers and associated compliance costs was far greater for small- and medium-sized enterprises. Costs also vary according to the intra-Community border being crossed. There are considerable discrepancies in the average costs per consignment, with Belgium and Italy representing two extremes. In the former case, partially as a result of the Benelux trade agreement, the costs of importing are around three times less than the import charge costs into Italy (Table 3.3). It is the Commission's central contention that physical barriers:

...impose an unnecessary burden on industry flowing from the delays, formalities, transport and handling charges, thus adding to costs and damaging competitiveness. (Commission 1985: 9)

Table 3.3 Administrative costs to firms per consignment (ECU)

	Imports	Exports
Belgium	26	34
Germany	42	79
France	92	87
Italy	130	205
The Netherlands	46	50
United Kingdom	75	49
Average	67	86

Source: Ernst and Whinney, 1988.

The purpose of customs procedures

Customs procedures are at present maintained for a number of reasons, the most important of which include:

1. Varying rates of Value Added Tax which are applied according to the destination principle (i.e. tax paid in the

country of sale) which necessitates border tax adjustments.
2. Road transport licences and quota restrictions are enforced at border controls.
3. Common Agricultural Policy compensatory amounts for certain agricultural produce are enacted at EC borders.
4. Variations in public health and safety standards necessitate health checks.
5. Bureaucratic formalities for statistical purposes.

Physical barriers are therefore maintained for legitimate reasons and are somewhat paradoxically reinforced by some Community policies that use internal frontier posts as a means of controlling common EC policies, such as on agriculture and steel. Nonetheless, the Commission's 1985 White Paper boldly states that:

> Our objective is not merely to simplify existing procedures, but to do away with frontier controls in their entirety. (Commission 1985a: 9)

In order for the Commission to eliminate internal frontier barriers and controls, the White Paper proposes a whole series of measures aimed at coordinating policies and approximating legislation. Notable achievements include the introduction of a uniform customs entry and transit document in January 1988. The Single Administrative Document (SAD) replaced a system where over 70 forms were used in the Community. Alongside SAD, a harmonized coding system was introduced in order to classify all EC trade. Notwithstanding these achievements, the Commission has to face a number of important obstacles in order to eliminate intra-Community border controls. For example, certain national protective measures do not fall within the Treaty of Rome. Security checks against terrorism and the illicit trade in goods are an important role for internal frontier posts. None of the aforementioned problems are unsurmountable, but the Commission needs to find alternative ways of tackling these difficulties in order to ensure that physical barriers are removed in their entirety.

TECHNICAL BARRIERS

Alongside physical barriers, technical regulations are rated by industrialists as one of the most important obstacles to intra-Community trade. In 1983 there were over 100,000 different technical specifications affecting intra-Community trade. Furthermore, technical regulations were proliferating at a rate of over 5,000 per annum (Colchester, Buchan 1990). Not only is the absolute number of technical regulations vast, but the field is constantly changing as a result of technological developments and increasing concerns for the environment and health and safety. The Commission regards the elimination of technical barriers as important as abolishing physical barriers (Commission 1985a). Indeed there is little point in removing obstacles at Community borders only to find the same obstacles being enforced within Member States.

There are three main types of technical barriers: national standards, national technical regulations and testing and certification procedures. All have an adverse impact on Community industries exploiting the full potential of the European economy. Furthermore, technical standards are particularly prevalent in the high-technology high-growth sectors, those areas of the economy the Commission has put great store in reviving as part of the '1992' process. Whilst national standards can have a beneficial impact in guaranteeing a minimum level of safety for the consumer and environment, they can also be used as a form of national protection against goods being imported from other Member States. Whether their impact is for good or bad, they fragment the Community market and inhibit Community industries from exploiting scale economies necessary to compete in the world economy. Removing these barriers is complicated by the diverse nature of the regulations which are operated and enforced in both the public and private sectors.

National technical regulations are perhaps the most obvious technical barrier. They are enacted by national parliaments in order to ensure minimum levels of standards in the areas of health, safety and the environment. However national standards, sometimes referred to as industry standards, often have the same barrier effect as technical regulations, despite their voluntary character. Private organizations, such as BSI (in Britain), DIN (in Germany) and AFNOR (in France), produce voluntary standards which are not legally binding but have a quasi-legal status because they are often adopted as reference standards by insurers, architects and government procurement

Table 3.4 Rank of importance of technical regulations to various industries

Rank order from the			Judgement of expert service of the Commission		
			Degree of importance		
			Great	Medium	Less
1.	Motor vehicles	68		X	
2.	Electrical engineering	66	X		
3.	Mechanical engineering	63	X		
4.	Chemicals, of which:	60			
	– pharmaceuticals		X		
	– other				X
5.	Non-metallic mineral products	56		X	
6.	Other transport equipment	55			X
7.	Food and tobacco	52	X		
8.	Leather	51			X
9.	Precision and medical equipment	50	X		
10.	Metal articles	50		X	
11.	Rubber products	50		X	
12.	Plastics	47			X
13	Wood and furniture	44			X
14.	Metals	41			X
15.	Office and data-processing machinery	41		X	
16.	Textiles	38			X
17.	Footwear and clothing	37			X
18.	Mineral oil refining	37			X
19.	Paper and printing	35			X
20.	Artificial fibres	31			X

Source: Commission 1988a: 51.

agencies. Finally, testing and certification procedures which are used to enforce technical regulations and register goods with the national standards institutes are, to a large extent, nationally based. In other words, one Member State will refuse to recognize the certification procedures enacted by other Member States. This can result in additional testing or even a barrier to market entry.

Despite the considerable importance attached to technical regulations by European companies, the Cecchini Report was unable to quantify their economic costs because of the complexity and the sector-specific nature of these barriers. A business survey commissioned for Cecchini's 'non-Europe' research did, however, ascertain for various industrial sectors how important the technical barriers were. Based on a survey of 11,000 business respondents throughout the Community, the survey was able to rank the importance of technical regulations to different manufacturing sectors (Table 3.4). Therefore, the costs to the European economy of technical barriers can only be outlined in a qualitative way. The profusion of different technical barriers increases company costs as a result of the unnecessary duplication in research and development costs, together with a loss of manufacturing efficiency associated with reduced economies of scale. Public authorities are also hampered by the associated duplication in the costs of testing and certification. Finally, the consumer pays as a result of the increased costs borne by industry. In order to remove these technical regulations, the Commission has developed a multi-dimensional strategy based upon three new policy instruments.

1. Mutual recognition

The Commission's aim is to establish throughout the Community the principle of mutual recognition, which results in any product that is lawfully manufactured in one Member State having access to all other Member States, subject to certain minimum safety standards. The principle of mutual recognition was established in the now famous ruling of the European Court of Justice in 1978, known as the Cassis de Dijon case. There then followed a whole series of further judgements that reinforced the principle of mutual recognition. One of the most celebrated examples was the German law on beer imports that prohibited beers brewed in other Member States on the grounds that they contained additives and therefore contravened German national 'purity laws'. At the same time, German breweries were producing beers for export with additives. The Court of Justice ruled that beers should not be prohibited on the grounds of purity laws and that the German Government had to recognize the principle of mutual recognition. As a consequence the German purity laws remain for those beers brewed and sold in Germany but, under mutual recognition, the market has been opened up to import additive beers, giving the consumer the right to choose. The principle of mutual recognition is the cornerstone of the new rules designed to remove technical barriers. Where the selective harmonization of regulations and standards is not considered essential from either a health/safety or an industrial point of view, immediate and full recognition of differing quality standards must be the rule. As such there is no obligation on the vendor to prove equivalence of a product produced according to the rules of the exporting state. Similarly, there is no obligation to submit such a product to certification procedures in the importing state.

Mutual recognition is but one, albeit the most important, weapon the Commission can now use to remove the impact of differing technical standards. However, governments can in a number of cases circumvent mutual recognition on the basis of Article 36 of the Treaty of Rome (HMSO 1967). This enables Member States to restrict, via technical regulations, trade in goods on the grounds of health and safety concerns. There is a general feeling amongst Member States that Article 36 is often used in a covert way to stop competitive entries into national markets. As a result, the Commission has elected in certain selected areas to adopt harmonization policies.

2. Selective harmonization

Article 100 of the Treaty of Rome enables the Council of Ministers to legislate for the approximation of Member States' laws that affect the functioning of the common market. This process is referred to as harmonization and has, in the past, been a notoriously bureaucratic, expensive and time-consuming process with little of real value being produced. Because of the unanimity required by the Council of Ministers, the practice of incorporating detailed and specific technical regulations to suit all twelve Member States led to considerable delays. However since 1985, with the prospect of majority voting under the SEA, the Commission has adopted a new approach to harmonization. Harmonization Directives now focus on 'codes of essential requirements' which establish a basic set of minimum standards. Having set the minimum standard, the Commission then leaves it to the manufacturers as to how best to satisfy these requirements. The new 'codes of requirements' are not exhaustively detailed Directives, they often cover broad product areas and have the advantage of harmonizing a wide number of products with limited product detail. Once a product manufactured in one Member State conforms to the essential requirements, it is then free to circulate throughout the EC. In other words, the mutual recognition principle will apply to technical standards so long as they conform to the 'code of essential requirements'.

In order to facilitate the mutual recognition of technical standards, the Commission has promoted European standardization bodies, such as the European Committee for Standardization (CEN) and the European Committee for Electrotechnical Standardization (Cenelec), to develop common industrial standards throughout the Community. CEN and Cenelec are comprised of industrial concerns and incorporate EFTA countries as well as EC ones.

3. The mutual information directive

The Commission also recognized the need to prevent new technical regulations replacing old 'harmonized' ones and so passed the Mutual Information Directive (Brealey, Quigley 1989). This obliges all Member States to notify the Commission of any new regulations or standards. If the Commission or any other Member State regard a new regulation as likely to have a barrier-inducing effect, the Commission has the power to freeze the new technical regulation for up to one year. Since 1985 this option has been used 40 times in response to a total of 450 notifications. Whilst it appears that the Commission is willing to accept considerable regulatory diversities, it will no longer tolerate Member States being able to keep out competing products on technical grounds alone.

THE COMMISSION'S PHILOSOPHY

In its attempt to remove the barriers represented by technical regulations, the Commission has adopted a series of innovative measures based upon the free market. Unlike physical barriers, technical regulations cannot simply be abolished. What the SEA has done is to promote positive integration within the realms of a new minimalist approach based upon competition. The cornerstone of the SEA's attempt to remove technical barriers is the principle of mutual recognition. As a consequence Member States will still issue national standards and norms for their own domestic industries but cannot prohibit competitive goods from other Member States that satisfy the 'codes of essential requirements', even where these goods fail to satisfy domestic standards. This will produce a strengthened competitive environment within which different regulatory systems will confront and compete with one another. Those countries that demand a really high standard, causing extra industrial costs, will compete with countries accepting a lesser standard, so long as they satisfy the essential requirements. It will then depend on the market, based upon consumer choice, to decide on the cost/quality trade-off when buying a particular good. As Curzon Price states:

> This is indeed an exciting prospect: governments submitting to market competition in this way will be a sight to see. And the beauty of it is there will be no need for tedious negotiations in Brussels, no need for ponderous majority voting, no need for a nanny Commission to oversee it all. It is all a matter of free choice – governments, parliaments and industrial pressure groups, trade unions and 'public opinion' can choose either to move with the market or live masochistically with self-inflicted wounds. (Curzon Price 1988: 17)

This trade-off between cost, quality and safety already exists. For example, a person buying a motor car has the choice to purchase a high-cost, high-safety vehicle – such as a Volvo – or a lower cost, but perfectly safe vehicle – like a Renault. What the legislation does enforce is the right of the consumer, as opposed to government, to choose the appropriate level in the cost/quality/safety trade-off by ensuring that all products are freely available throughout the Community.

A COMMON MARKET FOR SERVICES

The Commission also considers the establishment of a single competitive market in the service sector to be a necessary precondition for a return to economic prosperity. Indeed it is not possible to perceive of a single market without the free movement of services. In 1982 services accounted for 57 per cent of the value

Table 3.5 Percentage difference in prices of financial products compared with the average of the four lowest observations: selected countries and products, 1985.

	Germany	France	Italy	UK
Banking				
Consumer credit	136	105	n.a.	121
Credit cards	60	–30	89	16
Mortgages	57	78	–4	–20
Commercial loans	6	–7	9	46
Insurance				
Life	5	33	83	–30
Home	3	39	81	90
Motor	15	9	148	–17
Commercial	–9	153	245	27
Liability	47	117	77	–7

Source: 'The Economics of 1992', *European Economy*, No. 35, March 1988, p. 91.

added to the Community economy whilst manufacturing indu try contributed less than 26 per cent (Commission 1988a). Hithe to, progress on the freedom to provide services throughout the Community has been less successful than the progress achieved in ensuring the free movement of goods. This has resulted in considerable variations throughout the Community in the costs to consumers of various financial products. Table 3.5 highlights the severity of these variations which in some cases can be as high as 245 per cent above the average cost of the same financial product in the four least costly Member States. The Commission now regards it as critical to open up the whole services market, enabling not only subsidiary and branch plants to locate in other Member States but also the right to offer such services across frontiers without having to go through the expense of locating in the country of sale or satisfying national qualifying examinations. Again the principle of mutual recognition is applied to the service sector in order to remove those barriers designed to restrict market entry. The liberalization of the service sector applies not only to the traditional services, such as insurance and transport, but also to the financial services sector, which is in turn linked to that of capital movements. Emphasis is placed upon the need to free the circulation of financial products (Commission 1988d).

The Commission has again adopted a minimalist approach that is based upon competition whilst at the same time ensuring minimum standards. The guiding principle is that of 'home country control', which attributes the primary task of supervising the financial institutions to the relevant authorities in the Member State of origin. The Commission's aim is to establish a minimum harmonization of surveillance standards in order to ensure the free movement of services. As in manufacturing goods, it appears likely that the different regulatory systems will be forced into some form of competition.

Public Procurement

In the Commission's drive to remove technical barriers to intra-Community trade, it has focused attention on the public procurement activities of Member States. The large market represented by public procurement continues to be subject to discriminatory policies which favour domestic suppliers over foreign ones. This promoted inefficiency reduces competition and adds to the costs of industry. In 1986 public purchasing, which includes purchases at all levels of government and public enterprises, was worth ECU 530 billion in the Community of Twelve, equal to approximately 15 per cent of Community GDP (Emerson 1988). The public purchasing market is therefore larger than the ECU 500 billion market in intra-Community trade. A considerable portion of public purchases are undertaken without being put out to competitive tender. Many purchases also involve goods and services that are inherently non-tradable or are ordered on a scale too small to involve expensive contractual procedures and negotiations. Nonetheless the potential contractual part of public purchasing, often referred to as the public procurement market, was estimated to be a sizeable ECU 240–340 billion in 1986, equal to approximately 7 to 10 per cent of the EC GDP of Twelve (Commission 1985a).

According to Cecchini (1988), only a fraction of the public procurement market is awarded to other EC countries, representing in total around 0.14 per cent of the EC GDP. An investigation undertaken by Atkins (1988) for the 'costs of non-Europe' research, estimate the expenditure savings to be derived from a more open procurement policy in five EC countries (Belgium, France, Italy, Germany and the UK) could amount to between ECU 8 and 19 billion. Of this, ECU 4 to 8 billion is accounted for by what is referred to as the 'static trade effect', whereby public authorities purchase from the cheapest suppliers as opposed to domestic suppliers. This will in turn lead to increased competition throughout the EC as previously closed sectors are opened up to full market pressures. In the medium to long term, a restructuring effect would take place which would reduce the number of producers and significantly raise capacity utilization rates, which in those industries dominated by public procurement are notoriously low. For example, boilermaking for the electricity industry has a utilization rate of 20 per cent and for the locomotive industry utilization stands at around 50 per cent. The restructuring activities would occur over a relatively long period of time but could be worth between ECU 4 and 8 billion. Most importantly however, the Cecchini Report (1988) predicts that the high-technology, high-growth sectors will receive the greatest stimulus from the opening up of the public procurement market. The Atkins study did not cover defence, which in the EC represents a considerable proportion of public purchases. According to NATO sources (Vredeling 1987), some ECU 132.6 billion was spent on defence in the EC of twelve in 1985. Expenditure on weapons and missile systems represented 22 per cent of European countries' defence budgets (Table 3.6). The fragmentation of armaments industries, duplicating the costs of research

Table 3.6 Public procurement of weapons and missile systems in 1985 (Billion ECU)

	B	D	F[1]	I	NL	UK	EUR6	EUR12
Defence Budget	3.4	28.1	28.3	15.0	5.3	31.5	111.6	132.6
(as % of GDP)	(3.3)	(3.4)	(4.2)	(2.7)	(3.2)	(5.3)	(4.0)	(4.0)
Expenditure on weapons and missile systems	0.4	3.9	7.6	2.8	1.2	8.5	24.4	29.3
Potential Savings[2]								6.2

[1] French expenditure on weapons and missile systems is assumed to be the same proportions of the defence budget as in the United Kingdom.

[2] Assuming that the potential savings on this type of defence procurement are comparable to those estimated in the Atkins study for transport equipment other than motor vehicles.

Source: Commission 1988a: 59.

and development together with a comparable reduction in the efficiency of manufacturing, results in considerable extra costs. According to the Commission (Emerson 1988), total savings for the EC of twelve in 1985 could be as high as ECU 6.2 billion. Overall then, the EC economy could stand to gain from cost savings linked to the liberalization of public procurement practices. Including defence industries, this saving was estimated to be in the order of ECU 21.5 billion in 1985.

LIBERALIZING PUBLIC PROCUREMENT

The avoidance of competition within the public procurement sector has its rationale. Public purchases of goods and services can be used for a number of diverse objectives, notably for strategic reasons (defence, telecoms), employment reasons (regional policy) and development strategies (supporting new high-technology industries). In addition, the problem of removing protectionist tendencies is made more difficult by the complicated structure of the public sectors throughout the Community. Regulating public authorities as diverse as those in the UK and Italy will be both an expensive and time-consuming activity. For both historical and political reasons, the UK has a centralized purchasing system whereby 700 purchasing entities account for the bulk of public purchases. In both Italy and Germany, where a decentralized system of local government is both more accountable and powerful than in the UK, there are over 20,000 purchasing entities. To complicate matters further, the procedures for allocating contracts are often based upon restricted tenders or negotiations with individual firms.

The problems of trying to liberalize public procurement markets have been tackled on a number of occasions by the Commission, most notably in the 1970s when they produced legislation to 'open up' award procedures for public purchases. Directive 77/62/EEC tried to open the awarding procedures to Community-wide competition, whilst Directive 71/305/EEC coordinated awarding procedures in order to make the process transparent to potential bidders. This was to be achieved by advertising tenders in the 'Official Journal of the European Communities'. However, the Commission estimate that less than one ECU in four of public expenditure in the areas covered by the coordination Directives is actually advertised, reflecting both the difficulties of enforcing legislation in public procurement activities and a high level of infringement of existing laws.

It is fair to say that previous Community legislation concerned with public procurement has had a minimal impact on liberalizing the market and inducing competition. Faced with this limited success, the 1985 White Paper proposed a series of measures designed to tighten up the enforcement of current legislation and increase the transparency of awarding procedures

(Commission 1985a). It is important to note that none of these measures will apply to a selection of strategic concerns, notably defence. However, the Community proposes to extend the coverage of its new legislation to incorporate most markets currently excluded, including energy, transport, telecommunications and water supply. Most importantly, legislation exists to include the public purchasing activities taking place within the service sector. It has also reduced the threshold at which contracts fall within the scope of EC Directives, from one million ECU to ECU 700,000. Other measures include the ability of private firms to assert their legal rights under EC rules. In other words, companies will be able to sue public bodies if it can be proved that contracts were awarded in an unfair way. By ratifying the SEA, EC governments have committed themselves to liberalizing their public procurement practices, making decisions based on market factors such as quality, price and delivery as opposed to nationality. However the whole area is a highly sensitive one, as Curzon Price states:

...according to most people, government agencies which buy abroad are virtually committing high treason. (Curzon Price 1988: 18)

Again the SEA emphasizes competition and a liberalization of markets as a means of ensuring both the free movement of the factors of production and economic gain arising from public procurement practices. As the Cecchini Report eloquently states:

The negative consequence of closed and protective procurement is that in certain key high tech supply sectors where public authorities are the major purchasers, a symbiotic relationship has gradually built up between suppliers and buyers. This economic incest is a breeding ground for commercial deformities and deviant competitive behaviour. (Cecchini 1988: 20)

FISCAL BARRIERS

For a single market to function effectively, all impediments to the free movement of the factors of production have to be reduced to a minimum. One important barrier that helps to segment the

Community economy is the wide diversity in indirect tax rates, which effectively divide the Community into twelve separate self-contained fiscal units. Not only do the wide differences in indirect taxation distort competition, they also reinforce the physical barriers used to collect levies arising from these discrepancies. The Commission has long regarded the harmonization of indirect taxation as an essential and integral part of a genuine common market. Articles 99 and 100 of the Treaty of Rome provide the means for the Commission to propose legislation aimed at approximating indirect taxation. However, it was the second VAT Directive, passed in 1967, that firmly established the EC's intention to create a harmonized tax base.

The elimination of frontier barriers from within the Community means that fiscal barriers will have to be reduced. At present, the significant differentials in both the coverage and rates of indirect tax result in the de-taxing of goods destined for intra-Community 'export' and re-taxing them again on 'import'. In order to operate this rather clumsy system, it is necessary to have an elaborate system of frontier-related fiscal controls, dividing the Community up into twelve separate fiscal compartments. The key to removing these frontier controls rests on the ability of the Commission to reduce significantly the differentials in indirect taxation.

DISPARITIES IN THE RATES, COVERAGE AND STRUCTURE OF INDIRECT TAXATION

The sixth VAT Directive was partially successful in creating a common VAT base throughout the Community. In other words, broad agreement was reached on what items were to be considered as taxable. However, differences in coverage still persist, notably in the food, fuel, transport and small-trade sectors. More importantly, there are considerable discrepancies in the number and the level of VAT rates imposed by Member States. For example all Member States, with the exception of the UK and Denmark, apply more than one rate. In addition, the actual level of VAT varies enormously (Table 3.7). With the exception of the zero rate operated by the UK and Denmark, rates vary from one per cent in Belgium to 38 per cent in Italy. The standard rate of

Table 3.7 VAT Rates in the Community (1988)

	Reduced Rate %	Standard Rate %	Higer Rate %
Belgium[1]	1 and 6	19.0	25 and 25 +8
Denmark	-	22.0	-
France	2.1 and 4 5.5 and 7	18.6	33.33
Germany	7	14.0	-
Greece	6	18.0	36.00
Ireland[2]	2.4 and 10	25.0	-
Italy	2 and 9	18.0	38.00
Luxembourg	3 and 6	12.0	-
Netherlands	6	20.0	-
Portugal	8	16.0	30.00
Spain	6	12.0	33.00
United Kingdom[2]	-	15.0	-
Commission proposal	4 to 9	14 to 20	abolished

[1] An intermediate rate of 17% is also applied.
[2] These countries also refund tax paid at the previous stage on certain domestic transactions (ie they apply a zero rate).

Source: Commission 1988a: 61.

VAT, that used for the majority of purchases, varies from 25 per cent in Ireland to just 12 per cent in Luxembourg and Spain. It is not only the level and coverage of rates that vary between Member States, there are also discrepancies in the actual number of rates. The UK has one rate whereas Belgium has seven separate rates depending on the category of purchase, ranging from one per cent to 33 per cent. This results in wide variations in both the level and coverage of VAT. For example, food in the UK is zero rated whereas in Denmark it is liable to a 22 per cent VAT rate. As far as excise duties are concerned, coverage is fairly uniform when compared to indirect taxes (mainly on tobacco, alcoholic beverages and hydrocarbons). But whilst there is uniformity in coverage, the actual levies of excise vary enormously, considerably more than in the case of VAT (Table 3.8). For example, the rate of excise on cigarettes varies from ECU 0.12 per packet in

Table 3.8 Excise Duty Rates: Current Situation (1 April 1987) Proposals for Harmonisation

	Pure Alcohol (ECU per hl)	Wine (ECU per hl)	Beer	Cigarettes (ECU per 1000)	(ad valoren %)	Petrol (ECU per 1000)
Belgium	1,252	33	10	2.5	66.4	261
Denmark	3,499	157	56	77.5	39.3	473
Germany	1,174	20	7	27.3	43.8	256
Greece	48	0	10	0.6	60.4	349
Spain	309	0	3	0.7	51.9	254
France	1,149	3	3	1.3	71.1	369
Ireland	2,722	279	82	48.9	33.6	362
Italy	230	0	17	1.8	68.6	557
Luxembourg	842	13	5	1.7	63.6	209
Netherlands	1,289	33	20	26.0	35.7	340
Portugal	248	0	9	2.2	64.8	352
UK	2,483	154	49	42.8	34.0	271
Rates proposed	1,271	17	17	19.5	52 – 4	340

The taxes on cigarettes comprise a specific excise duty, the rate of which is given here for 1,000 cigarettes an ad valorem duty and VAT, the rate being shown here as a percentage of the retail price.

Source: Commission 1988a: 63.

Spain to ECU 2.76 per packet in Denmark. As far as alcoholic beverages are concerned, Denmark, Ireland and the United Kingdom have the heaviest taxation on beer, wine and spirits. The point which emerges immediately is that of the complexity, range, diversity and individuality of the present indirect rates in the EC.

THE PURPOSE OF THE EXISTING FISCAL BARRIERS

Under the present system of indirect taxation imposed upon intra-Community trade, fiscal barriers are an integral and indispensable part of the supporting administration. As we have already mentioned, the destination principle operates to ensure that the tax accrues to the country where the goods are finally consumed. This necessitates intra-Community trade being de-taxed on 'export' and re-taxed on 'import'. Fiscal barriers therefore reinforce the physical frontier barriers. For example, if a British manufacturer exports a product to Spain, it is the Spanish consumer who ultimately pays the VAT, not the British manufacturer. As a result, it should be the Spanish exchequer who receives the tax, not the British. The British Government therefore refunds the VAT paid by the British exporter and the Spanish Government tax the importer as the good enters Spain. Critically, the system relies upon the customs procedures adopted at frontier posts. The proof of export depends on the paper work completed during one of the many administrative procedures undertaken at the customs post. Only when a government receives the necessary paperwork will it issues a tax exemption on the good being exported. In the case of the British export to Spain, the situation is further complicated as a result of the product having to travel through France which will neither de- or re-tax the good. However, it is necessary for the transit country to ensure that the product is not sold in its own country free of VAT and thereby depriving the exchequer of income and distorting the domestic market. This is achieved by the paperwork at frontiers, with transit cargoes being 'checked-in' and 'checked-out' of a country.

The destination principle has the advantage of reducing any bias in intra-Community trade resulting from variations in indirect taxes. For example, the fact that the UK has a zero rating on children's clothes and Portugal has an 8 per cent VAT rating does not increase the competitiveness of British exports, which would be liable to the 8 per cent tax on entry into Portugal. However, the ability of VAT rates to distort intra-Community trade is recognized by Guieu and Bonnet (1987), who argue that domestic VAT policies are often discriminatory, with higher rates being applied to goods with little or no local content or production. This curtails imports from other Member States and re-directs the market to domestically produced substitutes. Finally, VAT and excise duties can be levied to reinforce domestic policies concerned with health, safety and the environment. The British Government's attempt to stimulate the consumption of lead-free petrol resulted in a reduced excise rate compared to that levied on leaded petrol. These policies are often considered to be part and parcel of a government's sovereign power and removing the right of individual Member States to set their own indirect taxes is a highly sensitive one.

THE COMMISSION'S PROPOSALS: 1987

In order to ensure the free movement of the factors of production, the Community considers it essential to remove the physical barriers at intra-Community frontier posts. However, there is no means of removing such posts if the rates, coverage and structure of indirect taxation remains. The existing system of indirect taxation is therefore a major impediment to the establishment of a truly integrated European economy. In July 1987, the Commission forwarded a package of seven draft Directives to the Council of Ministers with the aim of integrating indirect taxation throughout the Community.

VALUE ADDED TAX

The Commission's objective was to reduce, but not remove, the disparities between Member States' tax levels. The idea was therefore not to harmonize but to reduce disparities to such a level that they no longer provided the incentive to distort trade and competition. In order to support this approach to tax integration, the Commission cited the example of the USA where there are neither fiscal frontiers nor a complete harmonization of retail taxes between the states. Variations of up to six per cent can be tolerated without a significant distortion to trade flows. The approximation principle led the Commission to propose a number of rate brackets within which Member States would be free to set specific rates. The Commission's first proposal was for a two-band system involving a Standard rate (14 to 20 per cent) and a Reduced rate (4 to 9 per cent). The higher VAT rate which exists in six Member States and is applied to some luxury goods would have been abolished. The approximation principle would allow for a very significant degree of flexibility whilst at the same time removing the trade-distorting impacts of indirect taxation. To enforce approximation, it would have been necessary for the Commission to choose the appropriate band for each particular product. At present, the Commission propose that foodstuffs, energy products, water supplies, reading material and passenger transport be subject to the reduced VAT band.

Finally, the Commission proposed legislation that would result in VAT on intra-Community trade being treated in the same way as that which exists within one country's boundaries. In other words, VAT would be charged and collected in the country of 'export', whilst the corresponding 'import' tax would be deducted in the country of importation. However the final purchaser of the product would pay the VAT in the country of purchase at the rate applicable in that country. In order to ensure that the tax paid in the country of consumption did not end up in the country of export, an EC clearing house was proposed. This would refund to the country of consumption that tax collected by the exporting country, thus bringing to an end the existing practice of de-taxing intra-Community goods on 'export' and re-taxing them again on 'import'. More importantly, it would remove the fiscal demands placed upon frontier controls.

EXCISE DUTY

Since VAT is calculated on a product's price inclusive of excise rates, an approximation of excise rates could result in price differentials greater than that considered tolerable by the VAT bands. The Community therefore decided that excise duties should be harmonized. The rates proposed by the Commission are listed in Table 3.8 above. A number of proposals are now in front of the Council of Ministers but it is a complex process; not only the exact rates have to be decided upon but the exact product definition has to be agreed, such as the alcoholic content of wine, fortified wines and liqueurs.

IMPLICATIONS AND PROBLEMS

Lord Cockfield has always maintained that in signing the SEA and endorsing the Commission's drive to remove frontiers, Member States have committed themselves to removing fiscal barriers and that the only way to remove these barriers is by VAT approximation. However, fiscal barriers have proven to be amongst the most stubborn of all barriers to eliminate as a result of Member States being unwilling to cede the necessary authority to Brussels. The SEA endorsed the use of majority voting in the Council of Ministers on issues necessary to complete the SEM by 1992. Critically, under the SEA, tax legislation still needs to be passed by a unanimous vote in the Council of Ministers, thus ensuring the right of veto for any Member State that considers its vital national interests to be threatened. This has resulted in fiscal barriers being one of the most contentious issues to resolve in the White Paper programme. The preservation of the right of veto in the Council of Ministers has less to do with the exact details or ramifications of approximation than the perceived loss of fiscal sovereignty. Furthermore, Member States are legitimately concerned about some of the budgetary consequences of the Commission's proposals. In order to dispel such fears, the Commission adopted a policy of trying to limit the budgetary ramifications to a minimum for the maximum number of states. Under the original proposals, Denmark and Ireland, who have relatively high VAT rates, stood to loose a considerable portion of their revenue whereas Luxembourg, Spain and Portugal were in the fortunate position of standing to receive a significant increase in theirs. Most of the other Member States would have experienced marginal variations in their existing indirect taxation revenue.

The Commission's proposals to remove fiscal barriers are in marked contrast to the policy initiatives taken to eliminate the physical and technical barriers. In the latter case, the primary tool used to ensure free movement is the principle of mutual recognition, leaving it to free trade and the market place to remove barriers. In the case of excise duties, and to a lesser extent VAT, the Commission proposed the old-style harmonization of the 1970s and early 1980s. This, coupled with the fact that the Commission's proposals on taxation require unanimity in the Council of Ministers, means that fiscal barriers are going to be the most difficult barriers to remove and a real threat exists that, in the absence of agreement, the White Paper proposals will not be implemented in their entirety. The right of veto had brought a stalemate in the decision-making process by 1988, stimulating the British Government to propose an alternative mechanism to harmonization. Partially based on the mutual recognition principle, they proposed a system whereby goods would be free to move throughout the Community without first harmonizing VAT rates. Any VAT distorted trade flows would then flourish until market forces (for governments this would mean a loss of tax revenue) forced Member States to adopt more competitive rates. To the free-market faithful, this proposal was a fiscal version of 'mutual recognition' which prevented the need for harmonization. With a relatively low tax structure and the cost-penalty imposed on cross-Channel movements, which would in effect reduce competitive pressures on higher UK VAT rates, the British had a keen self-interest in promoting competition between tax systems. However, this enthusiasm did not extend to excise duties where the level of taxation is significantly higher in the UK than on continental Europe. For 'health reasons', the UK argued that variations in excise duties should be protected. This British proposal, which like the approximation proposal, needs a unanimous vote in the Council of Ministers, was supported by only one other Member State: Luxembourg. The Commission then made a number of other proposals in order to make the approximation principle more acceptable, such as widening the VAT bands so the Reduced rate could vary from 0 to 9 per cent. Interestingly, this greater flexibility in the band structure was partially a result of the UK's outspoken resistance to abolishing its zero-rated category on food and children's clothes.

THE COMMISSION'S PROPOSALS: 1989

By the end of December 1988, the Finance Ministers had rejected both the original Commission proposal, based on a Community-wide 'clearing house', and the British model of fiscal mutual recognition. Furthermore, the Commission recognized the folly of trying to harmonize such a diverse range of VAT and excise rates such as existed across the Community. However, the Commission did insist on the need to abolish the de- and re-taxation of intra-Community trade as this would negate the purpose and philosophy of a single market. However insistent the Commission was, the Finance Ministers in the Council were equally determined to reject any proposal that would remove their sovereign control over revenue collection. This resulted in a Community fudge that falls well short of the proposals first outlined in the 1985 White Paper. An agreement was reached whereby zero-rated VAT would be allowed to continue and the system of de-and re-taxing intra-Community trade would be allowed to operate 'for a limited transitional period'. Whilst the specific details of the Directives are changing all the time, some of the basic principles have been agreed upon. Most importantly, VAT rates will be brought in line with the original two-band classification (4–9 per cent and 14–20 per cent) proposed by the Commission. However, existing zero rates will be allowed to remain. As for the free movement of goods across boundaries, there will be no limits on the quantity of VAT-paid goods carried across intra-Community borders by Community citizens. Commercial 'exports' and 'imports' will continue the practice of zero-rating. However, this will in future be policed by a system of spot-checking invoices as opposed to border paperwork. Finally, the Commission plans to establish a series of minimum excise duties designed to reduce the present vast discrepancies. There will however continue to be a restriction imposed upon the amount of excise-bearing goods Community citizens can carry across borders.

Although the Commission stress the transitional nature of these proposals and re-state their long term objective as introducing a harmonized Community VAT system, there is no precise timetable attached to this 'transitional period'. Clearly the compromise between the Finance Ministers and the Commission does not comply with either the operational or philosophical objectives of the '1992' programme. For a single market to be effective, VAT on intra-EC trade has to be collected as though the Community were one country. For the foreseeable future, intra-Community trade will have a tax regime that differentiates it from purely national trade. This whole tax issue reinforces a point made earlier, that fiscal policies are considered to be part and parcel of a government's sovereign power and removing the right of individual Member States to set their own indirect taxes touches a highly sensitive political nerve.

MORE THAN JUST BARRIERS

The task of removing barriers to the free movement of trade appears detailed and technical but nevertheless fairly straightforward. As such, the 1985 White Paper was originally perceived to be a technical document rather than a visionary blueprint for greater European integration. '1992' can therefore be interpreted to be part of the functionalist approach to integration established by Jean Monnet and Robert Schuman. The Commission choose the issue of removing non-tariff barriers as it was considered to be a rather trivial and technical issue best left to the European technocrats like Lord Cockfield. Member States could therefore be persuaded to cooperate and pool resources over an issue perceived to be a rather small and functional step towards ensuring a more common market. However, the significance and effects of removing non-tariff barriers to the free movement of the factors of production were underestimated. It would appear fair to assume that many Member States signed the 1987 SEA without fully realizing the full economic and political consequences of doing so.

The Commission has long regarded frontier controls as the most potent symbol of the EC's continued fragmentation. The main thrust of the '1992' programme is therefore aimed at removing the barrier functions imposed at border controls. Borders not only represent the territorial limits of Member States, they also represent the spatial limits of a country's legal jurisdiction and its associated political economy. Removing border controls therefore implies much more than just eliminating customs formalities; it implies a long-term commitment to merging political economies and legal jurisdictions. Boundaries and their associated functions represent one of the most accurate barometers to the level of European political and economic cooperation (House 1980; Gibb 1985). Boundary functions (ie barriers) are a product and not a cause of differing economic, political and social structures. By agreeing to eliminate these boundaries, Member States are committing themselves to a programme whose primary objective is to merge economies, jurisdictions and, in the long term, political systems. The process of removing non-tariff barriers by the principle of mutual recognition, and thereby allowing diverse jurisdictions to compete with one another, will exert pressure for an overall equalization of Community law. This linkage is well illustrated by the removal of barriers to the free movement of people. The 1985 White Paper reiterated two fundamental rights first outlined in the Treaty of Rome concerning the freedom of individuals to cross from one Member State to another, and the freedom to enjoy access to professional activity throughout the Community. *Completing The Internal Market* states the Commission's aims as:

(1) the abolition of all police and customs formalities for people crossing intra-Community borders and,
(2) the removal of all restrictions on the movement of labour, establishing the freedom to exercise a profession or occupation within the Community, regardless of where any training or qualifications were received. (Commission 1985a: 14)

This seemingly simple task of removing barriers restricting the EC's 320 million citizens has considerable political ramifications. Not only are there the immediate and detailed problems concerning questions such as security, particularly those associated with terrorism, there is also the long-term issue of the treatment of non-Community citizens. The issue of immigration control touches at the very core of the sovereign rights of Member States: the right of parliaments to determine the racial composition of the nation. Although it is the individual right of parliaments to grant nationality, once an immigrant possesses an EC passport he or she is legally entitled to travel and work anywhere in the Community. Similarly when the border controls are removed, there will be an irresistible pressure for a common Community policy on visitors' visas. There would be little point in France imposing visa restrictions on South Africans if the UK had no equivalent restrictions. When intra-Community borders eventually lose their immigration function, a South African who entered Britain would then be free to travel throughout the Community, regardless of whether individual Member States impose visa restrictions or not. The seemingly technical issue of removing barriers to the free movement of people necessitates a common Community policy for visas for any country outside the EC. If there is a common visa policy, does this not imply some coordination of foreign policy? Equally, if Member States are going to rely less on border controls there will be a need to harmonize criminal law and policing procedures.

This example reiterates a point made earlier in this chapter, that it is not frontier formalities that create a barrier; it is the divergence in the social, economic and political conditions existing either side of the frontier. Without explicitly saying so, the Commission, by eliminating barriers and creating a 'Europe without frontiers', is establishing an environment that necessitates an equalization, if not harmonization, of jurisdictions. The beauty of the '1992' programme is that it is a self-policing system being propelled by competitive forces and enabling those very same forces to decide upon the appropriate regulatory system. Economic expectations of the SEM programme are therefore high. The economic vision associated with '1992' requires a vast political commitment by European citizens and their parliaments. The level of this commitment will be affected critically by the economic benefits, both real and perceived, emanating from the single market.

4.   The 'costs of non-Europe': rhetoric or reality?

The current chapter aims to evaluate the economic benefits arising from the internal market programme as predicted by the Commission and the Cecchini Report (1988), and to examine the probability of this programme achieving its desired objectives. There has been a great deal of hype and media rhetoric lavished on the '1992' programme and its ramifications for the British, European and world economies. At the same time, there has been a great deal of confusion, in both the public and private sectors, on what this programme is all about. There are of course very differing concepts of what '1992' means and what it is suppose to achieve. The central focus of this book is the friction that exists between the European visionaries who see '1992' as just one further step towards European integration, and the Euro-pragmatists who regard the EC as a powerful customs union and '1992' as a vehicle for promoting free-market principles. It is therefore very difficult to evaluate the potential economic benefits and overall success of the '1992' programme as its objectives, needed as a base to evaluate success, vary amongst the visionaries and pragmatists.

As soon as the SEA had been signed, the Commission was actively promoting European Monetary Union as an integral part of the SEM. At the European Council Meeting at Hannover in June 1988, it was agreed that:

... in adopting the Single Act, the Member States of the Community confirmed the objective of progressive realization of economic and monetary union. (Delors 1989: 3)

As a consequence, a 'Committee for the Study of Economic and Monetary Union' was established under the Chairmanship of the President of the European Commission, Jacques Delors. In Spring 1989, the Delors Committee made detailed proposals, the so-called 'three-stage plan', for European economic and monetary union (Delors 1989). At the same time the 'social Europe' programme was gradually taking shape, considered by many to be an integral part of the SEM. '1992' can therefore mean many things to many people. However there is one central tenet common to all these interpretations of what the SEM should and should not include: the liberalization of trade allowing for the free movement of goods, people, capital and services throughout the Community.

The economic legislation of the SEA involving the removal of all technical, physical and fiscal barriers has been accepted by all twelve Member States. In signing the SEA, Member States ensured the free movement of trade through the removal of non-tariff barriers. The 1985 White Paper and much of the SEA is uncompromisingly technical and pragmatic. It is a liberal-market solution to the European economy's problems. Both the Commission and the Cecchini Report claim the SEM will promote economic welfare gains throughout all Member States and benefit all Europeans. As Cecchini notes:

The failure to achieve a single market within the European Community has been costing European industry millions in unnecessary costs and lost opportunities... what is on offer is significant, inflation free growth and the creation of millions of new jobs. (Cecchini 1988: cover page)

It is this central premise that the present chapter examines and then critically evaluates. Those areas more problematic to the completion of the internal market, social legislation for example, are dealt with elsewhere in this book. However it is readily accepted that such an academic division over-simplifies the debate, with many people considering an active social policy as essential if the real benefits of the internal market are to be realized. Nonetheless, a critical examination of the economic benefits arising from the removal of non-tariff barriers is a necessary starting-point for an evaluation of the whole '1992' programme.

RESEARCH ON THE 'COSTS OF NON-EUROPE'

The 1985 White Paper and the 1987 SEA were based upon a variety of economic assertions concerning the benefits of achieving a fully integrated European market. The EC's economic rationale supporting these assertions arose from an unprecedented research programme, the so-called research into the 'Costs of non-Europe', launched by Lord Cockfield in 1986. The research, directed by Paulo Cecchini, was unprecedented on a number of accounts. Most notably the scope of the study was vast, incorporating most sectors of the European economy in the twelve Member States. In total, there were approximately 40 firms of private consultants working under Paulo Cecchini or Commission advisors. The end result was 16 considerable volumes containing in-depth studies into the benefits of an integrated European economy. The principal results were made available in the March 1988 special issue of the 'European Economy' Journal (Commission 1988a) and a Commission book, edited by Michael Emerson, entitled *The economics of 1992* (Emerson 1988). Finally, an overall summary of the findings was published in the form of the Cecchini Report (1988), entitled *The European Challenge: 1992*.

For the purpose of quantifying the benefits of an SEM, the research used two types of methodological investigation: microeconomic and macroeconomic. It then fused together these two different approaches to quantify the full economic benefits of an integrated market. Given the Report's and consultants' terms of reference, to investigate the costs of non-Europe, it is not altogether surprising that they all saw benefits arising from this integration, the costs of non-Europe being analytically identical to the benefits of completing the internal market. As a consequence, both the Commission and Member States justify the '1992' programme with the research and conclusions produced by Cecchini. However the Community commissioned this research programme after the SEA had been ratified. The economic legislation had been drawn up and the political decisions made before the impact of completing the internal market had been properly examined. It is therefore right to question the objectivity of a piece of research undertaken with the explicit purpose of justifying political and economic decisions already made. For example, when commenting on the 'costs of non-Europe' research, the Commission states:

> the political effort required to complete the internal market will be very considerable. Will it be worth the trouble? The findings of this study are in the affirmative. (Emerson 1988: 1)

Harsh criticism has subsequently been directed at the objectivity and accuracy of the Cecchini studies, for example:

> The Cecchini studies represent collectively one of the largest exercises in applied economic analysis ever undertaken ... but the Cecchini studies looked only at this [market fragmentation] possible cause and were determined to prove its importance. (Neuberger 1989)

and:

> Seldom in the history of social research have so many been paid so much to produce such negligible results. (Cutler 1989: 54)

The present chapter now goes on to examine and critically evaluate Cecchini's findings. The Report predicts very large benefits for the European economy, concluding that the total potential gain to the Community as a whole is likely to be in the region of ECU 200 billion (1985 prices), adding more than 7 per cent to the Community's GDP. This, the Cecchini Report predicts, will be unaccompanied by inflation and could create up to 5 million jobs. It is unnecessary to examine the details of each independent economic expert, consultant and research institute that supported Cecchini's study. For the purposes of the current study, the results of Cecchini's research can be divided into two broad categories: microeconomic and macroeconomic.

THE MICROECONOMIC ESTIMATES

The initial impact of eliminating non-tariff barriers will be felt at the most disaggregated microeconomic level. Companies and firms will be forced to re-think their development strategies as their costs of production decrease and overall competitive pressures increase. This should, in turn, lead to enhanced economies of scale as the competitive pressures of the market place restructure European industries. Broadly speaking, therefore, the microeconomic benefits arising from the SEM can in themselves be subdivided into two separate stages:

Stage one: gains from the removal of barriers affecting trade and overall production and

Stage two: indirect microeconomic gains arising from the 'supply-side shock' to the market as a result of increased competition.

STAGE ONE: BARRIER REMOVAL EFFECTS

The non-tariff barriers that have a direct impact on intra-Community trade are the physical, technical and fiscal barriers examined in Chapter 3. As these barriers are removed, the costs of importing and exporting within the Community will be reduced, resulting in lower overall prices. Released resources can either be used on alternative production or result in a greater demand for cheaper products. The Cecchini Report (1988) quantifies these benefits by measuring the direct costs arising out of the existing non-tariff barriers. The direct cost of frontier formalities, and associated administrative costs for the private and public sectors, was estimated to be in the order of 1.8 per cent of the value of goods traded within the Community. To this must be added the costs for industry of other identifiable barriers in the internal market (e.g. technical regulations) which are estimated, in opinion surveys of industrialists, to average a little over 2 per cent of those companies' costs. The combined total represents about 3.5 per cent of industrial value-added costs. However the impact of removing these barriers is essentially short-term; they will be once-and-for-all savings. As a consequence, the removal of non-tariff barriers – what the '1992' programme is all about – is predicted to generate an increase of around 2.5 per cent in the Community's GDP, equal to approximately one year's growth. It is the economic process that this initial action sets in motion that offers the real rewards expected from the SEM. As such, the success of this initial stage is critical to the SEM; it is that stage upon which all other subsequent economic benefits depend.

It is therefore not surprising that a number of theories have been put forward to question the predictions made of this initial stage, the most important of which is the likelihood that come '1992', the European economy will not be a single integrated entity but one within which non-tariff barriers still operate to fragment the market. The Cecchini study did not estimate what the effect of a partial removal of non-tariff barriers would be. All estimates were based upon the supposition that customs checks and frontier administrative procedures would be removed in their entirety. This is indeed critical to the functioning of the free market, as the Commission points out:

> ...all the essential barriers have to be removed, otherwise the last remaining barriers may on their own be sufficient to restrain competition. (Emerson 1988: 7)

Lord Cockfield's 1985 White Paper contained the now famous list of 300 policy proposals designed to eliminate non-tariff barriers. Although these were condensed to 278 proposals, some involve contentious issues where finding an agreement to suit all Member States is exceptionally difficult. This is particularly so in the case of fiscal policies where unanimity is still required in the Council of Ministers. Indirect taxation is likely to be one of the most difficult areas in which to implement the 1985 White Paper proposals. There is a very real likelihood that by the end of 1992, fiscal border controls will not have disappeared. But even in the situation where all the existing non-tariff barriers were removed, other barriers may still be effective in segmenting the Community market. This is a thesis put forward by Kay (1989), who argues that the existing fragmentation of the European economy is not the result of trade barriers of a kind which it is within the powers of the Commission to remove. The argument here is that the SEA will not create a semi-homogeneous market like that in the UK or

France. The central contention is that demand differs not as a result of barriers but as a result of habits, cultural preferences, climatic conditions and social preferences. These variations will be enhanced by the legislation designed to liberalize trade, as it will affect supply more that demand. Kay and Smith (1989) cite the British preference to drive on the left-hand side of the road, which is a product of a unique historical/industrial evolution and not an attempt to discourage foreign car imports. Nonetheless, it is an obstacle to the free movement of goods and parallel trade between markets. On a similar note, Geroski (1989) makes the point that the SEM will result in an extension of the diversity within markets as opposed to some form of uniformity. He argues that a basic flaw in the Commission's thinking on '1992' is the perception that a unified market will emerge by uniting diverse consumers in one market area. Therefore whilst '1992' will create a mass market of 320 million people, it will not create a market for mass-produced goods.

Another threat to the achievement of the internal market is the very real danger that border controls will not be removed. In 1985 West Germany and France joined the Benelux countries in an agreement designed to remove frontier formalities for people and goods. Under the so-called 'Schengen' agreement, frontier checks were to have completely disappeared by 1990. This had not been achieved because of German fears about drugs from the Netherlands and French worries about firearms from Belgium. The lack of enthusiasm for removing all frontier checks is now the subject of bitter controversy in the '1992' programme. Although the SEA commits all Member States to create a market 'without internal frontiers', in 1988 the British Prime Minister, then Margaret Thatcher, stated:

> It is a matter of plain commonsense that we cannot totally abolish frontier controls... if we are to protect our citizens and stop the movement of drugs, of terrorists, of illegal immigrants. (Economist 1988b)

Finally perhaps the most serious obstacle to the predicted gains to be had from the removal of barriers affecting production is the future success of the Commission's policies designed to liberalize the vast public procurement market. Throughout the 1970s the

Commission enacted legislation aimed at eliminating the discriminatory practices of public bodies choosing Community suppliers. The impact of this legislation has been disappointing, with the measures taken to enforce free competition failing to either liberalize the procurement markets or open up the procedures. As the Cecchini Report notes, the Community legislator has up to now proved no match for national and local purchasing bureaucracies. This highlights a central underlying issue supporting many of these criticisms, which is the restricted ability of legislation to eliminate all forms of discrimination. As a consequence, Kay argues that the spirit of '1992' is more important than the letter, noting that:

> The French Government prefers to buy from French producers, but the French consumers, faced with a wide range of potential suppliers, appear to do exactly the same. You can lead a horse to water, but you cannot make it drink or look into its mind and establish why it has refused to drink. (Kay 1989: 14)

Given the problems of policing open public procurement, it appears likely that public bodies will continue to discriminate between Community suppliers in their public procurement practices after 1992.

Overall then, there are serious doubts about the underlying policy hypothesis that an internal market will be completed. If some barriers were to escape effective elimination, it may negate the positive impact of removing other non-tariff barriers. It would certainly reduce the predicted gains arising from the removal of barriers affecting trade and production. Nonetheless, Member States have committed themselves to completing an internal market and it is on that basis that the following analysis proceeds. To recap then, the economic gains from stage one (Table 4.1), arising from the removal of non-tariff barriers, amounts to a net welfare gain of between ECU 74–91 billion (1985 prices), equal to a 2.2–2.7 percentage increase in Community GDP. So even when the internal market is completed and all the non-tariff barriers are removed, the economic benefits arising from this process will be equal to just one year's growth in a bad year. As the Cecchini Report notes of this stage one process:

Table 4.1 (Stage one) Microeconomic estimates of potential economic gains for the EC resulting from the removal of non-tariff barriers. [Based on 7 member countries at 1985 price]

		billion ECU	% GDP
1.	Gains from removal of of barriers affecting trade (eg frontier delays)	8–9	0.2–0.3
2.	Gains from removal of barriers affecting overall production (eg technical standards, public procurement)	57–71	2.0–2.4
3.	Gains from removing barriers (stage 1 and 2)	65–80	2.2–2.7
	For the EC of 12 (1985 prices)	74–91	2.2–2.7

(Based on 7 member countries at 1985 prices)
Source: Cecchini 1988: 84; Emerson 1988: 203.

> ...this is merely the primary effect, and thus only a minor part of the story explaining the environment of the European home market in the next decade. (Cecchini 1988: 73)

The real benefits arise from the indirect microeconomic processes enacted as a result of the removal of non-tariff barriers.

STAGE TWO: MARKET INTEGRATION EFFECTS

The key to understanding the Commission's estimates of the economic benefits arising from '1992' is the relationship that exists between removing non-tariff barriers and the creation of a new and pervasive competitive environment. In theory, the removal of non-tariff barriers will reduce the costs for goods and services and as a consequence, promote a growth in demand. This new demand, now within a single market, strengthens competitive pressures and leads to the restructuring of industry based upon new enhanced economies of scale. Inefficient industries will be forced to close down and new investment will be directed to those plants moving towards the optimal size. The gains resulting from the exploitation of economies of scale are estimated to be in the order of ECU 61 billion, at 1985 prices (Table 4.2). However market integration and enhanced competition

Table 4.2 (Stage two) Microeconomic estimates of potential economic gains for the EC resulting from market integration and competition. (Indirect micro-economic gains)

		billion ECU	% GDP
1.	Gains from exploiting economies of scale more fully	61	2.1
2.	Gains from intensified competition reducing business efficiency and monopoly profits	46	1.6
3.	Gains from market integration	*62–107	*2.1–3.7
4.	For the EC of 12 (1985 prices)	127–87	2.1–3.7

* The Commission notes that this alternative estimate for the sum of line 3 cannot be broken down between the lines 1 and 2.

(Based on 7 Member Countries at 1985 prices)
Source: Cecchini 1988: 84; Emerson 1988: 203.

lead to gains beyond those associated with the economies of scale. In particular, there will be considerable gains to be had from an overall rationalization of business activity. There are a whole series of inefficient business practices made possible as a result of weak market forces arising from market fragmentation. Over-manning, excess overheads and over-stocking result in what the Commission calls 'x-inefficiency', which refers to the inefficient allocation of human, physical and financial resources. 'X-inefficiency', together with excess profits and monopoly profits, arise from conditions of weak competition. The move towards a more integrated and competitive economy will remove these burdens (Fig 4.1) and bring gains estimated to be in the order of ECU 46 billion, or 1.6 per cent of the EC GDP. Overall therefore, the gains arising from market integration could be as high as ECU 107 billion or 3.7 per cent of the EC GDP, a sum substantially

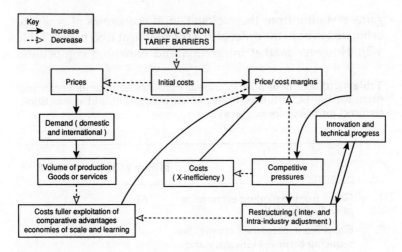

Figure 4.1 Integration and the effects of size of markets (*Source:* modified from Commission, 1988a).

larger than the direct microeconomic gains. However as they are dependent on the indirect microeconomic processes, the Commission considers the gains to be had from market integration will take several years to materialize. Furthermore, these gains are dependent on the central presupposition that economies of scale have not yet been reached and that increased competition will restructure European industries helping them to exploit greater economies and remove 'x-inefficiencies'.

Economies of scale, restructuring and 'x-inefficiency'

The 'costs of non-Europe' research commissioned Pratten (1988) to examine the potential economies of scale savings for the EC. The study shows that there are substantial unexploited potential economies of scale. Economies of scale can be defined as an increase in output proportionately larger than the associated increase in inputs, and hence leading to a fall in unit costs. Pratten in his detailed study of scale economies uses engineering evidence to examine the hypothetical minimum efficient technical size (METS). The results of his study are far too detailed to examine here. They covered a wide range of scale economies, such as production, research and development, business organization and finance, across a broad cross-section of industries.

The calculations show that for manufacturing industries, gains from enhanced economies of scale could be worth ECU 60 billion. Furthermore, given a doubling of overall production, unit labour costs for supplementary production could drop by an average of 10 per cent in car manufacturing and 20 per cent in aircraft manufacture. In more than half of all branches of industry, 20 firms of efficient size can co-exist in the Community whereas the largest national markets could only support four. The Commission therefore argues that only an internal market on a truly European scale can combine the advantages of technical and economic efficiency. The Commission estimates that about one third of European industry could profit from cost reductions ranging from 1 to 7 per cent, depending on the branch concerned. The aggregate cost-savings from improved economies of scale would amount to approximately 2 per cent of EC GDP.

The Commission's perception that economies of scale are present and unexploited in most sectors of the European economy has been criticized. Such criticism attacks the very substance of the '1992' programme, the rationale of which is to provide Europe's enterprises with markets equal to that of the American and Japanese. Furthermore the benefits of opening up the European market are not just connected with product costs. The Commission expect a wholesale restructuring of the European economy. A great deal therefore rests on the existence of unexploited scale economies. Neuberger (1989) produces evidence to argue that the EC does not in fact have smaller companies than either Japan or the USA, and that the fragmented EC market does not pose a serious obstacle to the formation of Community-wide firms. Using 'The Times Thousand' and 'The Financial Times 500' lists of the world's largest companies, Neuberger shows the EC to have a greater share of the largest industries compared with either the USA or Japan. In an examination of those companies with a turnover of more than 10 billion in 1986, it can be seen that the EC had more companies than America and double the number in Japan. Paradoxically, despite the poor performance of the UK compared to other EC economies, UK companies dominate the league of the largest European companies. Company size, economies of scale and economic vitality do not therefore go hand in hand. In another criticism of the scale economy argument leading to economic gain for the European economy, Geroski (1989) questions the relationship between size and efficiency. Simply put, Geroski argues that the major benefits of the SEM are those arising from extending product diversity as opposed to increasing the scale of production and imposing uniformity. He argues that:

> ...the benefits of scale economies can only be realized by product standardization, and this, in turn, means a reduction in the variety of goods offered for sale and in their degree of customization. (Geroski 1989: 33)

It will therefore rest with the market, and in particular the customer, to decide upon standardization or customization. The expansion of the market caused by the removal of non-tariff barriers allows for either one of these options to be chosen, but not both. Geroski considers it likely that the market will favour product diversification and the predicted economic gains arising from scale economies will not materialize.

Most authors critical of the Cecchini Report dispute the evidence put forward to support the idea of unexploited economies of scale. There exists much evidence to refute the contention that plant size effects productivity levels (Pratten 1988). The automobile industry is the most widely cited sector, used by both the supporters and detractors of the economies of scale argument. The experience of the UK car industry throughout the 1960s and 1970s highlights the problems associated with increasing size and efficiency. During this period a series of government-sponsored mergers took place, culminating in the establishment of the large British Leyland Group. The rationale behind these mergers was to increase the economies of scale in order to compete in an increasingly harsh environment. However, the end result was disastrous; not only was there a 40 per cent reduction in model styles, but the benefits of scale economies never materialized. In fact quite the converse; there was clear evidence pointing to substantial diseconomies of scale resulting from an unwieldy management structure. At the same time, as the European market became progressively more open throughout the 1970s and 1980s, the number and type of model variants increased. Large scale rationalization and product standardization did not take place.

The Commission's belief in the ability of the market place, through enhanced competition, to restructure industries has also been criticized. Many of the advantages associated with scale economies and the removal of 'x-inefficiencies' depend on the predicted industrial restructuring process. In a competitive environment, restructuring should depend on comparative advantage favouring the expansion of the most efficient firms. As the Commission notes:

> ... competition leads to the restructuring of industries, with inefficient plants closing and investment made in new plants.
> (Commission 1988: 196)

However, as the SEM programme began to materialize, there has been frenetic corporate activity based on mergers, alliances and trade agreements. Many large European companies lack competitive advantage but survive behind non-tariff barriers designed to distort competition. These companies, often referred to as national champions, are now facing a situation of real competition in which there will be losers and winners. In order to circumvent unfettered competition, European companies have entered into a bout of mergers and alliances on a scale hitherto unknown in the EC. Encouraged by governments not wishing to see the end of a national champion and the EC keen on exploiting Euro-Scales, European companies have rushed into agreements with likely competitors. The agreement between GEC, Plessey and Siemens is an example of national champions cooperating across a whole range of activities in order to exploit larger scale economies. But as Porter notes:

> These practices [mergers and alliances] threaten the very foundation of competitive advantage and the benefits of 1992.
> (Porter 1990: 24)

The Cecchini Report highlights competition as being the driving force behind innovation (Fig 4.2) and the gains to be derived from market integration. Indeed European consolidation, through mergers and alliances, is regarded by many as a step likely to enhance competition and increase the economies of scale. On the other hand, as Porter notes, 'the secret of competitive advantage is to compete', and much collaborative activity is based upon a damage-limitation principle: limiting competition in order to safeguard a particular niche in the market. If this latter hypothesis is correct and European firms continue to blunt the

Competition and Innovation

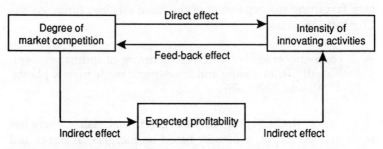

Figure 4.2 The relationship between competition and innovation (*Source:* Cecchini, 1988).

competitive edge through mergers, there is a very real chance that the perceived benefits from market integration will be illusory. The '1992' programme would then produce the one-off gains itemized in stage one and the one-off gains derived from restructuring; it would not, however, create the competitive environment deemed necessary for the European economy to compete effectively in the global economy.

Finally, in criticizing the ability of the gains achieved in stage one (derived from removing non-tariff barriers) to generate the economies of scale predicted in stage two, Cutler (1989) argues there is a fundamental inconsistency in the Commission's argument. As the predicted direct microeconomic benefits arising from the removal of non-tariff barriers are relatively small (Table 4.1 above), it would appear that these barriers do not in themselves represent a serious barrier to market entry. Consequently, if the gains to be had from enhancing scale economies are as great as the Commission predicts, European firms would have enlarged long ago. Cutler concludes that the removal of non-tariff barriers will not alter the economic environment to such a degree as to promote the realization of large-scale economies. Again, as in stage one, there are considerable doubts as to whether the Cecchini Report provides an accurate assessment of the benefits likely to arise from exploiting economies of scale more fully. The idea that there is a direct causal relationship between removing non-tariff barriers and being able to enhance scale economies is certainly open to question. As Pratten comments in the conclusion of his *Survey of the Economies of Scale*:

> ...estimates of the economies of scale are elusive and many of the estimates which are available are hedged around with qualifications. (Pratten 1988: 149)

In summary, the Cecchini Report predicts overall potential welfare gains by taking a microeconomic approach. The calculation is based upon the direct economic benefits to be had from removing non-tariff barriers and their indirect affect on enhancing business efficiency through competition. In the aggregate, for all sectors and all types of cost savings and price reductions, the study suggests total economic gains in the order of 4.5 to 6.5 per cent of GDP for the Community as a whole. At 1988 prices, for the twelve Member States, this amounts to a range of around ECU 170 to 250 billion. These estimates of economic gain have been criticized on a number of fronts and it would appear valid to question their basic underlying assumptions. However, in addition to the microeconomic gains associated with stages one and two, there were also macroeconomic estimates (stage three) based upon new business strategies and policy coordination initiatives. It is to these estimates that the present chapter now turns.

STAGE THREE: THE MACROECONOMIC CONSEQUENCES OF EC MARKET INTEGRATION

The Commission's calculations of the economic benefits arising from SEM deregulation include a macroeconomic assessment to supplement the microeconomic estimates. Focus is concentrated on the ability of the SEM to ease the macroeconomic constraints currently restricting the European economy, such as budget deficits, external balance of trade deficits and inflationary pressures. The Cecchini study includes a series of macroeconomic simulation exercises whose purpose is to give a time scale to the predicted benefits and to express the results in terms of other economic variables, such as employment considerations. Consequently the impact of the SEM, based on the results obtained from the microeconomic studies, can be grouped under four main headings, each having a different macroeconomic impact.

1. The removal of frontier delays and costs

The downward pressure on EC production will increase the competitiveness of imports from other Member States. This will lead to intra-EC trade being substituted for national goods and intra-EC imports taking the place of extra-EC imports (see Chapter 3). The end result should be an improvement of each Member State's terms of trade as import prices drop.

2. Opening up public procurement

According to Atkins (1988), the liberalization of public procurement will substantially reduce the average costs of investment spending and reduce production costs. Cecchini predicts big reductions in purchasing costs allowing governments greater financial room for manoeuvre.

3. Liberalization of financial services

It is predicted that the liberalization of this sector will allow for the wider availability of credit and a better allocation of financial resources. Both of these will lead to gains in productivity.

4. The supply-side effects

Business strategies will have to react to a new competitive environment, forcing companies into cost-cutting programmes involving rationalization and larger scale economies. It is also expected that productivity gains in the factors of production will produce overall cost savings. This may, in the short term, have a depressant effect on demand as labour is shed. In the medium to longer term, the Commission predicts overall employment gains.

The macroeconomic analysis suggests that completing the internal market will reduce inflationary pressures, ease Member States' budgetary constraints and produce activity-bolstering

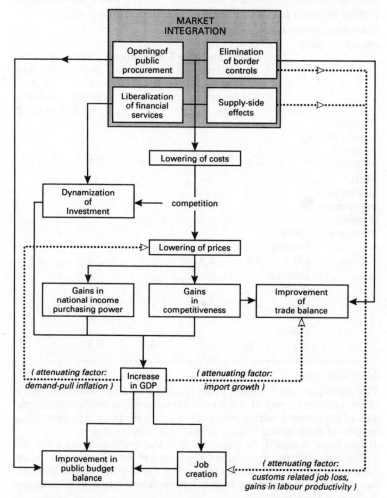

Figure 4.3 Principal macroeconomic mechanisms activated as a result of the single market (*Source:* Cecchini, 1988).

effects. Fig 4.3 outlines the principal macroeconomic mechanisms activated as a product of the SEM, and Table 4.3 lists the medium-term economic benefits of this process.

Table 4.3 (stage three) Macroeconomic consequences of completion of the internal market accompanied by economic policy measures (medium-term estimates for EUR12)

Nature of Room for economic manoeuvre policy used		Economic Consequences				
		GDP as %	Consumer prices as %	Employment (in millions)	Public deficit as % point of GDP	External balance as % point of GDP
Without accompanying economic measures		4.5	-6.1	1.8	2.2	1.0
With accompanying economic policy measures	Public finance (A)	7.5	−4.3	5.7	0	−0.5
	External position (B)	6.5	−4.9	4.4	0.7	0
	Disinflation (C)	7.0	−4.5	5.0	0.4	−0.2

Margin of error: ± 30%

The accompanying economic policy (public investment and reduction in direct taxation) is such that the room for manoeuvre created by completion of the internal market in respect of the public finance position (or in respect of the external balance or prices) is fully exploited.

It has been assumed, in this case, that the accompanying economic policy is so arranged as to exploit 30 per cent of the room for manoeuvre created by the fall in consumer prices. Full use of that room for manoeuvre would give unrealistic results (sharp deterioration in the external balance in particular.

Source: Commission 1988a: 165.

SUPPORTING POLICY INITIATIVES

The Commission regards the microeconomic benefits as being the basic minimum to be expected. It argues that the easing of macroeconomic constraints (inflation, unemployment, public and trade deficits) should, indeed must, be seen as additional growth material. On a similar note, Cecchini cites the exploitation of the room for manoeuvre, referring to the room created by the easing of macroeconomic constraints. The Commission then goes on to examine how the budgetary surplus created by the SEM could be used to generate economic growth. Whether Member States use the budgetary surplus to reduce the overall tax burden, promote large-scale European infrastructure projects or restore the level of public indebtedness, it will eventually translate into a spur for economic activity. The use of macroeconomic policies to stimulate growth in the EC economy is the final stage of Cecchini's assessment into the 'Costs of non-Europe'. However, the exact relationship between the easing of inflationary pressures, public and external balance constraints and enhanced economic activity depends on the economic policy measures taken, and in particular the macroeconomic coordination of these policy measures. The level to which the budgetary surplus, in other words the spare capacity in public spending, is used to stimulate the economy was simulated by Cecchini using three different policy scenarios (Table 4.3 above). According to scenario A, there is a full conversion of the budgetary gains into economic growth. Although this has a favourable impact on both employment and GDP (rising by 6 million and 7.5 per cent respectively), it leads to a significant deterioration in the external balance of payments (-0.5 per cent). Scenario B involves a cautious economic policy involving the removal of the external balance. Scenario C, that preferred by the Commission, is a half-way house between A and B. It involves a partial exploitation of the budgetary surplus whilst at the same time making slightly more than full use of the EC's external balance. Therefore if a specific macroeconomic policy that recognized the potential for faster growth is pursued, Cecchini predicts economic gains in the order of a 5 million increase in employment and a 7 per cent increase in the EC GDP.

   This then, is the end result of the Cecchini predictions concerning the full economic benefits to be derived from integrating the

European economy. As with the microeconomic predictions, the Commission's macroeconomic analysis has been criticized as conjecture with several fundamental weaknesses.

MACROECONOMIC POLICY COORDINATION

The essence of the Commission's macroeconomic assessment is that the removal of non-tariff barriers will reduce existing macroeconomic constraints, which will in turn lead to additional growth through government-induced reflation. It is the greater flexibility created by the internal market that will in theory bring substantial economic gains to the European economy. For example, at the end of stage two (microeconomic market integration effects) the Commission predicts an employment increase of 1.8 million jobs whereas at the end of stage three, this has increased to 5 million. But what are the chances of the twelve governments simultaneously agreeing to adopt a policy of reflationary expansion? An investigation into the macroeconomic consequences of completing the internal market was undertaken by Catinat (1988) for the 'Costs of non-Europe Research'. According to Catinat, the potential for additional government spending released as a result of the internal market amounts to approximately 3 per cent of the EC GDP. If the Community governments were to decide on spending all the extra money gained from market integration on reflating the economy, it would create a considerable expansionary programme. Neuberger (1989) compares such a programme with that of the British Labour Party's election manifesto in 1987, stating:

> At the 1987 general election, Labour's expansion programme to reduce unemployment by 4 per cent in two years involved increasing public spending by around 10 billion gross or three per cent of GDP. What the Commission is therefore proposing is a programme on the scale of Labour's programme at the 1987 general election for the whole of the EC. (Neuberger 1989)

However there are several reasons to doubt the proposition that Community-wide agreement will be reached to reflate the European economy. One cautionary note relates to the fact that the easing of macroeconomic constraints will take place in the medium to long term, variously described as six to eight years, and that governments will not actually realize that their budgetary position is significantly better at any one point in time. If the macroeconomic gains are gradually infused into the economy, as predicted by Cecchini, it seems unlikely that a reflationary response will be considered appropriate.

The reflationary policies predicted by the Commission are accompanying measures and not directly linked to the '1992' programme. In short, they are conjecture. But given the importance of such accompanying measures, what policies do the Commission forward to ensure that these policies are undertaken? Cecchini considers the SEM programme, with its impact on lessening the financial burdens of government, to be the driving force behind government-induced reflation. Neuberger, on the other hand, considers that expansionary policies will be made even more difficult as a result of the internal market, arguing that a truly free internal market will prevent individual Member States adopting reflationary policies. If one or two states adopt expansionary policies they will experience balance of payment problems, similar to the French experience in the early 1980s, as other states with restrictive policies constrain domestic demand and encourage export production. Throughout the 1980s, the West German balance of payments surplus and the British deficit were partially a result of such divergent economic policies. After following a policy of public sector constraint, the British Government eased its macroeconomic constraints and reflated the economy by reducing the tax burden, the main beneficiary of which was the West Germany economy. Therefore, a reflationary policy on the scale predicted by the Commission depends on a consensus amongst the twelve Member States to coordinate their macroeconomic policies. The chances of the Twelve simultaneously recognizing the desirability of reflation is rather remote. If for no other reason, any state that decided to follow a restrictive monetarist economic policy in the face of other countries reflating would in all probability experience a substantial balance of payments surplus. Therefore, in order for the European economy to achieve the potential gains envisaged by the Cecchini Report, some form of supranational coordination of economic and monetary policy is essential.

The predictions of economic gains from the stage three process are most circumspect. The macroeconomic policies assumed by Cecchini are not in fact part of the SEM programme. Nonetheless, they represent by far the largest gains in Cecchini's assessments into the economic benefits arising from the SEM programme. Paradoxically, these gains arise not from market integration or liberalization, but from government intervention. This in many ways contradicts the free-trade competitive ethos associated with the '1992' programme.

CONSEQUENCES FOR EMPLOYMENT

The success of the SEM programme in stimulating the European economy will be judged by a whole plethora of parameters, none more important than employment. As the Commission notes:

> among the various indicators of success, the most crucial today is that relating to employment. (Commission 1988a: 166)

As a consequence, the Cecchini Report consistently makes reference to the beneficial impact of the SEM on employment conditions throughout the whole of the Community. Indeed, employment generation is regarded as the most important benefit of the entire '1992' process:

> perhaps most important of all, is the medium-term impact of market integration on employment. With its injection of inflation-free growth, coupled with a loosening of the constraints on public exchequers in the Community's Member States, the European home market of the 1990s raises the prospect, for the first time since the early 1970s, of very substantial job creation. (Cecchini 1988: XIX)

The Cecchini Report predicts the level of this substantial job creation to be in the order of 5 million, when the relevant accompanying policy measures have been applied. As with the other benefits, the end total gain is derived from adding the cumulative totals from the economic processes taking place in stages one, two and three. The initial starting point for the SEM is the removal of non-tariff barriers which will produce gains in the efficiency of trade and production. However these gains in efficiency are dependent on the shedding of excess labour resources 'artificially' maintained by the fragmented market. Most of the microeconomic studies assume, but do not specifically quantify, that an increase in efficiency derived from a reduction in labour will have a positive social value as this labour is redeployed in other more dynamic sectors of the economy. There is however a real threat that in the short term, the EC economy will experience job losses that could have a serious impact on dampening demand. For example, job losses are expected in both the public (customs officers) and private (freight agencies) sectors as a result of removing physical barriers. While customs officers will still be required for non-EC trade, a majority of the 45,000 EC customs personnel will be affected. The Commission notes that:

The total impact on employment is initially slightly negative but in the medium term increases. (Commission 1988a: 19)

Whilst the magnitude of this 'slightly negative' impact is never specifically mentioned in the Cecchini Report, a table in a European Economy article (Commission 1988a), entitled 'illustrative profile of evolution of employment', indicates that it could be in the order of 500,000 over a period of one or two years (Fig 4.4). Stage two will also involve job losses as market integration promotes the adoption of larger scale economies, restructuring and the reduction of x-inefficiencies, specifically defined as over-manning. Estimates of the benefits associated with this economic process refer to competition leading to plant closures. Again the resources saved as a result of more efficient production units, resulting from scale economies being adopted in research and development, production and management, will initially have negative employment consequences. Almost all of the EC documents warn that the transition to a single market will involve a difficult adjustment process. Some job losses will be inevitable in the short term as industries are rationalized and restructured in the face of stiffer competition. Initially then, the single market will involve harsh dislocations and plant closures as the more efficient firms squeeze out the less competitive ones. The predicted benefits of the SEM do not mean immediate and equal gains for all. However, as the effects of the internal market start to

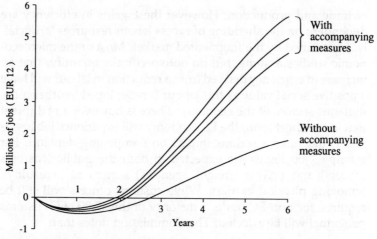

Figure 4.4 Illustrative profile of evolution of employment (*Source* Commission, 1988a).

bite, in terms of increased purchasing power, competitiveness gains and the initial lowering of prices, the Cecchini Report predicts an overall employment gain of 1.8 million jobs, 400,000 of which would be directly attributable to the opening up of public procurement practices. In the most optimistic of scenarios, stages one and two could create 2.3 million jobs. However as the Commission notes, even this improvement

> would not be sufficient to bring about any significant reduction in the current unemployment figure, since the unemployment rate would fall by only 1 to 2 percentage points in the medium term. (Commission 1988a: 162)

Even these quite modest predictions involve a number of assumptions that clearly inflate the predicted beneficial impact of the SEM on the employment market. One of the most optimistic assumptions is that resources released as costs will be effectively redeployed elsewhere in the economy. Fundamental to the Cecchini predictions on employment is the contention that labour released in the restructuring process will be re-employed productively. All estimates are based on this simple assumption of redeployment, although it is recognized there may be some time lag before this happens completely. This question of time lag is noted but not discussed, with the comment that:

...thus, in the short term, productivity gains might mean a degree of job loss, but this dip in employment would be progressively filled and then spectacularly built on. (Cecchini 1988: 97)

However, even with the most optimistic of assumptions, the employment gains achieved after stages one and two are fairly minimal, amounting to approximately 1.8 million jobs in the EC of twelve. As already stated, the beneficial impact of the SEM on the EC's employment structure will depend on the negative displacement effects of market integration being effectively redeployed productively elsewhere. The mechanism proposed by the Commission to ensure that this redeployment takes place is the adoption of coordinated macroeconomic policies, essentially that of reflation made possible by the easing of macroeconomic constraints. As far as employment is concerned, it is coordinated government action and not market integration that will bring widespread benefits to the workers of Europe. The facts speak for themselves. Without accompanying measures, the internal market is predicted to create an extra 1.8 million jobs. With accompanying measures, it could generate up to 5.7 million jobs. There is a real threat therefore that the predicted negative employment consequences of the SEM will be greater than assumed by Cecchini and in the likely absence of a coherent single macroeconomic policy, the labour resources released as costs will not be effectively re-employed productively in other parts of the European economy.

IS IT ALL A TANTALISING CHIMERA?

The continued fragmentation of the European economy throughout the 1970s and 1980s led to its weak position in many markets and the potential for cost savings arising from the rationalization of production and distribution structures. The Commission predicts that the completion of the internal market will have a significant and positive impact on the Community's economic performance and employment levels. Furthermore, this economic growth could in theory be achieved without inflationary risks or a deterioration in public finances. The underlying central assumption is that the removal of barriers will set off an economic chain reaction, maintained by vigorous competition, which will transform the Community's economic performance. As the Cecchini Report notes, by realizing the collective potential, the SEM will put Europe in a position of

> competitive strength and an upward trajectory of economic growth lasting into the next century. Such additional growth... is not a tantalising chimera. On the contrary, it is a firm prospect. (Cecchini 1988: XVII)

and

> What is Europe's greatest opportunity is within its collective grasp. In seizing it Europeans will not only do themselves justice now, but bequeath a legacy of durable wealth and stability to future generations. (Cecchini 1988: 106)

There is however much uncertainty about the implementation of the '1992' programme and the likely response from both industry and government to the opportunities and problems created. There are many inconsistencies and assumptions in Cecchini's analysis of the benefits arising from the internal market. These can be divided into three broad categories. First, there are the problems associated with measuring the potential benefits to be had from the removal of non-tariff barriers. Many of the microeconomic studies indicated only small initial benefits arising from free trade. Second, there is the problem associated with the causal assumptions taken for granted in the economic chain reaction instigated by the removal of non-tariff barriers. A significant proportion of the economic gains resulting from the internal market are dependent on multiplier effects predicted to arise from economies of scale and restructuring. The beneficial and positive impact of these processes has been questioned. Finally, and perhaps most seriously, is the assumption concerning the accompanying macroeconomic policy measures. It is at present difficult to assess the likelihood of a coordinated Community-wide macroeconomic policy taking place.

The Cecchini Report, together with Commission documents, clearly overestimate the benefits to be had from the internal market programme. The now notorious predictions of a 7 per cent increase in GDP and an employment gain of over 5 million are at the very top end of most reasonable expectations. These predictions are dependent on a successive series of assumptions, all multiplying the overall benefits of the SEM. In one of the few alternative estimates to Cecchini's Report, Neuberger (1989) predicts that the SEM will generate additional growth over the medium term of two to four per cent and a reduction in the level of consumer prices by an equal amount. This would be barely enough to bring the growth rates back to those experienced in the 1970s. Nevertheless, it is clear that the SEM will have some form of beneficial impact on the economic vitality of the European economy. Whilst the magnitude of this impact is open to question, the possibility of it moving the European economy on to a higher path is more problematic.

The purpose of the present chapter is not only to examine the predicted economic benefits on the internal market, but to evaluate the possibilities of the programme achieving its desired objectives. As far as the Euro-pragmatists are concerned, the internal market programme may turn out to be a disappointment with negligible economic benefits and the continued fragmentation of European economic space. And whilst these pragmatists consider '1992' to be a useful vehicle for promoting free trade, the substantial benefits of the internal market programme will only be recognized with considerable government intervention based on macroeconomic reflationary policies. On the other hand, '1992' has transformed the political momentum of the European Community. It has renewed the drive towards European integration, focusing the minds of European citizens, and broadening the minds of European business people on the opportunities available in an integrated market. The SEM is all about the compelling economic arguments for further European integration. For European visionaries '1992' has been an unbridled success. Whatever its end result it has already reactivated the drive towards European unity. It is in many ways too easy to get bogged down in criticizing the SEM in purely economic terms whilst at the same time forgetting the political momentum propelling the '1992' programme forward. Nonetheless, it is in these exact economic terms that the SEM programme has been sold to its Community citizens.

5. Towards a Social Europe

At the European Council held in Strasbourg in December 1989, all Member States except Britain adopted the *Community Charter of the Fundamental Social Rights of Workers*. This document was designed to 'form a keystone of the social dimension in the construction of Europe in the spirit of the Treaty of Rome supplemented by the Single European Act' (Commission 1990a: 3). Although the British government rejected what it saw as a radical socialist initiative likely to disrupt its vision of 'free-market' competition in a European Economic Community, the Charter was really a restatement of an old theme in the new context of the '1992' initiative. There has always been a strand of Community thought maintaining that a degree of social harmonization was essential to prevent unfair competition arising as a result of some Member States having more generous provisions than others. But, despite the efforts of the Commission to promote such harmonization from the 1960s onwards, governments generally felt that existing divergences in social standards did not substantially distort trade between them in a market which was not so 'common' as originally foreseen (Wallace, Hodges 1981). Besides, social policy was something that they wanted to keep mainly within the national sphere.

THE LONG HISTORY OF SOCIAL POLICY IN THE EUROPEAN COMMUNITY

Despite the predominance of economic actions in the development of the Community, there have always been much wider visions associated with the European idea. Some of the Community's original architects saw economic integration as a means of uniting European states politically rather than an end in itself. Such a political union, although not clearly defined, would deal with a whole range of matters including foreign policy, security and social affairs. The Schuman Declaration of 1950 which launched the ECSC was anything but a limited document concerned simply with efficient coal and steel production. Seen as the first step towards a 'European federation indispensable to the preservation of peace' (Schuman 1950), Article 46 of the ECSC Treaty also recognized that the creation of a common market for the production of these basic commodities would have to be balanced by social measures aimed at 'improving working conditions and living standards for workers' in these industries (Treaties 1987). Therefore, as the decline of these industries gathered pace, the ECSC funded a whole series of reconversion measures to cope with an associated increase in unemployment; since 1954, grants and loans amounting to more than ECU 10 billion have been made by the ECSC in this respect (Commission 1987a: 6). Similarly, in 1957 the Treaty of Rome establishing the EEC contained specific objectives of a social character. In admittedly general terms, Article 117 stated that 'Member States agree upon the need to promote improved working conditions and an improved standard of living for workers' and envisaged the 'harmonization of social systems' (Treaties 1987). Article 51, amongst others, gave some substance to this rather airy phrase by ensuring that migrant workers moving from one Member State to another would receive the social security benefits of the host country; in similar vein, Article 119 called upon Member States to apply 'the principle that men and women should receive equal pay for equal work'.

THE SOCIAL DIMENSION OF THE COMMON AGRICULTURAL POLICY

The much-maligned Common Agricultural Policy (CAP) – an essential requirement of the EEC Treaty – also has a social dimension rarely appreciated in Britain but widely accepted in the continental states. Article 39 of the Treaty laying down the basis for such a policy stipulated that 'a fair standard of living for the agricultural community' must be ensured and insisted that 'account shall be taken of the particular nature of agricultural activity which results from the social structure of agriculture'. When governments in Britain and the United States have attacked the protectionist aspects of the CAP, their continental counterparts in France, Germany and elsewhere have defended the CAP on various grounds, including those of a social character (Hill 1984; Wise 1989; 47–55). In these latter countries there has been a widespread concern, reinforced by electoral considerations, to preserve a genuine rural society in which farming continues to play an important role. There has long been a desire to stem, if not stop, the flow of people off the land, thus preventing the creation of ever larger rural zones with dwindling populations, ageing farmers, abandoned land, dilapidated buildings, decaying villages, and deteriorating scenic quality. Long before the idea gained much ground in Britain, planners and politicians in continental states – not least in West Germany with its much vaunted attitudes to economic efficiency – were prepared to defend the notion that agricultural policy had to be concerned with more than the production of food at the lowest possible cost. Thus, the CAP was seen as an instrument of social policy as well as one of food production. People were encouraged to perceive the small farmers of regions like Bavaria and the Massif Central as 'guardians of nature' who not only produced material things to eat and drink, but also preserved beautiful landscapes and settlements to help restore human spirits jaded by the demands of urban industrial life! The needs of threatened farming communities could thus complement the needs of stressed urban populations in some sensible social harmony. In the words of one high-level French government report, there should be no reluctance about giving 'financial aid to farmers who provide the Community with a free service in preserving its natural heritage' (Secretariat d'Etat 1983: 69).

In truth, this financial aid – excessive as it may seem to those in English-speaking countries – has not stopped the continuation of a relentless rural exodus across the European Community and an associated deterioration of the fabric of agrarian society. Whatever critics of the CAP might think, its social elements have not made it immune from market forces. The clash between the 'social' and 'economic' dimensions of EC agricultural policy has frequently manifested itself over the years in a multitude of ways. For example, the so-called 'lamb wars' which broke out periodically between Britain and France during the 1980s highlight this 'social versus economic' tension. These conflicts were triggered off when French sheep farmers blocked, by one illegal means or another, the importation of British sheepmeat into France. Sometimes the French government would help their farming constituents by insisting on extremely strict and time-consuming checks on the carcasses as they arrived at the ports. Such actions infuriated the British who saw them as a flagrant violation of the basic 'economic' demand that there shall be free trade and competition across national borders within the Common Market. To defend their actions, the French made a number of arguments some of which had an overt 'social' character (Raux 1984). For example, they made the point that imports of relatively cheap lamb threatened the already precarious livelihoods of many French sheep farmers who were struggling to survive in some of the country's poorest regions which were suffering serious depopulation. The destruction of such small farms and the rural society they supported was all the more unacceptable to many in France in that UK producers were only able to 'flood' the French market because they imported large quantities of cheap New Zealand lamb into the UK. In other words, the British were demonstrating a socio-economic preference for the interests of their 'kith and kin' in the Antipodes rather than accepting the principle of 'Community preference' which was designed to protect the living standards of EC farmers. How legitimate was it, argued defenders of French sheep farmers, to allow the societies of those with few, if any, employment alternatives to be destroyed by the interests of a relatively small number of privileged New Zealand sheep ranchers who enjoyed exceptional productive conditions of space and climate that few could compete with in an open market? In their view, the social implications of economic competition between small producers and large producers could not be ignored, especially in a Community where unemployment was a serious problem (Fig 5.1).

But the most obvious 'social dimension' of the Rome Treaty was contained in Article 123 which called for the creation of a European Social Fund (ESF) in the following terms:

In order to improve employment opportunities for workers in the common market and to contribute thereby to raising the standard of living, a European Social Fund is hereby established....it shall have the task of rendering the employment of workers easier and increasing their geographical and occupational mobility within the Community. (Treaties 1957)

The ESF, discussed more fully below, began to function in 1960, providing funds to help retrain redundant workers and resettle

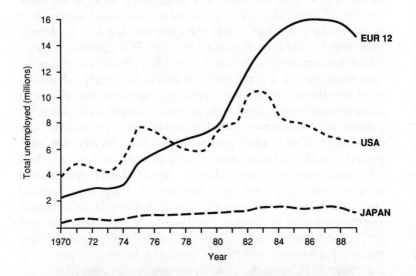

Unemployment Rate (%)			
	EUR 12	USA	JAPAN
1970	1.5	4.8	1.1
1975	3.2	8.3	1.9
1981	6.7	7.5	2.2
1983	10.0	9.5	2.6
1986	10.8	6.9	2.8
1987	10.6	6.1	2.8
1988	10.3	5.4	2.5

Figure 5.1 Unemployment trends in the EC, Japan and USA, 1970–89 (*Source:* Eurostat, 1975–90).

them in other areas where employment was available. Continuing the earlier work of the ECSC, it also assisted in maintaining the incomes of workers whose employment was 'temporarily reduced or suspended'.

Admittedly, these early steps in the development of Community social policy were limited, but they established a precedent and legal basis upon which to build. Moreover, they demonstrated an awareness that not all would be 'winners' in the building of a common market and that some social measures would be necessary to help the 'losers' in order to preserve a social consensus in favour of European integration. This has always been an essential element in the argument for a European 'social dimension'. But in those early days there was a predominant assumption that liberalization within a common market would lead to economies of scale and economic growth from which the greater number of Community citizens would benefit; in effect, an essentially liberal economic policy would be the best social policy as well.

The early days of the EC were indeed associated with unprecedented levels of economic growth; consequently, there was little pressure to enlarge the social aspects of the Community's work. The free movement of manual workers, if not their professional counterparts, was satisfactorily achieved by a range of Community measures relating to social security provisions. The Social Fund was helping workers adversely affected by change in coal, steel and other industries. The 'guidance' section of the European Agricultural Guarantee and Guidance Fund (EAGGF) was assisting farmers adapt to new circumstances. National legislation was coping with other social matters. What more was there for the EC to do?

Growing Pressure for a more Comprehensive Community Social Policy.

In the late 1960s, however, some began to argue that the drive to economic integration required a more forceful social policy articulated at Community level. At the European Council in The Hague in December 1969, Chancellor Brandt of West Germany submitted a memorandum on social policy which stated that coordination of economic integration with social harmonization was vital, not least in view of the social upheavals that had disturbed many EC countries following the 1968 'May events' in Paris. Furthermore, renewed efforts to move towards Economic and Monetary Union (EMU) required a counterbalancing set of social policies to protect those likely to suffer from such a development. These EMU initiatives were being made as the objective of moving towards a genuine common market was being thwarted by a range of national economic divergences, including differing rates of growth and inflation (Lodge 1989b: 311). If a truly integrated 'economic space' was to be built, it would inevitably provoke fears of falling further behind in the poorer peripheral regions; consequently, the Community should also build a European 'social space' to counter such anxieties.

However, somewhat paradoxically, increased monetary instability, inflation and other socio-economic divergences impeded rather than impelled progress towards EMU and related social policies. It was not until 1973 that further impetus for a more substantial social dimension came when the United Kingdom, Ireland and Denmark entered the Community. The first two countries in particular brought with them the worry that a common market generates economic forces favouring those countries lying in its geographical centre. Moreover, the British government, bruised from its bitter struggle to overcome Britain's reticence about the European idea, wanted to demonstrate to its sceptical electorate that the Community had a 'human aspect' concerned with more than just budgetary balance-sheets and 'butter mountains'! Thus at the Paris summit of October 1972, to which the new members in waiting were invited, the Community's leaders called for initiatives in social, environmental and consumer affairs as well as stating their determination to

> ...strengthen the Community by establishing an economic and monetary union, the guarantee of stability and growth, the foundation of their solidarity and the indispensable basis for social progress, and by ending disparities between the regions. (Venturini 1989: 16).

Out of these grand declarations of intent two concrete commitments of a social character emerged: first, the creation a Community regional policy to be supported by a special fund; secondly,
the drawing up of a social action programme for the Community.

THE EUROPEAN REGIONAL DEVELOPMENT FUND

The regional policy of the Community is studied in detail in
Chapter 7 as one of the more tangible and geographical aspects of
a developing social Europe. However, it is appropriate here to
point out how it fits into the overall development of a 'European
social dimension'. Policies designed to promote regional development in less-favoured areas are intrinsically 'social' in character in that they advocate governmental intervention to mitigate
what are seen as the adverse effects of 'free market' forces. They
are underpinned by a belief that it is unacceptable for people in
poorer regions to lag too far behind others in terms of social and
economic welfare. A variety of reasons explain the growth of
regional policy, but a moral sense of seeking social justice is
certainly one of them. The Treaty of Rome was rather vague
about moving towards greater spatial equality in social welfare,
but the preamble to the Rome Treaty setting up the EEC
expressed the signatory states' general desire to reduce '...the
differences existing between the various regions and the backwardness of the less favoured regions' (Treaties 1987).

In 1973, the enlargement of the Community to include countries such as Britain and Ireland which, like Italy, both had problem regions on the geographical peripheries of the Common
Market, reinforced the case for an EC regional policy. Clearly,
these new Member States could perceive national advantage in a
common policy diverting Community resources to their
depressed areas. Thus, in 1975 the Council eventually established the European Regional Development Fund (ERDF). Although
this Fund was small in relation to the scale of the regional divergences within the Common Market, it grew steadily both in
absolute terms and as a proportion of the Community budget,
rising from 4.8 per cent of total EC spending in 1975 to 9.6 per cent
in 1989 (Commission 1989d). The entry of the relatively poor
Mediterranean states – Greece in 1981 followed by the Iberian

countries in 1986 – further reinforced the role of regional policy in the Community's overall 'social dimension', as did the fears of peripheral areas which felt threatened by the potentially centralizing effects of the drive towards a single European market by the end of 1992 (Chapter 7).

THE DEVELOPMENT OF A SOCIAL ACTION PROGRAMME FOR THE COMMUNITY

In January 1974 the Council, also responding to the goals set by the 1972 Paris Summit, adopted a resolution on a Social Action Programme (SAP) which set out 20 ways of achieving three major goals:

1. the attainment of full and better employment in the Community;
2. the improvement of living and working conditions so as to make possible their harmonization while the improvement is being maintained;
3. the increased involvement of management and labour in the economic and social decisions of the Community, and of workers in the life of the enterprises in which they are employed. (Venturini 1989: 16)

The Commission welcomed this first serious attempt 'to draw up a coherent social policy setting out in a purposeful way the initial practical steps on the road towards the ultimate goal of European Social Union' (Commission 1974: 2). However, these eloquent phrases foundered on the rocks of the economic recession that deepened following the enormous increases in oil prices from the mid-1970s onwards. As Member States fell back on national responses to decreasing growth rates, increasing unemployment and rising inflation, this comprehensive plan disintegrated into a series of piecemeal actions. Thus, public awareness of any social dimension to Community activities remained limited as disputes over trade proliferated in a far from common market showing little sense of social solidarity faced with the problems of 'stagflation'. So-called national 'trade wars' over products such as apples, lamb, milk, beer, wine, and citrus fruit were widely reported in the mass media, increasing public hostility towards the Community. In the United Kingdom, the isolation of these 'social' initiatives from public debate was intensified by the long-running conflict over British 'contributions' to the Community budget which did immense harm to the image of the Community until its resolution at the Fontainebleau summit of 1984 (Shackleton 1989).

The discussion so far suggests a model of the Commission being the champion of social policy with Member States vetoing initiatives on economic grounds. However, this oversimplifies the complex relationships and decision-making processes within the Community. The subtle interplay which actually exists between the Commission and Member States on the economic and social dimensions of Community life is well illustrated by a brief review of the efforts to create a common policy in transport.

THE COMMUNITY'S COMMON TRANSPORT POLICY

The Treaty of Rome recognized the importance of transport to the establishment of an integrated European economy. Transport is an important industry in its own right, employing over 15 per cent of the Community workforce and representing more of the EC's GDP than agriculture. However, it is more vital to the functioning of a truly integrated and free market than these figures suggest. A Common Transport Policy (CTP) is necessary in order to achieve one of the primary objectives of the Rome Treaty: the free movement of the factors of production. The importance attached to transport was duly reflected in the Treaty, with a CTP being one of only three policies specifically mentioned in Article Three. The rules for operating a CTP include a number of special provisions exempting transport from the scope of the common market. In other words, the CTP does not have to adhere strictly to the free-market principles based on competition. It was therefore agreed that certain limited exemptions to competition would be tolerated, particulary those concerned with public service obligations and regional development strategies. Overall however, the Treaty of Rome focused on the establishment of a CTP to be organized in accordance with free market principles.

The Commission's 1963 Schaus Memorandum, named after the first EC Commissioner for transport M. Lambert Schaus, proposed an ambitious policy aimed at eliminating all obstacles preventing the development of a free market in transport. The 1963 Memorandum concentrated on the removal of national discriminatory policies and rates, the elimination of all policies distorting transport movements and, most importantly, the creation of 'healthy competition' in its widest scope. In this instance, the Commission proposed a policy based on competition and the 'free market' which Member States found unable to accept. Given the diversity in the structure, regulatory controls and objectives of the different transport policies adopted by Member States, it was perhaps unrealistic to assume immediate unification based on competition. Member States were genuinely concerned with the economic and social implications of adopting a policy that removed their considerable regulatory controls. Consequently the Council of Ministers, that EC institution responsible for ratifying legislation, never reached a consensus on the Memorandum. The Council's failure to establish a set of ground rules needed to operate a coherent transport policy reinforced the trend amongst Member States to adopt measures that were purely national in character.

The Commission continued its attempt to establish a CTP based on competition with the 1973 Memorandum stating its aims as:

> the development of a common transport market based on the principle of the free play of market forces subject to correction only in exceptional circumstances. (European Study Service 1989: 12)

The measures proposed by the 1973 Memorandum were similar to the Schaus Memorandum. There was however a slight shift of emphasis in order to allow Community intervention in the planning and financing of an integrated transport network so that resources could be put to their best possible use. Nonetheless, the 1973 proposals met with the same fate as the 1961 Memorandum. Again, the point of contention was the introduction of competition in an industry with considerable social obligations heavily regulated by Member State governments. In an attempt to stimulate the Council of Ministers into action, the Commission, on 24 October 1980, forwarded a list of priority projects and an associated timetable to the Council. Indeed numerous attempts were made by the Commission to instigate some action leading to the development of a CTP. In each event, the Council did little more than adopt a very limited number of topics and declared itself ready to discuss matters further.

Formulating the CTP has suffered from the conflicting philosophies of 'social intervention' and 'liberal free trade'. For Member States to accept the original Community proposals, based on free market principles, would have involved a major change in attitude and, more seriously, the threat of economic dislocation. The polarization between the need to liberalize transport and harmonize the conditions of competition has been the major source of conflict in the development of the CTP. These conflicting philosophies were reflected in the Treaty of Rome's lack of direction. The Treaty did not forward a grand design, it proposed policies based on free-market principles that could be waived in a number of circumstances. This left plenty of room for debate as to what the CTP should and should not include. For example, as late as 1974 it was undecided whether or not a CTP had to be committed to a common market in transport. Some Member States argued that the general provisions of the Treaty of Rome did not apply to transport. It was only in 1974 that the Court of Justice ruled in favour of the Rome Treaty, considering the Treaty to be universally applicable.

This lack of direction resulted in the laborious harmonization negotiations aimed at liberating the technical, fiscal and social obstacles to the creation of a CTP. Although there are over 170 agreements in the transport sector, most relate to areas of marginal importance. Exceptions to this rule are the 'social' policies developed by the Commission, and subsequently passed by the Council, concerned with harmonizing the working conditions of goods vehicle drivers. The primary aim of the so-called 'tachograph legislation' is to remove the distorting influence of different regulatory systems on the transport sector. However, the legislation is explicitly social in character, ruling that:

A driver must not drive more than 9 hours in a day...After 4.5 hours driving, whether continuous or accumulated, a driver must take a break of at least 45 minutes,

and

A driver must have a minimum weekly rest of 45 consecutive hours. (Department of Transport 1987: 2)

The tachograph regulation is a rare example of transport legislation, with an explicit social dimension, being passed at the Community level. In 1988, over 40 Commission proposals stood before the Council of Ministers, some of which had been there for over ten years, the end result being over 30 years of inaction, with the most characteristic feature being its failure to affect the transport policies and markets of Member States. Reflecting the real frustration over this inaction, the European Parliament took the Council of Ministers to the European Court of Justice for failing to provide policies in the sphere of international transport. In May 1985, the Court of Justice found the Council of Ministers guilty of failing to fulfil its obligations under the Treaty of Rome. However by the end of that year, following the publication of Lord Cockfield's White Paper on *Completing the Internal Market*, the Council of Ministers agreed to create a free market in transport by 1992.

THE EUROPEAN SOCIAL FUND

Although stagnation and national conflict characterized the Community during much of the 1970s and early 1980s, slow movement, albeit disjointed, did continue towards social goals. The grand phrases about attaining 'full and better employment' (above) would have seemed ludicrous to any unlikely listener in the growing masses of EC unemployed (Fig 5.1) , but tiny steps were still being taken. For example, the Social Fund continued to grow both in scope and the financial resources at its disposal, as the Commission urged reluctant Member States to give more substance to their grand declarations.

From its very limited beginnings in 1960 (see above) the ESF developed in pursuit of two main goals:

1. to help cope with changes arising as a result of Community policies (eg retrain persons wishing or forced to leave the agricultural, textile, or clothing industries);

2. to help cope with the problems endured by certain regions or certain sections of society such as migrant workers (since 1974), young unemployed (since 1975), women (since 1978) and disabled people.

These wide goals permitted applications for support from a great range of public and private bodies. To meet the growing demand, the Fund's budget was regularly increased both in absolute terms and as a proportion of the Community's budget (Commission 1989d; Shackleton 1989). Between 1973 and 1989 the amount available to the ESF rose from ECU 249 million (5.5 per cent of the EC budget) to ECU 3232 million (7.2 per cent of the EC budget).

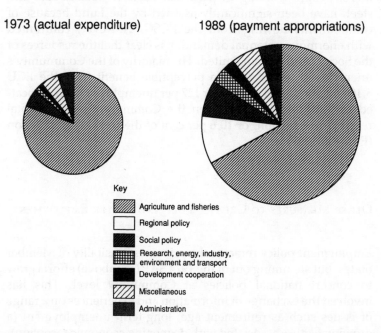

1973 (actual expenditure)   1989 (payment appropriations)

Key

Agriculture and fisheries

Regional policy

Social policy

Research, energy, industry, environment and transport

Development cooperation

Miscellaneous

Administration

Figure 5.2 Division of the EC budget 1973 and 1989 (*Source:* Commission, 1989d).

Inevitably, potential needs outstripped available resources as unemployment in the EC10 grew from 2.6 million in 1973 to 6.5 million in 1980 to 12.4 million in 1984; with the addition of Spain and Portugal in 1986 the total for the EC12 exceeded 16 million by 1987 (Fig 5.1). The fact that the ESF was still only securing some 7.2 per cent of the Community budget in 1989 whilst agriculture was obtaining some 67 per cent also underlines the limited scope of these social efforts (Fig 5.2). Indeed, it is hard to refute the charge that the Social Fund was part of an essentially 'cosmetic' policy designed to give the impression that the Community was tackling these increasingly severe problems, whereas little of substance was in fact being achieved to counter growing mass unemployment.

Such criticisms can be mitigated by pointing out that the Social Fund was meant to complement rather than replace national social policies (which is not the case for agricultural policy where the Community assumes overwhelming responsibility). Furthermore, people working in particular sectors, notably coal and steel, have been significantly assisted by the Fund because of commitments flowing from the ECSC. However, confronted with enormous potential demand, it is clear that the resources of the Social Fund remain limited. The majority of the Community's unemployed would feel no perceptible benefit from the ECU 3,100 million (2,046 million: or 127 per unemployed head) allocated to the Fund in 1987 when the Community's jobless total reached 16.1 million, or 10.6 per cent of the working population (Eurostat 1989).

OTHER MEASURES TO CREATE 'FULL AND BETTER EMPLOYMENT'

Employment policy remains the prime responsibility of Member States, but stemming out of the 1974 SAP (see above) efforts grew to concert national policies at Community level. This has involved the exchange of information and experiences on a range of issues such as retirement age, long-term unemployment (a growing feature associated with deepening economic recession), and local job-creation schemes. More specifically, a European

Centre for the Development of Vocational Training was established in Berlin to improve and harmonize levels of vocational training. Representatives of governments, employers, workers and the Commission work together in this Centre to build the basis for Community resolutions on matters including training for new technologies and the preparation of young people for work. The Social Fund cooperates with these activities, notably on the question of youth employment which has become an increasingly prominent aspect of the Community's efforts to promote a social Europe. For example, in 1976 the EC's Ministers of Education adopted a resolution to improve young people's preparation for work, whilst in 1978 the European Council agreed that the Social Fund should pay special attention to work-creation schemes for those unemployed under twenty-five years old. But all these efforts have still not created a genuine common vocational training policy to match the development of the Single European market.

The very general aim of improving living and working conditions has long underpinned a number of Community activities, despite the limited legal basis provided by the founding treaties. Linked to the ECSC, Safety and Health Commissions were set up for the coal (1957) and steel (1965) industries, while the Euratom Treaty (1957) laid down minimum standards regarding protection against radiation. Following the adoption of the Social Action Programme in 1974 (see above) a series of Directives in similar mould laid the foundations for harmonized efforts to improve working conditions. In 1974, an Advisory Committee on Safety, Hygiene and Health Protection at Work was set up to assist the Commission in formulating proposals for these matters. This led to the adoption of an action programme in 1978 which produced Directives to protect workers from the dangers of physical, chemical and biological agents at work, namely: exposure to lead, asbestos, cadmium, vinyl chloride monomer and other carcinogenic substances (Venturini 1989: 20 & 117).

Equality of treatment for both men and women has also been a major theme of the Commission's drive to develop the EC's social dimension. From 1975 onwards a succession of Directives were implemented enshrining the principles of equal pay for equal work, equality of access to employment, vocational training, promotion and social security rights. Special attention was also

paid to the rights of pregnant women and mothers to retain their
jobs whilst enjoying adequate maternity leave, as well as the
need to promote sexual equality in practice as well as in law
(Venturini 1989: 19).

The quest to promote a communal improvement in living and
working conditions also extended into the realms of working
hours and statutory holidays. In 1975, a Council resolution
(which recommends rather than requires) called upon the Member
States to introduce a 40-hour week and 4 weeks paid holiday
as standard practice (Venturini 1989: 20). To move from recommendation to concrete action on such matters within a Community that has a wide variety of working and recreational traditions is
an immense undertaking, the wisdom of which many would
question. To assist such efforts, yet another EC body – the European Foundation for the Improvement of Living and Working
Conditions – was set up in Dublin in 1976. As unemployment
rose during the recession, it, and other EC organizations, turned
attention to the contentious issue of work-sharing. As books with
titles like *The collapse of work* (Jenkins, Sherman 1979) received
much publicity, the Council called upon the Commission in 1979
to get representatives of both employers and employees to examine jointly the possibilities of reorganizing work by: reducing the
amount of overtime, introducing flexible retirement, reducing
the annual volume of work, extending annual holidays and training leave, and developing part-time and temporary work (Commission 1988f: 5). However, unlike the Directives related to
matters of health and sexual equality at work, this effort to lighten
people's working load and introduce greater flexibility in working patterns was based on a voluntary approach. Not surprisingly, nothing of great note emerged on these questions as Member
States contented themselves by making general declarations of
intent at Community level, while retaining firm control of policy
specifics within national institutions.

THE DEMOCRATIZATION OF ECONOMIC LIFE

The ideal that all those involved in the productive process should
participate in the making of decisions affecting their working
lives has long had its adherents in the European Commission.

There has been some success in setting up bodies which bring together representatives from all sides of industry at a remote Community level, but attempts to impose more democratic structures at company level have achieved very little (Venturini 1989: 21; Lodge 1989b: 312). At the European level a network of committees has grown up over the years within which representatives of employers and employees meet to express their opinions and assist in the formulation of EC proposals. Some of these bodies were expressly required by the founding treaties, notably the Economic and Social Committee (ECOSOC), the European Social Fund Committee and the ECSC Consultative Committee. However, most have developed in 'ad hoc' fashion in order to bring the various 'social partners' into the policy-making process.

The ECOSOC is the most obvious symbol of this desire to bring the 'economic' and 'social' dimensions of EC life together in a single consultative body, but in truth its influence on Community decision-making has been small and largely invisible to the mass of working people. It has a rather crude tripartite structure composed of 'employers', 'workers' and those representing 'other activities' (eg farmers, consumers etc.), none of whom are elected. The 189 members, who can hardly be expected to cope adequately with the extremely wide-ranging and numerous issues dealt with by the Community, are appointed, in 'corporatist state' fashion, from lists drawn up by the member governments. As a sort of microcosm of interest groups within EC society it produces worthy reports which doubtless have some effect on proposals formulated by the Commission. Nevertheless, its members, appointed rather than elected, can hardly provide a substantial democratic input into the deliberations of the Community. The manifest inadequacies of the ECOSOC have, in part, been compensated for by the multitude of specialist advisory committees already mentioned. For example, there are joint labour and management committees for certain industries such as textiles and construction, committees to advise on socio-economic matters relating to transport, foodstuffs and so on. But the closed world of appointees to these numerous bodies, operating away from public gaze, has not injected a vigorous social-democratic component in Community life. Not surprisingly, therefore, numerous Europe-wide pressure groups have sprung up outside of ECOSOC's limited confines.

Following social unrest throughout western Europe in 1968, union pressure for a more meaningful Community social policy grew. The idea of 'worker participation' had received a very public airing in the May 'uprising' in France where youthful exuberance and idealism had severely shaken the French state and stirred unions into action. Thus in May 1970, the first EC conference on employment pulled together the Member States' employment ministers, as well as delegates from the Commission and the two sides of industry. Out of this emerged yet two more advisory bodies: the Standing Committee on Employment and the Tripartite Conferences within which the 'social partners' (employers and employees) and 'decision-makers' (Member States, Council and Commission) seek to consult each other on broad social and economic issues in an effort to concert their objectives. Predictably, little of real significance emerged from these bodies, again notable for their anonymity as far as the general public were concerned. The Council did adopt some Directives on workers rights, notably in relation to mass dismissals, company takeovers and bankruptcies, but discussion and proposals far outweighed decisive action (Teague 1989: 58). In frustration, the European Trade Union Confederation (ETUC) threatened to withdraw in 1978 unless something concrete emerged from these deliberations; nothing did, and the Tripartite Conferences consequently lapsed. In truth, despite the Commission's best efforts to build a consensus based on 'integrationist' principles designed to overcome the traditional antagonism of capital and labour, on crucial issues such as work-sharing and the generation of employment the viewpoints of employers and employees could not be reconciled in some sort of 'corporatist' compromise.

The idea of involving workers more fully in the affairs of their company was central to the Commission's approach to social policy. During the 1970s it proposed a series of draft Directives and resolutions relating to company organization, including measures to increase employee participation. The most significant in this context of 'democratizing' economic life at local level were the draft Fifth Directive, first proposed in 1972, and the so-called Vredeling Directive, named after the Commissioner then in charge of Social Affairs. These proposals aimed to introduce formal consultation and information procedures into larger, especially transnational, companies within the Community, but fierce opposition from employers ensured that they were never adopted by the Council (Teague 1989: 65).

WHY DID THE 1974 SOCIAL ACTION PROGRAMME ACHIEVE SO LITTLE?

The 1974 Social Action Programme produced some limited piecemeal results, but clearly discussions far outweighed decisions during the 1970s and early 1980s. The reasons for this are varied. First, faced with the intensification of social problems during the economic recession, Member States fell back on national, rather than Community, responses to these difficulties; the relatively prosperous shied away from financing social schemes of primary benefit to their poorer partners, while the relatively poor countries were wary of being burdened with costly, restrictive social measures. Such responses were intensified as the Community struggled to absorb the UK, Ireland and Denmark in its first major enlargement during the 1970s. In particular, the enormous problems of absorbing a reluctant Britain, increasingly embittered by its 'contributions' to the EC budget, swamped social issues. The fact that unanimity was required in the Council for any proposals in this area also contributed to the stagnation of EC social policy.

Most fundamentally, however, a clash between the philosophies of the Commission on one hand and those of Member State governments on the other hindered progress. The former, always keen to promote a 'European' dimension, favoured a 'harmonization' approach to social policy. Essentially, this involved examining procedures in the various Member States to find the 'best practices' on employment and then drafting Directives designed to pull everyone upwards. Definition of 'best practice' tended to be in terms of an 'integrationist' philosophy whereby the conflicts between capital and labour would be resolved within democratic company structures in a 'social-market' economy. In truth, the codetermination model established in West Germany and the Netherlands, elaborated with French notions of 'worker participation', loomed large in the Commission's thinking. Predictably, the problems of transferring employment practices across frontiers proved greater than the Commission anticipated. In the words of one labour lawyer:

We cannot take for granted that rules or institutions are transplantable...any attempt to use a pattern of law outside the environment of its origin continues to entail the risk of rejection....The conclusion is clear: rules relating to the power relations in the industrial relations systems and also in society as a whole will be the most difficult to transplant... (Blanpain 1985: 7)

SOCIAL POLICY AND COMMUNITY REVIVAL DURING THE 1980s

In 1981 a socialist government came to power in France under President Mitterrand. Britain was not the only country in Europe where those on the Left had misgivings about what was seen as the excessively 'economic' orientation of a Community where the interests of business seemed paramount; similar sentiments were widespread in the new French political majority. This, coupled with a desire to pull the EC out of the fractious stagnation into which it had sunk, led France's new government to issue a memorandum on the creation of a 'European social area' which would have three main objectives:

1. to place employment problems at the heart of Community social policy;

2. to increase the 'social dialogue' between employers and employees at Community, national and company level;

3. to improve consultation and cooperation on matters of social protection. (Fabius 1984; Vandamme 1984)

There was little immediate response to this appeal. Indeed, France subsequently made its own ultimately ill-fated effort to spend its way out of the recession in traditional Keynesian manner. Nevertheless, a major Community government was now proclaiming its support for a social Europe, thus increasing the potential to turn an era of indecisive discussion into an era of action.

The chances of tapping this potential grew following the crucial European Council held at Fontainebleau in June 1984, when a series of long-running, debilitating disputes were resolved. In particular, Britain's quarrel with its partners over 'contributions' to the EC budget was settled and the barriers which lay in the way of the entry of Spain and Portugal into the Community were lifted, thus releasing energies to respond to new challenges and embark on a programme of revival (the origins of the '1992' project can be traced back to this period). At the same time a new European Commission took office, significantly headed by Jacques Delors, a powerful French socialist politician who had played a very prominent ministerial role in the Mitterrand governments of the early 1980s. It was not coincidental that the Fontainebleau summit also approved a new social action plan based upon the deliberations of the preceding Council of Ministers for Social Affairs which concluded that;

> the Community will not be able to strengthen its economic cohesion in the face of international competition if it does not strengthen its social cohesion at the same time. Social policy must therefore be developed at Community level on the same basis as economic, monetary and industrial policies. (Venturini 1989: 26)

This reinvigorated desire to create a 'balanced' Europe found expression in the action programme presented by the new Commission to the European Parliament at the beginning of 1985 (Commission 1985b). It had four major aspects:

1. The creation of a single internal Community market by the end of 1992 to finally achieve the 'common market' goal of the Rome Treaty. While this goal was 'economic' in character and responded to the perceived need to compete effectively with the USA and Japan in a revived world economy (see Chapters 2 and 3), Delors's Commission also pointed to the 'social' benefits of increased growth and employment which, hopefully, would flow from its realization.

2. The preparation and ratification of a Single European Act to complement the founding treaties which no longer provided an adequate basis for Community action. This Act would promote far more than the single market project alone. It would also extend the Community's social actions via a range of provisions relating to improvement of the working environment, social dialogue and promotion of

'economic and social cohesion' across the Community. It was eventually signed in February 1986 and entered into force in July 1987 after ratification by the parliaments of all the Member States (Commission 1986a; and Treaties 1987).

3. The development of the so-called 'Delors package' which was presented in February 1987 (Commission 1987b). This set of proposals was full of social implications. Not only did it deal with reform of the CAP (bring its costs under control) and revision of the Community's finances (find new resources for the EC budget), but proposed the coordination of the three structural funds (the ESF, the ERDF and the EAGGF-Guidance Section), as well as a doubling of the funds at their disposal, in order to pursue social objectives more effectively.

4. The revival of the moribund 'social dialogue' between representatives of employers, employees and government. As we have seen, these had all but broken down at Community level as the recession had deepened. Again the driving hand of Jacques Delors was apparent as the so-called 'Val Duchesse' talks (named after a chateau in the Brussels suburbs) got going in 1985, bringing the so-called 'social partners' together to discuss the employment implications of macroeconomic policy, the single market and new technologies (Teague 1989: 70). Fundamental differences between the two sides soon became apparent as the European employers' organization (UNICE) saw the meetings as no more than a forum for discussion, whereas the European trade unions (ETUC), more in tune with the Commission's desires, wanted these talks to lay down a basis for Community legislation. Clearly, the enormous complexities of conflicts between capital and labour cannot be achieved in such a rarefied setting far from the numerous factory floors of the Common Market.

THE SINGLE EUROPEAN ACT AND SOCIAL POLICY

It is clearly a misconception, stemming from the enormous emphasis placed on the '1992' deadline, that the Single European Act is simply concerned with the creation of a Single European Market. In fact, it is a much more comprehensive treaty dealing with foreign, defence and social affairs as well as the much publicized economic issues. Articles 21–3 dealing with 'Social Policy' require action over a wide, if not clearly delineated, field. Article 21 ordains that the EEC Treaty must be supplemented with a number of provisions, including the following:

1. Member States shall pay particular attention to encouraging improvements, especially in the working environment, as regards the health and safety of workers, and shall set as their objective the harmonization of conditions in this area, while maintaining the improvements made.

2. In order to help achieve (this) objective, the Council, acting by a qualified majority on a proposal from the Commission, in cooperation with the European Parliament and after consulting the Economic and Social Committee, shall adopt, by means of Directives, minimum requirements for gradual implementation, having regard to the conditions and technical rules obtaining in each of the Member States.
    Such Directives shall avoid imposing administrative, financial and legal constraints in a way which would hold back the creation and development of small and medium-sized undertakings.

3. The provisions adopted...shall not prevent any Member State from maintaining or introducing more stringent measures for the protection of working conditions compatible with this Treaty. (Treaties 1987)

What is noteworthy in this Article is the commitment to qualified majority voting and the specific reference to legally binding Directives rather than 'Recommendations'. Directives leave the Member States some legislative discretion in how they achieve an agreed Community objective, but do not allow them to ignore that aim. Some concession to the sort of fears about bureaucratic interference expressed by the British government (see above) is evident in the reference to small and medium-sized enterprises, but the commitment to establish acceptable minimum standards across the Community is clear. However, Article 22, which deals with the more contentious issue of employee participation in the affairs of the enterprises for which they work, is far more circumspect, reflecting British and other reservations in this regard:

> The Commission shall endeavour to develop the dialogue between management and labour at European level which could, if the two sides consider it desirable, lead to relations based on agreement. (Treaties 1987)

There was nothing here to send shivers down the backs of directors in British boardrooms or raise the eyebrows of German, Dutch and French employers familiar with formalized cooperation procedures in industrial relations!

Article 23 underpinned a belief in the indivisibility of 'economic' and 'social' phenomena by laying down what was thought to be necessary to develop 'economic and social cohesion' in the Community:

> In order to promote its overall harmonious development, the Community shall develop and pursue its actions leading to the strengthening of its economic and social cohesion. In particular the Community shall aim at reducing disparities between the various regions and the backwardness of the least-favoured regions. (Treaties 1987)

The Member States go on to commit themselves to 'conduct' and 'coordinate' their economic policies so that these general aims are achieved. The linkage to the '1992' project is specifically made by requiring that 'the implementation ...of the internal market shall take into account (these) objectives'. More specifically still, the role of the Community's various 'Structural Funds' (ERDF, ESF and EAGGF-Guidance) is restated with a commitment to decide a package of measures to pursue these aims in the run-up to 1992. Such a package was to be subject to unanimous decision in the Council, but thereafter 'implementing decisions related to the European Regional Development Fund shall be taken by the Council, acting by a qualified majority...'. In fact, these SEA commitments did lead fairly quickly to a decision to double spending on the Structural Funds by 1993 and concentrate at least 80 per cent of these resources in the poorest regions of the Community (Commission 1987c; Commission 1990a).

Clearly, the SEA incorporates a desire to build a 'social dimension' into the Community's activities to counter the potential human costs of economic liberalization within a single market. But, equally evidently, there is enough ambiguity and imprecision in many of its provisions to allow national governments to contest the degree of social interventionism at a European level. As the single market develops and its effects become more evident, mighty battles will be fought over the nature of social Europe. The fact that all Member States except the UK signed the Social Charter in December 1989 indicates that the current is presently flowing in favour of the 'social marketeers'. But the Charter was only a 'solemn declaration' with no direct legal consequences. There have been plenty of these in the long history of attempts to develop a meaningful social policy at Community level, but the list of concrete achievements stemming from them is not very impressive. It remains to be seen whether the Social Charter provides a solid base for the introduction of tangible measures which really do affect the lives of workers throughout the Community, not least those threatened by increased competition in the Single European Market. This central issue, which will colour much of the Community's activity during the 1990s, lies at the heart of the following chapter.

6. A Social Charter for a European Social Market?

The European Commission, backed by a majority in the European Parliament, was determined that the move towards an integrated EC 'economic space' should be matched by the development of a corresponding 'social space' based on fundamental employment rights applicable throughout the single market. It was

> convinced that 1992 will be a success only if both sides of industry are involved in it. A social consensus is an essential factor in maintaining sustained economic growth. Europe cannot be built against the opinions of the employers or of the workers or of the general public, and efforts must be made, as the Commission has been stressing since 1985, to prevent distortions of competition from leading to forms of social dumping. (Commission 1989a:1)

The term 'social dumping' entered the '1992' debate to articulate fears that economic liberalization in the single market could be used to weaken social protection of workers competing for jobs in a more 'laissez-faire' international environment. There was a strong feeling in labour circles, forcibly expressed by the European Trade Union Confederation (ETUC), that Community action would be necessary to prevent companies playing one group of national workers off against another in an effort to minimize costs and remain competitive. The potential ability of companies, freed from national shackles on capital investment movements in a genuine common market, to force workers to accept reduced pay and conditions is considerable. Unions and political leaders in richer states like West Germany and Denmark where high wages, wide social security provisions, good working conditions and relatively heavy taxation prevail, suspect that investment – and jobs – could drift away from them towards countries where income expectations are lower, social provisions far less protective and environmental legislation less restrictive. In effect, ruthless competition in an unregulated market might lead to 'social dumping', a rather imprecise, but increasingly used concept to describe the potentially adverse effects outlined above (Boyer 1988).

During the 1980s the social dumping thesis gained ground for several reasons. First, the entry of Greece, Spain and Portugal into the EC widened the gap in social standards enormously, thus increasing the possibilities of trade, price and wage wars (see Tables 6.1–6.5 and Fig 6.1–6.2). Secondly, the internationalization of business, with multinational companies devising trade and investment strategies which straddled national boundaries, made the potential for social dumping practices ever more actual (Wadley 1986). Thirdly, the successful promotion of the single European market project drew consideration of such social matters out of esoteric conferences into more open public debate as people began to assess the costs and benefits of '1992' to them. The creation of some Community-wide social rights began to look less like the product of meddling 'Eurocratic' minds divorced from reality, but something of tangible benefit to workers in all Member States (Willis 1989). Supporters of this thesis had varying ideas on who would be the losers. Some feared that the wealthier countries would lose jobs and see their standards undermined, whilst others feared that poorer regions would never be able to raise their standards as they fought to compete with more powerful areas by constantly cutting prices and wages. Another tendency was to worry that the whole Community could suffer from unregulated competition. Peripheral countries might start the process of price-wage reduction to increase their exports or reduce import penetration of their previously protected home market. This in turn could provoke a retaliatory lowering of prices and incomes in the core states which might destabilize the

Community's economy as a whole in a deflationary spiral. Profit margins would be reduced along with purchasing power, tax yields would decrease, investment in new products and technology could dry up as managers and governments became obsessed with cost-cutting to maintain short-term advantage in a shrinking, but increasingly competitive market (Teague 1989: 77–80).

Table 6.1 Expenditure on social protection in EC member states as a percentage of national GDP, 1984.

Netherlands	33.2%
Denmark	30.5%
Belgium	30.2%
W.Germany	29.4%
France	28.0%
Luxembourg	27.0%
UK	23.9%
Ireland	23.0%
Italy	22.4%
Spain	17.0%
Portugal	15.7%
Greece	n.a.

Source: Eurostat 1989.

Table 6.2 Comparative industrial labour costs per hour in EC member states, 1984.

	PPS	ECU
Belgium	16.04	13.09
W. Germany	14.52	14.14
Netherlands	14.47	13.59
France	13.40	12.17
Luxembourg	13.24	10.96
Italy	13.24	10.39
Ireland	10.67	8.79
UK	10.12	8.84
Denmark	9.26	11.90
Greece	8.21	3.97
Portugal	4.7	2.29
Spain	n.a.	n.a

PPS = Purchasing Power Standard.
ECU = European Currency Unit.

Source: Eurostat 1989.

Table 6.3 Average hourly gross earnings for manual industrial workers in EC member states, 1986 (current PPS).

	PPS (Purchasing Power Standard)
Denmark	9.18
Luxembourg	9.03
Netherlands	8.54
W. Germany	8.48
UK	8.40
Belgium	8.17
Ireland	7.58
Italy	7.28 (est)
France	6.46
Spain	6.42 (est)
Greece	5.01
Portugal	3.55

Source: Eurostat 1989.

Table 6.4 Structure of labour costs in EC member states 1984 (% of total cost).

	Direct costs (%)		Indirect costs %	
	Basic salary	Other payments	Social security contributions	Other costs (eg train -ing)
France	52.6	16.1	27.7	3.6
Italy	54.2	19.4	26.4	6.9
Netherlands	55.8	17.3	24.1	2.8
Belgium	54.9	20.3	23.7	1.1
W. Germany	56.0	20.7	21.0	2.3
Portugal	58.6	16.5	18.0	6.9
Greece	61.0	20.0	18.0	1.0
Luxembourg	69.0	14.8	14.8	1.4
UK	71.3	11.8	14.4	2.5
Ireland (1981)	73.7	10.4	12.9	3.0
Denmark	83.6	8.8	5.7	1.8
Spain	n.a.			

Source: Eurostat 1989.

Table 6.5 Unemployment rates in EC member states (1983–87).

	1983	1984	1985	1986	1987	1988–7 average
Spain	17.8	20.6	21.9	21.2	20.6	20.4
Ireland	15.2	17.0	18.5	18.3	18.0	17.4
Belgium	12.6	12.6	11.7	11.8	11.6	12.1
UK	11.2	11.4	11.5	11.5	10.6	11.2
Netherlands	12.5	12.5	10.5	10.2	10.0	11.1
Italy	9.0	9.5	9.4	10.6	11.0	9.9
France	8.2	9.8	10.3	10.4	10.6	9.9
Greece	9.0	9.3	8.7	8.2	7.9	8.6
Portugal	7.7	8.4	8.5	8.2	6.8	7.9
Denmark	9.5	9.2	7.6	5.8	5.9	7.6
W. Germany	6.9	7.1	7.3	6.5	6.4	6.8
Luxembourg	3.6	3.0	3.0	2.6	2.7	3.0
EC 12	10.0	10.8	10.9	10.8	10.6	10.6

Source: Eurostat 1989.

In addition to the potential costs of ruthless price competition, adherents of the 'social dumping' thesis felt that an excessively deregulated 'Europe without frontiers' might lead to large companies devising strategies which intensified the geographical division of the Community's labour market into two distinct spheres (Gibb, Treadgold 1989: 75–82; Lipietz 1988). In the core areas of the internal market, companies could intensify the location of more sophisticated, high-salaried production tasks, whereas the poorer peripheries would continue to accumulate labour-intensive, lowly-skilled and poorly-paid jobs. Such an economic division could lead to serious political divisions in the Community which might ultimately threaten the effort to build political and economic union among its Member States.

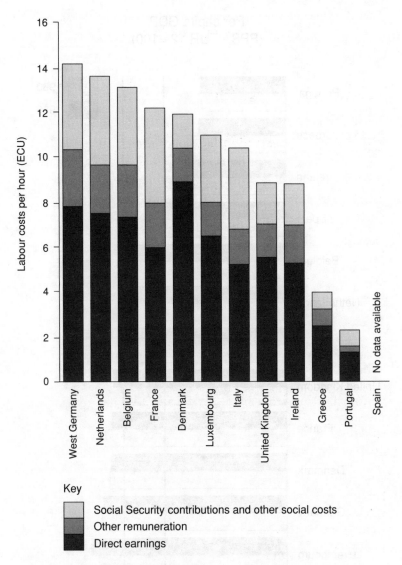

Figure 6.1 **Structure of industrial labour costs in EC countries, 1984.**
(*Source:* Commission, 1988h; Eurostat, 1990b).

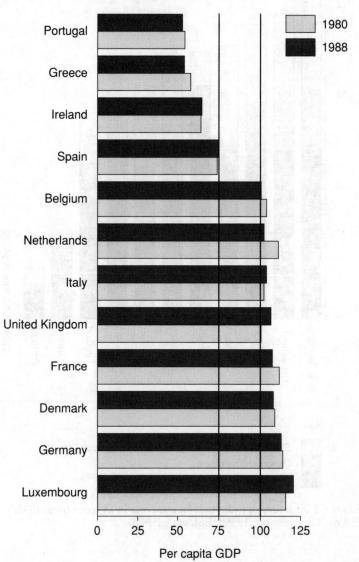

Figure 6.2 Gap between EC countries in terms of GDP per capita, 1980–8 (*Source:* Eurostat, 1975–90).

THE SOCIAL CHARTER

A conviction that fears of social dumping in the single market were not unfounded led the Commission to formulate the *Community Charter of the Fundamental Social Rights of Workers* which was accepted by all Member States except Britain in December 1989 (see previous chapter). The relationship of this so-called 'Social Charter' to the '1992' project was explicitly recognized by Mrs Vasso Papandreou, EC Commissioner for Social Affairs and Employment:

> efforts towards completing the internal market in 1992 have highlighted the importance of this social dimension. It is not simply a question of ensuring freedom of movement for persons, together with goods services and capital. It also contributes to improving the well-being of Community citizens and in the first place workers. The construction of a dynamic and strong Europe depends on the recognition of a foundation of social rights. A political signal given at the highest level was crucial. (Commission 1990a: 5)

Mrs Papandreou insisted that this initiative did not mean that 'we want to impose a uniform order in the EC'. On the contrary the Commission was 'aware that there are different attitudes, different historical developments, different cultures, different conditions...(and)...we don't want to over-regulate from Brussels' (Commission 1989b:2). She stressed that the principle of 'subsidiarity' should apply in the social field so that what can best be done at local level should be done at local level, what can best be done at national level should be done at that level, and then only those things best done at European level should involve Community action. Thus, there was no reason why many of the Charter's aims could not be achieved by action at national, regional or local levels. However, to win widespread support for the single market it was essential that the Community's leaders – that is the governmental heads of Member States – give a very visible 'political signal' to ordinary people that they were not only concerned to construct a 'businessman's Europe'; hence the importance of getting the European Council to accept the much publicized 'Social Charter' in December 1989.

This Charter had no legally binding consequences, but was a 'solemn declaration' laying a foundation upon which a programme of Community legislation could be built. In the words of Jacques Delors, the President of the European Commission:

> It is a solemn declaration and lays down the broad principles underlying our European model of labour law and, more generally, the place of work in our societies. It incorporates a foundation of social rights which are guaranteed and implemented, in some cases at the level of the Member States or at Community level depending on the field of competence. But it cannot be put into practice without the active participation of the two sides of industry. (Commission 1990c 3)

So the Social Charter was not a rigid legal prescription to be applied in some homogenizing manner across a diverse Community, but an attempt to win mass allegiance for the ideal of European integration by defining some basic minimum rights in the world of work including:

> freedom of movement of EC citizens within the Community;
> equitable wages sufficient to enable a decent standard of living;
> rights for part-time and temporary workers;
> improved living and working conditions involving the progressive Community-wide harmonization of holiday periods and so on;
> adequate social protection for both those in and out of work;
> freedom of association and collective bargaining;
> the right to vocational training;
> equal treatment for men and women;
> adequate participation of employees in the affairs of the companies that employ them;
> satisfactory health and safety at work;
> protection of children and adolescents at work;
> proper retirement pensions;
> the integration of disabled persons into the world of work.

Many states – notably West Germany with its 'social market' model – already had legislation which met, or exceeded, most of the requirements of the Social Charter. The aim of the Charter was not to undermine such Member State legislation nor to harmonize all national social policies. Rather it sought to lay down some 'fundamental social rights' which would establish basic minimum conditions (which individual countries could exceed if they so desired) and encourage movement towards 'best practice' in the Community. Thus, where necessary, the Commission would propose common legislation to ensure that no group of workers in any EC country be left far less protected than their counterparts elsewhere in the Common Market. In this way 'fair' as well as 'free' competition would be achieved in the single market.

The Commission also saw social policy as contributing to, rather than hampering, economic efficiency. It argued that social consensus, along with market competition, was a vital ingredient of sustained economic growth and job creation. Obviously, this approach clashed with the basic tenets of right-wing economists who blamed the relative economic stagnation of EC countries during the 1970s and 1980s on the systems of social protection and labour organization associated with the growth of post-war 'welfare states' (Commission 1988h: 57). The EC's declining proportionate share of international markets, its relative slowness in adjusting to new technologies, and its rapidly growing unemployment problem (see Chapters 2 and 5) were attributed, at least in part, to its extensive social welfare provisions which not only led to high labour costs and reduced competitiveness, but encouraged resistance to change in a world where the ability to adapt rapidly was a key to economic success. Whilst recognizing some elements of truth in these arguments (hence its proposals for greater competition in a single market), the Commission insisted that social policy and 'workers rights' could be used to combat 'Eurosclerosis' rather than aggravate it. In the most general sense, this argument maintains that a contented labour force, given a clear sense of participation in its company, is more likely to generate long-term economic efficiency than one which feels alienated from its employers and prone to disruptive industrial actions. More specifically a 'productive social policy' of the sort envisaged by the authors of the Social Charter could point to things like investment in training and improved working conditions as elements of social policy leading directly to increased economic efficiency. Clearly, the Commission was determined to build a social dimension which not only had a 'moral' foundation based on notions of equity (however difficult to define in precise terms), but which was also rooted in the belief that social policy and economic policy were not in some sort of inevitable conflict or 'zero-sum' game where one could only win at the expense of the other.

REACTIONS TO THE SOCIAL CHARTER

In adopting this strategy the Commission enjoyed the broad support of most Member State governments and the European Parliament. The general consensus was that European economic and political unity could not be based simply on laissez-faire competition within a common market. Unbridled competitive forces could engender serious social conflicts and lead employ-ers, employees and the general public to reject the larger objec-tive of European union. Free competition, whilst desirable, had to take place within a market where there were rules to ensure 'fair play' and mitigate social tensions which could create political instability. Thus, in 1988 the socialist French Prime Minister, M. Rocard, confirmed his government's commitment 'to the princi-ples of the free market, tempered by the claims of social justice' (Rocard 1988). Such sentiments are to be expected from a socialist leader but it is important to note that the majority of Member State governments, whatever their political leanings, supported the general contention that the single market should be a single social market. For example, the 'right-wing' conservative govern-ment of Germany under Chancellor Kohl accepted the Social Charter like the 'left-wing' socialist government of France under President Mitterrand. Whatever their precise appreciation of the questions involved – and this clearly does vary – they shared a basic 'social market' philosophy common in continental Europe. When the Commission talked of defending and developing a 'European social model' – distinct from those found in the USA, Japan and the communist world – integrating elements of free-market capitalism and welfare-state principles most national gov-ernments could respond positively to the general idea, whatever their reservations on particular points. Similarly, when the Greek President of the European Council, addressing the European Parliament in 1988, stressed the need to match the '1992' single economic area with a 'single social area', he struck a responsive chord amongst the majority of MEPs (Commission 1988g: 169). In fact, the European Parliament, with Socialists forming its dominant group in the late 1980s and early 1990s, had espoused the social Europe concept with enthusiasm and was constantly chastizing the Commission, and, more particularly, the Council, for the delay in turning the many EC social policy proposals into legislative action!

BRITISH RELUCTANCE TO ACCEPT THE SOCIAL CHARTER

However, this general consensus in favour of social Europe amongst the leaders of Community states did not include the British Conservative government of the 1980s and early 1990s. It felt very uncomfortable with what it was apt to dismiss, sometimes with good cause, as vague 'rhetoric'. Moreover, it was more prone to look towards the USA (and in some ways Japan) for 'social models' able to generate economic success. That is why the UK government, unlike all its partners, refused to accept the Social Charter in December 1989, seeing it as a way in which 'bureaucratic, socialist' practices would be reintroduced into Britain by the 'back door of Brussels' (Thatcher 1988). Mrs Thatcher's Conservative government had spent a decade reducing what it saw as excessive trade-union power and government intervention in the economy; it feared that the Social Charter might reverse this process of economic liberalization and deregulation. It felt that employers would become more reluctant to take on workers if they feared a burden of strict legislation on equitable wages, working hours, benefit contributions and so on. Thus, it was argued, the social objective of greater employment would be jeopardized by misguided social policies. Typical British 'Euroscare' stories were conjured up to reinforce such fears; for example, statements that baby-sitters would require formal contracts of employment whilst boys and girls would be prevented from delivering newspapers were widely circulated in the media!

So, wedded to a strong 'free-market' ideology, the 'Thatcherites' in Britain's Conservative Party rejected the assumptions of the social dumping school. Firm believers in the benefits of market liberalization, deregulation and open competition, they mounted a battery of counter-arguments. What was wrong, they insisted, with investment shifting from high-wage, high-cost economies to those with lower standards? Was there any more efficient way of generating growth and employment on Europe's poorer peripheries? Surely, this was a better way to transfer resources from richer to poorer areas than cumbersome, bureaucratic, interventionist regional policies? Such policies had remarkably little effect on the basic geographical pattern of socio-economic disparities in post-war Europe and cast serious doubts on the efficacy of government intervention in shaping socio-economic outcomes (Wise, Chalkley 1990). Rather than entangle employers and employees in common European legislation, let them compete in social as well as economic terms; if Spanish car workers were prepared to work longer hours for less pay and shorter holidays than their German counterparts in order to attract investment from Volkswagen, why put obstacles in their way?

In the run up to the adoption of the Social Charter this ideological clash between a social protectionist approach and a belief in the virtues of labour market deregulation became increasingly open. The British government, under the dominant leadership of Mrs Thatcher, strongly opposed a series of socially protective proposals from the Commission. While other Member States were prepared to accept the general thrust of these proposals, albeit with modifications, the British adopted an uncompromising stance. Very different ideas on job creation and social justice lay at the heart of this debate. For the UK government, increased employment depended on freeing the labour market from all the rigidities which successive waves of social legislation had built into it, notably in the post-war 'welfare states'. Employers would not employ if discouraged by a deterrent mass of legislation on pay, dismissals, hours of work and so on. During the 'Thatcher era' of the 1980s, such a policy had been vigorously pursued in Britain. The Commission, along with other Member States, agreed that greater flexibility was required in labour markets, but were not prepared to seek this at the expense of rights for workers. Indeed, it hoped to win flexibility by providing employees with sufficient social protection against the fears associated with job loss (Commission 1987d).

The opposition of the British government to these social-market initiatives was stiff; even the most unbinding of 'recommendations' were resisted. For example, its attitude to the proposed 'Recommendation on the Reduction of Working Time' can be cited. This recommendation, which had no binding legal force, was put forward in the early 1980s in response to growing unemployment and the perceived need for more work-sharing. However, the UK government, firmly opposed this limited initiative on the grounds that it would be the 'thin end of the wedge' leading to ever more bureaucratic, socialist interference with British labour market procedures (Welsh 1987).

But Not Simply 'Britain versus the Rest' on Social Europe

The British government's refusal to sign the Social Charter and its clear ideological opposition to many of the EC's social policy initiatives often made it seem yet another simple case of Britain fighting a lone 'anti-European' battle. In reality the picture was more complicated. Diverse countries and interest groups in an intricate interrelated network of Community and national institutions sought to impose their views on the many and complicated social issues involved. Just as British governmental opposition to the Social Charter did not represent the views of all in Britain, so the general accord expressed by other national governments did not signify complete unanimity on these social issues elsewhere. In fact there was a fairly widespread feeling that many governments found it convenient to hide behind Britain's (and more especially Mrs Thatcher's) skirt on these questions (Le Monde 1991: 73–8). How convenient to court political favour by making grand declarations of generous social intent in the sure knowledge that the UK government could be counted on to block concrete and potentially costly proposals! A closer look at some of the real complexity which lay behind an excessively simplistic 'Britain versus the Rest' scenario illustrates again the enormous difficulties of translating general social Europe ideals into concrete realities in the developing single market.

THE SOCIAL CHARTER AND THE LEFT IN BRITAIN

The hostile reaction towards the Social Charter emanating from Britain's government and business circles – but not its Trade Unions – was a variation on an old theme. Debates about the European Community in Britain have traditionally been couched in essentially economic terms with a reluctance to get drawn into wider forms of social and political union. Back in the 1950s and 1960s there were innumerable analyses of the potential economic costs and benefits of UK membership. Efforts were made to draw up some kind of gigantic financial balance sheet to help decide whether entry into the Community would make Britain richer or poorer. Issues like the price of food and the business gains to be made from access to a larger market dominated discussion at all levels of society. The widespread use of the term 'Common Market', or insistence on saying European Economic Community, betrayed this propensity to perceive the EC in uni-dimensional economic terms. The '1992' project reinforced this tendency by emphasizing the creation of a single European market, the business opportunities therein and the economic growth it is expected to generate. Only the Liberals and their successors in the Liberal Democratic Party have long felt comfortable with the wider aspirations of the drive towards European unity and the broadly social-market philosophy which was a major guiding force.

However, the Social Charter highlighted a significant change in some British attitudes to the Community. The Labour Party and trade unions in the UK had often been at the forefront of opposition to EC membership from the early 1960s to the late 1980s. But in September 1988, Jacques Delors, President of the European Commission and a prominent member of the French Socialist Party with lengthy ministerial experience, made an address at the annual conference of Britain's Trades Union Congress in Bournemouth (Delors 1988). This event symbolized a sea change in how the majority on the left of UK politics viewed the European Community. Hitherto, perceptions of it being a rich man's capitalist club notorious for such things as 'feather-bedding farmers' at the expense of the poor British consumer and draining investment from Britain's remoter regions into the Common Market's core areas dominated British left-wing attitudes to

European integration. However, a shift was taking place towards acceptance that there were social aspirations associated with the moves towards European unity which could help workers within the UK.

Several factors lay behind this change. Many Labour MEPs departed for the European Parliament implacably hostile to the Community, but cooperation with socialist colleagues from other Member States clearly had a 'Europeanizing' effect as the potential benefits of combined European action in the social field became apparent to them. Furthermore, a succession of Conservative electoral victories in the UK from 1979 onwards had been associated with a marked decline in the influence wielded by organized labour in British society. Contact with counterparts from Member States where such things as employee participation in the management of companies was legally ingrained led some to see Community legislation as a means of checking further erosion of trade union and worker rights within the UK. Awareness of the growing inadequacy of national action alone to counter the power of transnational businesses, ever more able to shift investment capital from one country to another in search of labour, also played a role in the change of European mood on the left of British politics. These forces eventually led the Labour Party to abandon its pledge to withdraw from the Community and begin to champion European social causes resisted by the Conservative government. A speech in September 1988 by Mr Kinnock, leader of the Labour Party, to the Socialist Group of the European Parliament clearly marked this strategic change. Echoing sentiments long held by continental colleagues he challenged the view that the single market 'will exclusively and inevitably be an open space for the operation of New Right economics'; he continued:

> Every one of our (socialist) movements in every one of our countries has, by a variety of means...made constant efforts to civilize the operation of markets and make economic activity compatible with human security. In some respects, the relative comfort and safety of modern life is due to the success achieved by socialists and others who realize that life is too important to be left to the dictates of demand and supply. That

is the spirit in which we must approach the new scale of
market operation. (Kinnock 1988)

Thus, the artificial separation of 'economic', 'social' and 'political'
aspects in the process of European integration was slowly beginning to break down in more and more British minds. This conversion to a fuller concept of the 'European idea' was sometimes
admitted with extraordinary candour; for example, the Labour
MP Bryan Sedgemoor, on the left of the party and erstwhile
opponent of the EC, argued to the House of Commons in June
1990 that 'it is time that left-wing members regarded the European Community as a stunning opportunity' (Economist 1990a).
Obviously, not all of Mr Sedgemore's party colleagues, including
stalwarts like Tony Benn, shared this enthusiasm. Nevertheless,
the statement did reflect a fundamental shift in overall Labour
Party thinking. Long-time Labour pro-Europeans were aston-
ished by the change of mood; one of them, Giles Radice,
described it as '...one of the most astonishing transformations in
British political history...'(Economist 1990a). Liberal Democrats
and pro-European Conservatives such as Edward Heath were no
longer so isolated as a more comprehensive vision of the Community spread across more of the British political spectrum.

ATTITUDES OF THE EC's 'SOCIAL PARTNERS' TO SOCIAL EUROPE

In explaining the UK government's opposition to the Social Charter (see above), the broad ideological clash confronting those who
thought that social interventionism in the economy was essential
to promote justice and political-economic harmony with those
who believed that it introduced burdens which stifled the economy and, ultimately, social welfare has already been highlighted.
Our discussion of attitudes towards the Social Charter on the
British Left, not to mention the social-market devotees in Britain's
pro-European Centre parties, has already indicated that the
broad dividing line between these two camps did not extend
neatly down the English Channel. The same big debate, and
elaborations of it, ignored national boundaries and can be found
to a greater or lesser extent in all Community countries.

For example, major elements of the debate opposing the UK
government to the Commission and others (see above) were

ritually played out in discussions between what are known as the EC's 'social partners'. Just as employers and employees organize themselves into distinct bodies like the British CBI and TUC at national level, so equivalent EC organizations exist. The main employers' body is the Union of Industries of the European Community (UNICE after its French initials) set up in 1957 before any other at the very onset of the the EEC (those on the Left would think it significant the capital interests were immediately organized to play a Common Market game which suited them!). Its principal task is to seek to influence Community policy-making and inform national members of relevant EC developments. The European Trade Union Congress (ETUC) is the trade union equivalent of UNICE. It was not formed until 1973 (again it is interesting to note the way in which 'labour' followed 'capital' in the usual reactive fashion of 'social' actions responding to those of an 'economic' nature). This body brought together all the socialist and social-democratic trade unions in the EC, with its main members being the German DGB, the French CFDT and the British TUC. However, several major unions remained outside the ETUC, most notably the communist organizations like the CGT in France, the CGIL in Italy and the Spanish Workers Commissions. Despite this fragmentation of the labour response to the EC, those bodies which do belong to ETUC have gradually become more integrated and ready to accept Community action as an awareness has grown that national unions need to cooperate across state borders to defend their interests in a business environment increasingly shaped by multinational companies. The importance of public enterprises has also been recognized by the Community institutions in conferring the status of 'social partner' on the European Committee for Public Enterprises (CEEP) as well. Inside the machinery of Community policy-making these three major social partners – the UNICE, the ETUC and the CEEP – enjoy equal status. In effect, this means that they are represented on the multiplicity of advisory committees which link national governments, interest groups, specialist agencies and others into the overall Community system of government. For example, they will inevitably participate in the deliberations of the Economic and Social Committee as well as more specialist bodies like the Standing Committee on Employment. Moreover, they will also be found on the governing boards of bodies like the

European Centre for Vocational Training on the European Foundation for the Improvement of Living and Working Conditions (see Chapter 5).

Most importantly, these major representatives of capital, labour and the public sector meet regularly in the so-called 'Val Duchesse talks' where they set up working parties to examine a whole range of socio-economic issues (see Chapter 5). When confronted with the Commission's efforts to promote a 'European social space', the reactions of these social partners mirror the disputes that have taken place between the UK and those who are pressing to strengthen Commmunity social policy. Thus, the business leaders of the whole Community list a number of priorities in UNICE's 'Agenda for Europe' which would not offend the thrust of British Conservative Party policy in recent years (Brewster, Teague 1989: 126). First, they echo the UK government's demand for a genuine internal EC market: in the words of their secretary-general they want

> a strong and coherent Community, with its energies directed towards enterprise and innovation and enjoying healthy economic growth upon which depend employment, living standards, working conditions and social security. (Le Monde 1991: 74)

But in line again with British governmental thinking in the 1980s they firmly resist the Commission's drive to build social policies to complement it. Instead they urge the creation of a more favourable climate for enterprise, a reduced burden of 'social' legislation on employers, a general 'rolling back' of state intervention to liberate entrepreneurial energies and so on. Finding the term 'social dumping' devoid of meaning, they rejected most proposals to harmonize or coordinate social policies across the Community (except in certain very limited fields like occupational health and safety); again the words of its Secretary-General would not sound out of place in the mouth of a British Conservative politician:

> let the accent be on dialogue and adaptability. Centralization, harmonization and European legislation in the social field would create new rigidities and further reduce our ability to

compete and pay for the society we want. (quoted in Brewster, Teague 1989: 127)

Predictably, the response of the ETUC to the '1992' and social Europe programmes in the Val Duchesse talks and other Community bodies is very different. Whilst accepting the single market objective, albeit with more reservations than UNICE, it argues that a European social dimension is essential for all the reasons that have already been rehearsed above. Thus, whilst many employers across Europe wanted local wage settlements, the ETUC pressed for collective bargaining at a European level if necessary. Whilst European company leaders sought to reduce the constraints of social legislation, European union leaders advocated a growth of Community-wide regulation to protect workers in the new, competitive single market. The Social Charter was very much a reflection of ETUC aspirations.

So the enduring confrontation between UNICE and ETUC over the Community's economic and social dimensions in the Val Duchesse context was very similar to the battle that the UK government had with the Community on the same issues, but it reveals that the real argument behind some very generalized public rhetoric was by no means a simple nationalistic one of 'Britain versus the Rest'. In the more concealed and serious debate in the many corridors of Community power, the evidence up to the present suggests that employers have been more successful than trades unionists in defending their interests in the Community's decision-making system. Thus the programme to create a single market has surged ahead on the basis of concrete EC law, whilst the proposals to build a social Europe have dragged behind and encounter the utmost difficulty in being translated into legislative action. There is nothing new about this as a brief examination of the fate of the Commission's so-called 'Vredeling Directive' illustrates.

This proposed Directive, which first appeared in formal draft form in 1980, was designed to guarantee a basic right for employees to be informed and consulted about company policy which might affect their working lives (see Chapter 5). As such it fell into a long-established effort by the Commission to develop a 'European social model' managing economic activity. The employers in UNICE were extremely hostile to the proposal, whereas the

ETUC was emphatic in its support (Brewster, Teague 1989:133–7). The latter argued that Community legislation was urgently required, given the scale of industrial restructuring that was being effected by multinationals across Europe and often entailing dramatic job losses (see Chapter 7). However, the ability of ETUC to mobilize support for its case was far outweighed by the forces which UNICE was able to muster. National employers' organizations like the CBI employed all their lobbying skills to block the Directive; even the German employers' federation, used to worker consultation procedures, rejected the Directive. Furthermore, the leaders of American and Japanese multinationals, which would be much affected by Vredeling's proposal, mounted an enormous campaign to stop it. For example, the Commission was directly threatened with a reduction of US and Japanese investment in the EC if this proposal became law. Similar pressure was applied to all the other public and private pressure points in the Community system of decision. Despite its best efforts, the ETUC could not marshall its members so effectively, nor did it enjoy the same financial resources. Thus when the issue was debated in the European Parliament, a journalist was able to describe the following scene:

> On Tuesday taxis swept up to the Parliament building bearing the most formidable galaxy of professional lobbyists Strasbourg has seen... (whereas)...the union lobby consisted of a couple of pleasant individuals from the European TUC handing out leaflets. (quoted in Brewster, Teague 1989:136).

As a result of all this pressure, an important element of the attempt to construct a European social space to match its fast-integrating economic space was indefinitely shelved. Those wanting to enlarge the EC's social dimension will have to find ways of becoming as effective in Community politics as those moulding its economic shape.

ATTITUDES TO SOCIAL EUROPE IN THE EUROPEAN PARLIAMENT

One body which has increasingly been looked to in order to find ways of strengthening the EC's social dimension is the European Parliament, long the 'poor relation' of the Council-Commission-

Parliament institutional trio at the head of the Community's political system. A survey of Parliamentary attitudes to EC social policy initiatives provides further elaboration of how the single market-social Europe issue is seen across the Community. Whatever the real limitations of this democratically-elected forum, its public debates clearly reveal the divergences and convergences of interest which are also played out in the more confidential confines of the Commission and Council as well as the Community's intricate network of committees meshing national and sectional bodies into the EC system.

The EP is widely regarded as a 'talking shop' with little power to influence the critical policy-making dialogue between the Commission and the Community's final decision-making body, the Council of Ministers. However, whatever its relative marginality to the key centres of EC power, its ability to mould Community policy has been steadily growing (Chapter 1) and is far from negligible; about 50 per cent of its amendments to policy proposals now find their way into the finally adopted Community law and this proportion is likely to increase (Lodge 1989a: 58–83; Pinder 1991: 34–9).

Those wanting a strong Community social policy have often criticized the Parliament's past performance (Le Monde 1991: 75) and lamented its failure or reluctance to provide effective support for the various social Europe initiatives during the 1970s and 1980s (see Chapter 5 and discussion of the Vredeling Directive above). However, the much publicized '1992' programme to create a single market sparked off a major movement in the EP to reinvigorate the idea of a complementary EC social space. The Socialists, who already formed the largest EP grouping, led this revolt against what they saw as the unbalanced 'Thatcherite' liberalism underpinning the single market initiative, but MEPs from other parties (for example those of a Christian-Democratic tradition) also supported this effort to balance 'economic' and 'social' aspects of EC policy. This pressure helped lead to the Commission's proposal for a Community Charter of the Fundamental Social Rights of Workers (the so-called Social Charter) even though the Parliament was largely ignored during its final formulation in 1989. However, it was consulted on the Commission's action plan to draw up specific proposals to put the Social Charter into effect. In due course the EP's Committee on Social

Affairs, Employment and the Working Environment produced the so-called van Velzen report on this action plan (European Parliament 1990a). This report, which was eventually adopted by a majority vote in the Parliament, represented an enthusiastic endorsement of the most comprehensive kind of social Europe concept. Typical of its numerous demands was one which wanted the Commission to propose, by the end of 1990, a Directive 'on the reduction of working hours with a view to a 35 hour week'. Furthermore, it demanded that the fate of this Directive should be decided by the Council on the basis of qualified majority voting (Article 118a of the EEC Treaty amended by the SEA) so that a small minority of Member States opposed to such measures could not block a measure acceptable to most countries (the UK Conservative government was clearly uppermost in many minds on this point). Amongst the mass of demands there were many others destined to provoke criticism that the social engineering aspects of the report reflected obsolete utopian ways of thought; for example, the call 'to ensure that at least half those receiving aid from the European Social Fund are women' might be motivated by the best of intentions, but the bureaucratic costs of trying implement what some would reject as a sexist measure would doubtless be high and of dubious efficacy.

The plenary session debates in the European Parliament obviously reflected the usual ideological divisions on the issue with those on the Left making pleas to implement the Social Charter with the same sense of urgency being applied to the single market programme; as the words of Mr McMahon illustrate, none were more passionate than Labour MEPs from supposedly isolated Britain:

> The social dimension is important. It is particularly important for those who come from the United Kingdom where trade union rights are being denied, where workers are being sacked in the North Sea (sic) because they are fighting for safety and trade union organization. In the city of London people are sleeping in cardboard boxes because of the social policies of the (UK) government supported by Lord O'Hagan and his friends.... When we see what has happened in the United Kingdom in the last eleven years, my God how we need a social dimension! We need Europe to come like the cavalry to the rescue. (European Parliament 1990c: 222)

Although Lord O'Hagan, a British Conservative MEP, was personally attacked in McMahon's speech, he actually exemplifies the point that many towards the Right in the EP did not reject the social Europe concept with the vehemence of many of their national counterparts; he declared:

> I am strongly in favour of the single market but a single social market. You cannot have a single social market without legislation to help workers and to help citizens. (European Parliament 1990c: 32)

His major criticism of the approach adopted by the Socialist group in the Parliament – shared by others on the moderate Right – was that its proposals were too many and often too impracticable to have any hope of success. Rather than drawing up vast plans of action with little sense of priority a more methodical pursuit of a limited number of precise pieces of legislation appropriate for the European level 'would actually affect and alter the lives of our citizens'; thus:

> This Parliament is not adapting to the modern requirements of what we are meant to be doing in the new emerging European Community where we have to have a social market to make 1992 work. (European Parliament 1990c: 221)

Others towards the Right shared similar views. Thus Mr Suarez Gonzalez, a Christian-Democrat MEP from Spain noted

> the curious spectacle of how dissatisfied the liberals (ie, non-socialists) feel with what the Commission is doing on social issues. I am not referring to the position of the more ideologically interventionist, more equalizing, more progressive sectors – if I may use these terms – but to liberal thinking in today's Europe. There is unanimity in the Parliament that the Commission really must stop fussing about empty terminology and get down to harmonizing social legislation....The workers of Europe are not going to believe it is so difficult to make the effort over social harmonization when they see even the width of lawnmower wheels being harmonized. (European Parliament 1990b: 185)

Of course behind the assumed 'unanimity' referred to in the above extract there were sharp divergences of opinion behind the general feeling that some sort of EC social policy was required. Indeed speeches that would have been warmly endorsed by British Conservative ministers were made by MEPs from a number of Community countries. For example, M. Le Chevallier from France criticized the drawing up of lengthy catalogues of social proposals which allowed the Parliament 'to indulge its dema-gogic fanaticism' and which took 'no account...of the state of social legislation in the different Member States, which prevents harmonization aligned with the highest standards if the social budgets of some Member States are not to explode' (European Parliament 1990b: 87). Others expressed reservations which were akin to those emanating from the UK government and employ-ers' organizations like UNICE. Mr Nielson of Denmark stressed that it was 'crucial' to 'respect the different approaches and tradi-tions in the Member States'; thus for example:

> Wages and working hours are some of the matters upon which...the Community has no powers to take decisions. In some countries they are settled by legislation. In Denmark we have a long-standing tradition by which the two sides of in-dustry negotiate agreements on them. It is important to up-hold this principle, because the agreements impose a system of joint responsibility....The Community cannot and must not take over this role. We must respect different traditions and hold back from any action to centralize and bureaucratize the decision-making process. We must have flexibility. It is essen-tial to avoid decisions on matters of detail within the Commu-nity framework. (European Parliament 1990c: 36)

Whilst some Danish MEPs were worried that the consequences of the Social Charter would disrupt their national system of labour relations and threaten their ability to compete (talk of an imposed 35-hour week horrified them as much as conservatives and liberals in other Member States), others were worried that harmonized Community social policy might undermine their 'Nordic model' of social welfare. Mr Sandbaek of the EP's 'Rain-bow' group was very emphatic on this point. After explaining the distinctiveness of Denmark's social security system based on high taxation financing generous benefits 'not tied to employment record', he insisted:

We will not in any circumstances accept a situation in which rights and entitlements under Danish agreements can be set aside by an EC Court in Luxembourg. If there are to be common rules, it must be clearly and unequivocally stated that they are minimum rules, under which all countries are free to go further in the direction of social protection. We will never approve a procedure under which EC Directives can invalidate our own standards. (European Parliament 1990c: 30)

Then, in a direct reference to the drive to eliminate national barriers in the single market, he stated:

The most immediate threat to the Nordic model, however, is the planned abolition of the frontier between Denmark and West Germany, which will make it impossible to collect the higher taxes and duties needed to fund our system of social provision. We therefore want the frontier to be maintained. (European Parliament 1990c: 30)

This belief that harmonization of social security at EC level was not essential in the single market was supported by a Danish academic analysis which concluded:

Neither the analysis of the principle of subsidiarity, nor the analysis of the 'social dumping' argument call for extended social security decision-making at Community level. The extent to which an ex-ante harmonization of social security is required for the effective operation of a single market seems to be smaller than is often thought. (Petersen 1991: 513)

Whilst many Danes, and others in wealthy northern countries, feared that the Community might dilute their social security systems, MEPs from southern Europe saw social Europe as another means to transfer resources to the EC's peripheries in order to improve living conditions. Thus, Mr Ephremidis, a Greek from the Left Unity group, spoke of the urgency of implementing a social programme to match the single market and so avoid political disruption; failure to do so would place 'a time-bomb...underneath this union which will explode, in the form of social upheaval'; he continued:

> I wish to refer to a specific example of what is happening in my country: for three months the government has been butchering social security rights, the right to a decent wage for workers, and is even blocking their demands and their industrial action by resorting to the courts, labelling them untimely, illegal and so forth. (European Parliament 1990c: 37)

Irish voices from the Community's northwestern periphery echoed the sentiments of their southern brethren at the bottom end of the EC's socio-economic welfare ladder. Mr de Rossa of the EP's Left Unity group was one of many who accused their national governments of mouthing soothing sentiments on social Europe to soften the harder edges of the single market programme, whilst in reality they were happy to hide behind the UK government's outspoken opposition to it; thus:

> Few issues have generated as much hypocrisy as this one has. From the outset it has been used as a placebo to placate workers and their representatives and lead them to believe that they were not being left behind in the drive towards the single market.
> The final version of the (Social) Action Programme was a pale shadow of what it could have been. What was worthwhile of what remained was optional and unlikely to be implemented. And even at that, the timetable was too vague and constantly edged off the agenda by commercial aspects of the single market project....
> It is clear from their own briefing document that the strategy of the Irish Government was to dilute and stall on the Social Charter Action Programme behind the scenes but not to take 'too prominent a defensive posture' in public lest they be accused of 'reneging on the agreement' and of 'sharing the ideological position of the UK'. (European Parliament 1990c: 223–4)

Mr de Rossa was in no doubt about what needed to be done to turn social Europe rhetoric into some form of reality:

Irish and European trade unions need to get their acts together to counter the more successful efforts of employer organizations to dilute and delay the Action Programme on the Social Charter....It is time that the Left majority in this Parliament who (sic) genuinely supports a worthwhile Social Charter decided to withdraw support for other aspects of the legislative programme until firm guarantees are given on the content and implementation of the Action Programme. The Trade Union movement needs to raise the level of awareness of employees concerning the impact of an internal market without a social dimension on their job security and working conditions. Only when industrial policy and social policy is as much an election issue as the common agricultural policy will governments and the Council take it seriously. (European Parliament 1990c: 223)

Thus, debates in the European Parliament reflected a range of diverging and converging interests over the Community's social dimension which tended to be hidden by the UK government's much publicized refusal to sign the Social Charter accepted by all the other Member States. However, the majority of MEPs expressed dismay, even anger, that the Commission's Action Programme, designed to give precise substance to the Charter's general aims, was meeting such resistance in the Council of Ministers. There was also harsh criticism of a Commission that was seen as being far too weak in pressing for its objectives. The Parliament's Report on the Commission's Social Action Programme (European Parliament 1990a) deliberately outlined 'almost 100 concrete proposals' thought necessary to supplement the Commission's proposals and produce a 'worthy counterpart to the (1992) White Paper' (European Parliament 1990c: 26). It also wanted such a programme to be decided in the Council of Ministers by an extended use of the qualified majority voting procedure (as for the single market programme) rather than allow individual Member States to block progress by insistence on unanimity: in other words, the procedures laid down in Articles 100A and 118A of the SEA. MEPs were perfectly aware that the Council's readiness to adopt majority voting for single market measures (although key areas like taxation and monetary union were exempt from this procedure) was not matched when it came to social policy proposals.

The greater reticence of Member States to concede national sovereignty in the social as opposed to the economic dimension of EC policy was noted elsewhere by the EP. The rapporteur of an EP Committee report on the social action programme noted the enthusiasm with which national governments supported the EC's 'subsidiarity' principle (ie; devolving government functions to the lowest appropriate level) when it came to social policy, but their lack of interest in it when economic matters were at stake:

> There is incidently something strange about the concept of subsidiarity, for the emotion with which it is referred to in discussions about the social dimension is in stark contrast with the lack thereof in discussions about economic and monetary subjects. As though the orientation of the economy might not be extremely decisive for the culture of a Member State. (European Parliament 1990c: 26)

Mr van Velzen detected the same inequality of approach concerning competition policy. He criticized what he saw as a tendency of the Commission and Council to apply EC competition laws in a purely 'economic' context without reference to social policy. This was unfortunate because:

> In my view, competition ought to be fair and in no way should social policy be used as an instrument for acquiring a stronger competitive position. At the present time major differences in social policies very often obscure the competition situation. I would therefore urge those people who find the concept of competition important to view it in relationship to sound instruments in social policy. (European Parliament 1990c: 26)

However, despite this majority Parliamentary pressure to promote the social Europe concept, the implementation of the single market project sped ahead at a far greater pace. In late 1991 the Commission was able to report that of the 282 measures in the single market programme well over 200 had been adopted by the Council, using qualified majority voting to get quick decisions, and that 168 were in force. This was five years after the 1985 White Paper, three years after the entry into force of the SEA and one year ahead of the '1992' deadline. In stark contrast, the Community's social action programme flowing out of the SEA and the Social Charter was limping along extremely slowly. By mid-1991 the Commission had drawn up a mere 18 concrete proposals out of the 48 envisaged in the social action programme (Commission 1991a). These measures encountered stiff resistance in the Council of Ministers, particularly from the UK. This resistance focused on both the substance of the proposals (see above) and the means of deciding upon them. Whilst some were prepared to accept that qualified majority voting should be the norm in the social policy area (as for much of the single market), others, led pugnaciously by the British government, were insisting on unanimous agreement in the Council before social measures could be passed. Thus, as the end of 1991 approached, there was virtually nothing of substance related to the Social Charter converted into concrete EC legislation (Economist 1991a: 80). The contrast between a 'fast track' approach to the single market and a 'reluctant crawl' towards social Europe could not have been sharper.

BROAD PRINCIPLES AND SPECIFIC PROVISIONS IN EC SOCIAL POLICY

We have seen that divergences over the Community social policy cannot be oversimplified into a question of 'Britain versus the Rest'. However, it is a fact that the British Conservative government of the 1980s and early 1990s led the campaign against what some saw as the excessive centralization of social policies at European level. Its particularly strong stance in this regard was highlighted by its solitary refusal to sign the Social Charter. Whatever the detailed substance of each debate about a proposed EC social measure the British style stood out in clear ideological opposition. This distinctive British governmental approach to EC social policy – and other Community matters – could also be detected in another significant way. Whereas most Member States were happy to sketch out broad visions and then get down to the somewhat messier, conflict-ridden process of working towards them, the British tended to be dismissive of such grand general schemes. For example, Mrs Thatcher – then Prime Minister – had her continental counterparts reaching for their advanced English dictionaries when she described their plans to move towards a single currency as belonging to the realm of 'cloud-cuckoo-land' (Economist 1990b: 57). Her reaction was true to a long-standing British tradition (deeply ingrained in both major parties) of discomfort in face of the big 'European idea'; hence the failure to join the various European Communities in 1950 and 1957, the refusal to join the European Monetary System fully in 1979 and, of course, the rejection of the Social Charter in 1989.

Those states signing the Social Charter were more ready than Britain to set grand general objectives and then negotiate specific policy details afterwards. They were happy to accept the broad principles within it before dealing with the concrete proposals of the Commission's Social Action Programme that was to follow. Commitment to a broad ideal did not prevent them bargaining hard over the precise shape of particular policies and attempting to employ the Community principle of 'subsidiarity' to their own national advantage. This latter principle, much promulgated by the Commission, states that the Community only seeks to take common action when set objectives (in this case those of the Charter) can be reached more effectively at European rather than national, regional or local level. Of course, there will always be argument about what is the most 'effective level' for action; but most accept this as the normal democratic process to be pursued within the Social Charter's broad guidelines. Nobody expected that this process would be easy, given the enormous diversity of national, regional and sectoral traditions within Europe's would-be 'social space'. Even the notion of 'subsidiarity', seen as a way of recognizing the varied socio-economic geography of the Community and refuting the charge of excessive centralization, is challenged by those who preferred the concept of 'complementarity'. This latter idea envisages cooperation between different levels of government in the pursuit of social aims, rather than a neat division of labour between them.

HARMONIZATION OR MUTUAL RECOGNITION IN THE FIELD OF SOCIAL POLICY?

More fundamentally, there was also the question of whether EC social policy should be based on the principle of 'harmonization' rather than that of 'mutual recognition'. Traditionally, the Commission's approach to such issues had been to seek a harmony of national practices. However, this tactic had yielded few results in the social field, or indeed any other, as proposals proved unable to make headway against a diversity of national practices and interests. So the Commission had switched progressively to the idea of mutual recognition of national systems, subject to a minimum standard acceptable across the Community. This strategy, adopted in the drive to create a single market (see Chapter 3), could also be applied in the effort to create a European 'social space'. In 1986, the Belgian presidency of the Council of Ministers put forward the idea of building up a 'minimum body of Community social provisions' to prevent such things as 'social dumping' in the single market (Commission 1988h: 61–2). This would involve agreement on a package of basic social rights which national systems would eventually have to accept, but not try to enforce complete harmonization across the very varied economic and social circumstances. This was increasingly seen as undesirable as well as impossible in such a diverse Community.

One such 'basic right' would require formal procedures to ensure that employees are consulted about the affairs of the company in which they work. This obligation could be met and elaborated upon in a variety of ways depending on national, regional, local or sectoral conditions. In other words, the Commission 'argues in favour of developing the social dialogue to allow better management of the diversity and flexibility of situations' (Commission 1988i: 8). So, following agreement on such fundamental principles, Member States could mutually recognize their different practices, and workers moving from country to country would have to accept them. Of course, even agreement on such principles is not easy; in 1989, Britain refused to accept those incorporated in the Social Charter despite their general character. But the other Member States were able to accept its broad guidelines more easily, expecting that they could then negotiate within them to produce a complex blend of Community harmonization and national mutual recognition of social policies operating at different levels. Indeed, the Commission set up a steering group of the so-called 'social partners' (ETUC, UNICE and CEEP – see above) in 1989 and invited them to formulate some proposals on employee participation in company affairs (Le Monde 1991: 74). Following the almost symbolic 'top down' gesture of the Social Charter, the Commission was trying to trigger off a 'bottom up' process whereby those directly concerned devise acceptable forms of workers' consultation in companies which could then form the basis of EC legislation.

IMPLEMENTATION OF THE SOCIAL CHARTER

The Charter was not a detailed set of European regulations that were to be imposed on the Member States by 'Eurocrats in Brussels'. Indeed, the Charter itself stated that:

> It is more particularly the responsibility of the Member States, in accordance with national practices, notably through legislative measures or collective agreements, to guarantee the fundamental social rights in this Charter and to implement the social measures indispensable to the smooth operation of the internal market as part of the strategy of economic and social cohesion. (Commission 1990a: 20)

In language which clearly indicated the will not to relinquish all control of social policy to Community institutions, the Charter also requires that the Commission

> submit as soon as possible initiatives which fall within its powers...with a view to the adoption...as and when the internal market is completed...of those (social) rights which come within the Community's area of competence. (Commission 1990a: 20)

Thus, within this restraining framework, which once again explicitly linked progress on creation of a European social space to success in completing the single market, the Commission began the process of drawing up concrete proposals to give effect to the Charter. This process is a dynamic one that still has far to go, but a selective indication of what is to come can be given under the main headings of the Charter (Commission 1990d).

1. Freedom of movement

In order to guarantee every worker the right to freedom of movement throughout the Community, the Commission would continue its efforts to eliminate obstacles arising from such things as non-recognition of qualifications and inability to avail themselves of social security benefits when they move from one country to another.

2. Employment and remuneration

To ensure, amongst other things, that workers, 'in accordance with arrangements applying in each country', receive 'a wage sufficient to enable them to have a decent standard of living', the Commission will propose a Directive setting minimum requirements for part-time working, fixed-term working, casual work, etc.

3. Improvement of living and working conditions

In order that 'the conditions of employment of every worker of the European Community shall be stipulated in laws, a collective agreement or a contract of employment', the Commission would propose a Directive to require written proof of an employment contract. Part of such a contract would give the 'right to a weekly rest period and to annual paid leave, the duration of which must be progressively harmonized in accordance with national practices'.

4. Social protection

To ensure that 'every worker shall have the right to adequate social protection...and enjoy an adequate level of social security benefits', the Commission would make a 'Recommendation on convergence of Member States' objectives in regard to social protection'.

5. Freedom of association and collective bargaining

To protect the rights of employers and workers 'to constitute professional organizations or trade unions of their choice for the defence of their economic and social interests', as well as 'the right to strike, subject to the obligations arising under national regulations', the Commission would insist on developing 'the dialogue between both sides of industry at European level' and produce 'a communication on their role in collective bargaining, including collective agreements at European level'.

6. Vocational training

The Commission would, amongst other things, propose measures to meet a basic requirement of the Charter that 'every worker of the European Community ...have access to vocational training...throughout his working life'.

7. Equal treatment for men and women

To assure 'equal treatment' and develop 'equal opportunities' for both sexes, as well as enabling them 'to reconcile their occupational and family obligations', the Commission would prepare a third action programme on equal opportunities for women, make recommendations on the protection of working women during pregnancy, maternity leave, child care and so on before drawing up relevant legislative proposals.

8. Information, consultation and participation of workers

To achieve the Charter's requirement that 'information, consultation and participation of workers must be developed along appropriate lines', the Commission would draw up proposals relating especially to workers in undertakings of European or transnational scale as well as proposals on equity sharing and financial participation by employees.

9. Health protection and safety at the workplace

To ensure that 'every worker must enjoy satisfactory health and safety conditions in his working environment, the Commission would propose minimum health and safety requirements in a range of sectors so as to achieve further harmonization of conditions in this area while maintaining the improvements made'.

10. Protection of children and adolescents

In order to achieve the Charter's aim of ensuring that young people are not used as cheap labour to the detriment of their education and training, the Commission, 'without prejudice to rules as may be more favourable to young people...(and)...subject to derogations limited to certain light work', would propose a Directive 'approximating the laws of the Member States on the protection of young people in regard to employment' which insisted, amongst other things, that 'the minimum employment age must not be lower than the minimum school-leaving age and, in any case, not lower than 15 years'.

11. Elderly persons

To ensure that every retired worker must have sufficient resources to afford 'him or her a decent standard of living' as well as 'medical and social assistance specifically suited to his or her needs', the Commission would propose an action programme to support pilot projects, exchanges of information, etc., and highlight the problems involved by organizing a 'Year of the Elderly' in 1993.

12. Disabled persons

To attain the Charter's objective of entitling 'all disabled persons . . . to additional concrete measures aimed at improving their social and professional integration', the Commission would prepare a third Community action programme on integration and equality of opportunity for the disabled, including a Directive to promote better travel possibilities for workers with disabilities hindering their mobility.

This selective outline of the Commission's strategy to implement the Charter highlights some crucial points. First, there was no intention of trying to centralize all aspects of social policy at Community level; there were numerous references to the need to respect national practices and so on. Secondly, much of the action envisaged at EC level was designed to encourage rather than compel movement towards more coordinated policies. Hence, the plans to have a 'Year of the Elderly', to set up a 'European agency' to provide scientific and technical support in the fields of safety, hygiene and health at work, to establish an 'employment observatory' for the Community to forecast trends in labour supply and demand with a view towards marrying workers and jobs more effectively across the single market, and so on. Thirdly, where the Commission did believe that Community law was required, it usually formulated its legislative proposals in the form of a Directive rather than a more rigid Regulation. Whereas EC Regulations are directly enforceable laws, identically formulated and applicable throughout all the Member States without the need for any intervening national laws, Directives are more flexible and allow account to be taken of different national traditions and varied socio-economic conditions. Although they are also legally binding, they lay down the intended results of EC legislation, leaving it to individual Member State governments to produce the precise national laws by which these aims will be achieved. Thus, a Directive may lay down minimum health and safety standards to be attained in workplaces throughout the Community, but allow each individual state government to devise the most appropriate local means of achieving the common end. It is important to grasp this element of spatial flexibility in the Community's legal structure, which helps mitigate criticisms of a monolithic centralist mentality in Brussels insensitive to geographical variety. Other elements of the Commission's action plan to implement the Social Charter were based on Recommendations and Opinions, for example in the fields of child care and the progress of countries towards ensuring an 'equitable wage'. These Community instruments are not legally binding, but are designed to put political pressure on governments to move towards Community objectives.

Thus, implementation of the Charter is not going to be some simple process of 'imposing' social policy on Member States from an all-powerful Community bureaucracy in Brussels. Obviously, the process of putting it into effect is going to be long and hard with many opposing viewpoints emanating from different groups in all Member States. Furthermore, there is no guarantee that its objectives will be achieved. It was not long before this became apparent.

PROPOSALS FOR PART-TIME AND TEMPORARY WORKERS

In the summer of 1990 the Commission presented three draft Directives to eliminate 'distortions of competition' within the Community arising from the different entitlements of part-time and temporary workers in different countries (Local Government 1990a). The basic principle underlying the Commission's proposals was that there should be a Community framework ensuring a minimum of consistency between the various forms of open-ended contracts in the different Member States. This meant: first, employers should have to bear the same types of costs (obviously the actual sums would differ from country to country) when they employ part-time and temporary workers; secondly, that there should be movement towards the best practice in Europe rather than a reduction in standards. The aim was to prevent employers in one country from undercutting prices and tenders of employers in another country by treating this particular group of workers markedly less well than elsewhere in the Common Market. To this end, the draft proposals required:

> the elimination of provisions leading to unfair competition (differences in social protection of part-time workers, paid leave, etc.);
> that workers in part-time and temporary employment should have the same access to vocational training, social services and so on as those enjoyed by full-time workers employed for an indefinite duration;

that such workers should also be taken into account in the
setting up of workers' representative bodies;
that any clauses preventing the conclusion of a contract of
employment for temporary work should be made null and
void;
that such workers enjoy the same health and safety conditions
as other workers and not normally used for work requiring
special medical provision.

Apart from the health and safety proposals, these provisions
would also apply to seasonal workers, but not to those who
worked for less than eight hours a week (those employing children to deliver newspapers in Britain could relax!).

The response of the UK government to these proposals was
predictably hostile, given its ideological commitment to reducing
governmental intervention in workplace activities (see above). It
argued that by increasing employers' costs as well as the administrative burdens of 'needless regulations', the number of part-time
and temporary staff in the UK would be reduced along with
labour market flexibility. In a memorandum to this effect, the
Department of Employment also maintained that the proposal
would thus discriminate against women and the disabled who
form a large part of the part-time/temporary workforce; a pointed
riposte to the claim that such measures were designed to protect
such exposed sections of the workforce (Local Government
1990a). The British government also challenged the legal basis of
the Commission's claim that such measures should be adopted
by qualified majority vote in the Council of Ministers (Article 21 of
the SEA: see above). In its view, issues relating to the rights and
interests of employees should be subjected to unanimous voting
in the Council.

As these proposals were put forward in 1990 there were more
than 14 million part-time and some 10 million temporary employees in the Community, making up nearly a quarter of the employed population (ie, excluding employers, self-employed and
family workers). Britain had the third largest proportion – 29 per
cent – of its workforce in this category and they had a relatively
poor deal in comparison with 'best practice' in the Community.
For example, if applied in the UK, the proposals would require a

reduction in the qualification period for entitlement to employment protection rights. Furthermore, all workers working more than eight hours per week would be brought into the National Insurance system however little they earned. In addition, there would have to be equal rights of access to non-wage benefits at work such as training.

Although, the British government and many employers resisted these proposals, the Trades Union Congress (TUC) supported them. In its view it was not simply a matter of granting basic rights, but encouraging the development of a skilled workforce. It argued that the crisis in the British labour market related to lack of skills and low productivity. Any move towards mitigating a two-tier labour market by establishing equal rights of training and employment conditions was to be welcomed. There were plenty of sources of cheap labour and goods outside of the Community, including in Eastern Europe; why encourage the growth of industries based on cheap labour within the single market? This approach was in tune with those prevalent in the Commission and most Member State governments which felt that the future of the EC lay in developing highly-skilled, highly-productive and highly-paid workforces, although there were obviously divergences of view to be found right across the Community.

Proposals on Working Time

Similar arguments met other proposals flowing out of the Commission's Action Programme to implement the Social Charter. For example, in July 1990 the Commission presented a draft Directive on working time which aimed to provide workers with a basic 'safety net' for daily and weekly periods of leave (Local Government 1990b: 11). In summary, the proposals required a minimum daily rest period of 11 out of 24 hours; a least one rest day a week; night workers should not work more than 8 hours in 24 and be forbidden overtime. Certain exceptions would be allowed, mainly in seasonal work, provided that compensatory leave was granted within reference periods of less than 6 months. Other exemptions would include farmers, some long-haul transport workers and those in sections of the oil industry.

Table 6.6 Statutory regulation of working time in EC states 1991.

Country	Working Week	Overtime	Nightwork
Belgium	40 hours	65 hours per 3 months	20.00–06.00
Denmark	no legislation	governed by collective agreement	no legislation
Germany	48 hours	2 hours/day for up to 30 days/year	20.00–06.00
Greece	5-day week 40 hours in private ind.	3 hours/day 18 hrs/week 150hrs/year	22.00–07.00
Spain	40 hours	80 hours/year	22.00–06.00
France	39 hours	9 hrs/week 130 hrs/year	22.00–05.00
Ireland	48 hours	2 hours/day 12 hrs/week 240 hrs/year	no legislation
Italy	48 hours	no legislation	24.00–06.00
Luxembourg	40 hours	2 hours/day	No general legislation nursing mothers & pregnant women 22,00–06,00
Netherlands	48 hours	0.5 to 3.5 hours/days	20.00–07.00
Portugal	48 hours	2 hours/day 160 hrs/year	20.00–07.00
UK	no legislation	no legislation	no legislation

Source: Commission 1991b.

Despite the far from radical character of these proposals, with flexibility built in to take account of special cases, the British government once again led the the attack on them by arguing that they would be too rigid and add to costs. Unlike other Member States, the UK had no statutory regulations on working times, believing that these were matters best left for negotiations between employers and employees (Table 6.6). The fact the UK had the highest proportion of night and shift workers in the Community and would find itself under pressure to make legal changes intensified the government's resistance. The Commission pointed out that no amendments to national legislation would be required as long as local collective bargaining agreements upheld the Directive's provisions, but the familiar criticisms of costly centralized bureaucracy persisted in British governmental and business circles, highlighting an opposition which was not entirely restricted to Britain.

On the other hand, the European Trade Union Confederation (ETUC), reflecting views also prevalent amongst representatives of labour in the UK, strongly criticized the Commission's proposals as an 'empty shell' (Local Government International Bureau 1990b: 11). It felt that the Commission was too concerned to avoid confrontation with the British government by setting unambitious objectives and being excessively flexible about the need for legislative changes. Thus, it was trying to persuade the European Parliament to amend the Commission's proposals by introducing more restrictive rules such as a maximum working day of 8 hours within a maximum working week of 40 hours. In all Member States except Britain, limits were already set at this level or were even stricter, so the Commission's proposals did little to move towards 'best practice'. The ETUC was also concerned by the large number of exceptions in the draft Directive, feeling that they should be negotiated between the relevant management and union representatives rather than defined by an EC law.

PROPOSALS ON PREGNANT WORKERS AND MATERNITY LEAVE

Predictably, in the autumn of 1990, a proposed Directive to protect pregnant women at work and those who had recently given birth again provoked the usual hostile response from the British government (Commission 1990e; Local Government 1990c:10). This measure was designed to entitle pregnant workers to at least

14 weeks of leave on full pay with no loss of pay or promotion prospects. Employers would have to find alternatives to night work for such women, who would also be exempt from work in the fortnight before birth. If employers decided to extend night work beyond the minimum of 14 weeks, they would have to pay 80 per cent of the full wages. Amongst other things, these proposals would entail a substantial increase in entitlement to paid leave in Britain. Under UK law pregnant workers were entitled to only 6 weeks of maternity leave on 90 per cent of full pay, a further 12 weeks on an agreed reduced sum and, subject to the approval of the employer, a further 22 weeks without remuneration. In relation to existing UK practice, the draft Directive would also greatly relax the conditions relating to unfair dismissal due to pregnancy. Thus, the Conservative government condemned the proposal on the grounds that it would increase costs and discourage employers from taking on young women staff. In its view, far from improving female rights, it would reduce employment and consequently discriminate against women! The Labour opposition, in contrast, deplored what it saw as yet another isolated and backward British stand on such matters.

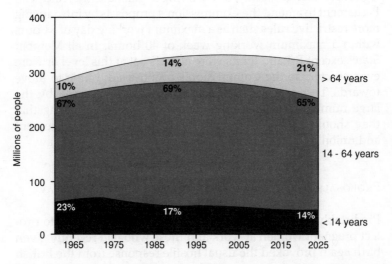

Figure 6.3 Evolution of the EC's demographic structure, 1961–2025 (*Source:* Commission, 1988f).

The Commission, as usual, tried to strengthen the moral basis of its social proposals by appeals to economic logic as well. It pointed out that only 1 per cent of the 52 million female workers in the Community were pregnant at any one time, so costs would not be raised unduly. Furthermore, it related the initiative to falling birth rates and shortages of skilled labour in the EC (Fig 6.3 and 6.4). Most Member States had fertility rates below replacement level and some were heading rapidly towards absolute

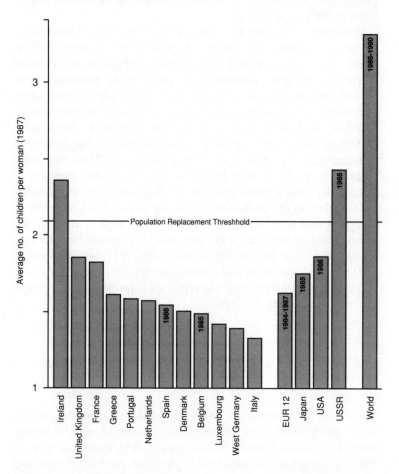

Figure 6.4 Average number of children per woman in EC and elsewhere, 1987 (*Source:* Commission, 1990b).

population decline; for example, the population in former West Germany was expected to shrink from 61 million to 47 million by 2030, a drop of nearly a quarter (Financial Times 1990). Similar trends were discernable elsewhere, even in the 'Catholic' southern Mediterranean countries such as Italy and Spain. Such major demographic changes made it imperative to encourage women, especially those with skills, both to stay in the workforce and have children; hence the draft Directive. Social policy was thus presented as an economic investment as well as a moral imperative in the single market.

Eventually in November 1991 a somewhat diluted Directive on pregnant women was finally adopted in the Council despite strenuous opposition from Britain and reservations felt in other countries. The UK government abstained in the qualified majority vote on the question, still opposed in principle to Community encroachment on such social matters, but unable to apply a veto. Thinking that such matters should be decided by unanimity, British ministers were considering a challenge to the legality of the Council's decision in the European Court. However, their resolution to do so was being weakened by the prospect of potentially hostile public opinion. A UK general election was due to take place in the six months following this decision on maternity rights and Conservative MPs were reportedly worried that votes could be lost if their government was seen to be opposing an improvement in working women's rights (Guardian Weekly 1991a:3). Despite the talk of democratic deficits in the Community system, public opinion clearly does impinge on EC policy-making in a variety of ways.

IN CONCLUSION: SINGLE MARKETS, SOCIAL CHARTERS AND POLITICS

The Social Charter was a clear 'political signal' from the highest Community level that a 'European social area' should be strengthened to counterbalance the fast-integrating 'economic area' of the single market. Whatever the particular national differences of interest and emphasis, the majority consensus throughout the EC favoured this approach. But in Britain, its adoption by the other eleven Member States without the accord of the UK government highlighted major ideological clashes about the future character of the European Community. On one side, many British Conservatives saw the Charter as part of an attempt to reintroduce bureaucratic socialism into Britain via the 'backdoor of Brussels'. In her 'Bruges speech' of September 1988, when the Commission was drawing up its Charter proposals, Mrs Thatcher, then Prime Minister, emphasized her determination to protect the achievements of the 'Thatcherite revolution':

> we have not successfully rolled back the frontiers of the State in Britain, only to see them re-imposed at a European level, with a European Superstate exercising a new dominance. (Thatcher 1988: 4)

Such sentiments flowed out of a tradition which saw the 'free enterprise' economic elements of the '1992' project as an adequate basis upon which to build European unity; talk of developing a European 'social space' ignored 'the lesson of the economic history of Europe in the 1970s and 1980s'. For Mrs Thatcher this lesson was that a 'state-controlled economy is a recipe for low growth...(whereas)... free enterprise within a framework of law brings better results'. The framework of law she had in mind would rid the market place of barriers hindering open competition rather than build up a European edifice of workers' rights:

> our aim should not be more and detailed regulation from the centre...(but)...to deregulate and remove constraints on trade. (Thatcher 1988: 6)

Mrs Thatcher's reading of the SEA had clearly focused on its requirement for a single internal market and ignored, or underestimated, the sections on 'social and economic cohesion'. However, opponents of her government's approach to the EC were reading developments differently. The Labour Party's traditional hostility to the Community was changing to enthusiasm as the Commission strove to give renewed substance to the stagnating 'social dimension' of European integration. In the words of Mr Kinnock, unrestrained 'market power' would have detrimental consequences for 'civil rights and environmental conditions, individual opportunities and collective provisions' (Kinnock 1988: 3). In signing the Social Charter, eleven Member State governments – of various political colours – had indicated their broad agreement with this view despite their particular differences over detail and precise implementation of general objectives.

Observers of this debate, aware of Europe's complexity and the subtlety of Community processes, can easily conclude that both sides overstated their case. The Thatcherite spectre of an all-powerful, corporatist European 'superstate' ready to 'extinguish democracy', made far too light of the power wielded by national governments within the Community's supranational institutions (Chapter 1). For example, the Commission had been trying to promote forms of worker participation throughout the Community since the 'Vredeling' Fifth Directive had been proposed in 1972 (see Chapter 5). However, although most Member States required some kind of formal employee involvement in company affairs, countries such as Britain had successfully blocked even the most general type of EC regulation in this area. Similarly, the broad and legally unbinding provisions of the Social Charter gave enormous scope to member governments to resist, amend and find very flexible solutions adapted to national, regional and local conditions. Many years of complex negotiations involving numerous institutions and interest groups at both European and national level are clearly in store before strong social policy linkages cross the frontiers of the Common Market. Thus, while some on the Right of British politics gird themselves to fight the paper dragons of a would-be socialist superstate, some on the Left are in danger of lurching from simplistic opposition to a 'rich-man's club' to naive enthusiasm for a vision of social Europe where an equitable balance of power between employers and employees in an increasingly European and international economy will apparently deliver 'productive and socially just solutions' (Kinnock 1988: 6).

In truth, the balance between 'economic' and 'social' policy in the future European Community will depend, as always, on the political balance of forces within its intricate interlocking network of European, national and, in some cases, regional institutions. This obvious fact can be too easily overlooked in European debates dominated by crude '1992' deadlines and simplistic visions of a 'Europe without frontiers'. The precise policies that emerge from the general guidelines of the Social Charter will be shaped by a very pluralistic process involving the various EC institutions, some regional bodies, big business, representatives of organized labour and, above all, 12 or more national governments operating together in the Council of Ministers. In the past, the balance of these forces has produced a European Community which has emphasized economic integration based on free-market competition. But the socially protective aspects of the CAP, maintained as a result of the political pressure farmers have been able wield, are clear evidence that there are no inevitable outcomes to the interplay of economic and social forces in the Community. The following chapter on a long-established social aspect of EC activities – regional policy – provides further insights into the importance of analysing the inter-relationships between the Community's economic, social and political dimensions.

7. Regional policy in the European Community

Policies designed to promote regional development in less-favoured areas are intrinsically 'social' in character in that they advocate governmental intervention to mitigate what are seen as the adverse effects of 'free market' forces. Although economic arguments about full use of human and physical resources also underpin regional development strategies, a moral sense of seeking greater social justice is usually present in some form. This sense may have its roots in some egalitarian ideal or simply be a more pragmatic belief that it is unwise to allow people in poorer regions to lag too far behind others in terms of social and economic welfare. Thus, the development of a Community regional policy provides a chance to assess the success of efforts to build one element of a European social dimension in the past. In so doing, some indication can be obtained of the difficulties facing those trying to put flesh on the bones of the Social Charter.

The preamble to the Rome Treaty setting up the EEC expressed the signatory states's general desire to reduce 'the differences existing between the various regions and the backwardness of the less favoured regions' (Treaties 1987). This rather vague formulation reflected the fact that most of the original Member States were content to pursue regional goals at a purely national level with little desire to create a common regional policy for the Community as a whole. Therefore, the pursuit of greater regional equality through government spending programmes and controls on the geographical location of investment was kept jealously within the geographical framework of national territories for many years. EC governments, to the left and right of the political spectrum, had diverted resources from richer to poorer areas in pursuit of greater regional equality and social harmony within their separate national frameworks, but balked at the idea of doing it together on a Community scale. Of the original 'Six', only Italy with its Mezzogiorno problem was really interested in a Community regional policy; the other members, not keen to contribute to common funds which would be channelled towards the Italian south, were determined to keep regional development in national hands.

In 1973, the entry of the United Kingdom, Ireland and Denmark into the Community strengthened the hand of the Italians, as well as the Commission, which also wanted an effective EC regional policy. Clearly, these new Member States could perceive national advantage in a policy diverting Community resources to their depressed areas. Thus, in 1975 the Council eventually established the European Regional Development Fund (ERDF). The entry of the relatively poor Mediterranean states – Greece in 1981 followed by the Iberian countries in 1986 – further reinforced the role of regional policy in the Community's overall 'social dimension', as did fears that the potentially centralizing effects of the drive towards a single European market by the end of 1992 would weaken still further the situation in peripheral areas and those especially dependent on traditional industries (RIDER-IRIS 1989). The Commission's 1985 White Paper which promoted the single market project recognized the validity of these worries in stating that:

> Economic integration, by increasing the possibilities for human, material and financial resources to move without obstacle towards the most economically attractive regions, could lead to an increase in regional disparities. (Commission 1985a)

These anxieties were recognized in the 1986 Single European Act which contains an important section concerned with the 'Economic and Social Cohesion' of the Community (Treaties 1987). Within it the long-held aim of 'reducing disparities between the various regions and the backwardness of the least favoured regions' was re-stated. Furthermore, the Commission was required to draw up comprehensive new proposals to reinvigorate Community regional policy in the new context of the developing single market (Article 130, A/B). In 1988, these proposals were converted into policy by the Council of Ministers with a commitment to double the EC's Structural Funds (ERDF, ESF and EAGGF-Guidance) by 1993 when the single market was due for completion. Moreover, these increased development resources were to be geographically concentrated on the poorest parts of the Community rather than scattered widely throughout all Member States including those at the richer end of the EC wealth scale. However, before assessing the impact of such actions, it is necessary to have an idea of the scale of the disparities the EC has always committed itself to reduce.

REGIONAL DISPARITIES IN THE EUROPEAN COMMUNITY

The gap between the richest and poorest parts of the Community remains very great. Indeed it has increased over the years as enlargement has brought in new Member States from the southern and northwestern peripheries of western Europe. In 1990 the exceptional incorporation of what was East Germany into the EC further widened the disparities that the Community has always wanted, in theory at least, to reduce. One major indicator used by the EC to measure these divergences is GDP per capita. To allow comparisons between regions in different Member States, GDP data are converted first into a common unit of account (the ECU) and secondly into a common purchasing power standard (the PPS, a unit of measurement that expresses for each country the price of an identical volume of goods and services, thus allowing comparisons of real purchasing power between countries and regions in a way which simple income statistics do not). EC statisticians also relate GDP data to the average population of a region in order to reduce distortions when making comparisons between regions of different size. Nevertheless, even when all these moderating calculations have been effected, an enormous gulf separates the most and least prosperous areas of the Community.

First, a significant divide exists at a national level. On the one hand, Spain, Ireland, Greece and Portugal had (1988) a per capita GDP in PPS less than 75 per cent of the EC 12 average (Eurostat 1990a). On the other hand, the other eight Member States all had a per capita GDP above the Community average. West Germany and Luxembourg had a GDP per head more than twice that of Greece and Portugal (Fig 6.2 above). This basic situation had changed little in relative terms during the 1970s and 1980s. Certainly, there was no real evidence of the widest gaps closing. For example, wealthy Luxembourg, situated in the Community's economic core, moved further ahead during the 1980s to exceed the EC average by more than 20 per cent in 1988, whilst Greece rejoined Portugal at the other end of the scale with a per capita GDP little over half of the Community norm (54 per cent).

At a regional level, the gap between the most and least prosperous areas becomes even wider (Table 7.1). Hamburg, with a GDP per capita (PPS) 82 per cent above the EC 12 average in 1988 lies at one extreme followed closely by Gronigen in the Netherlands (80 per cent), whereas parts of Aegean Greece are to be found 60 per cent below the average along with several other southern Mediterranean regions not much better off in Spain and Portugal (Fig 7.1). Of course, these extreme values should be treated with caution, particularly at the upper end. For example, Hamburg is a geographically small region of overwhelmingly urban character where activities with a high value-added are concentrated, often generated by commuters who work, but do not live, in the area. Likewise, the very high value for Groningen in a Northern Netherlands area of generally moderate prosperity can be explained by the extraction of highly valuable natural gas in this region. However, even if these extreme values are eliminated, the problem (assuming it is viewed as such) of regional disparities in the Community remains enormous.

In general, the disparities between regions in each country are usually smaller than those between Member States. However, some remarkable divergences within national territories persist. In Italy, the deeply ingrained division between North and South persists, with a GDP per capita nearly 20 per cent above the EC average across the former region (38 per cent above in Lombardy) and around 30 per cent below it in the Mezzogiorno (40 per cent below in Calabria). In Spain, regional per capita GDP ranges from

Table 7.1 GDP per capita 1988 for selected regions.

Country		Region	GDP per capita (PPS) (EC 12 = 100)
West	(highest)	Hamburg	182
Germany	(lowest)	Luneburg	77
Luxembourg		whole country	121
Denmark	(highest)	Copenhagen	128
	(lowest)	East	91
France	(highest)	Ile-de-France	164
	(lowest)	Corsica	76
UK	(highest)	Greater London	165
	(lowest)	Northern Ireland	80
Italy	(highest)	Lombardy	138
	(lowest)	Calabria	59
Netherlands	(highest)	Groningen	180
	(lowest)	Flevoland	67
Belgium	(highest)	Brussels	155
	(lowest)	Hainaut	78
Spain	(highest)	Balearic Iles	111
	(lowest)	Extramadura	50
Ireland		whole country	65
Portugal	(highest)	Lisbon	70
	(lowest)	Norte	42
Greece	(highest)	Sterea	67
	(lowest)	North Aegean	40

Source: Eurostat 1990a.

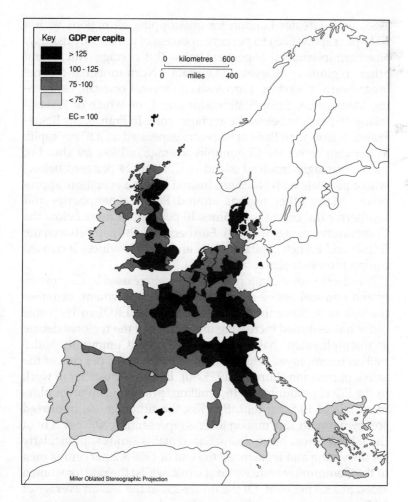

Key — GDP per capita
- > 125
- 100 - 125
- 75 - 100
- < 75

EC = 100

0 — kilometres — 600
0 — miles — 400

Miller Oblated Stereographic Projection

Figure 7.1 Regional variations in GDP per capita in the EC, 1988 (*Source*: Eurostat 1990a).

50 per cent to 100 per cent of the EC average, with the highest values in the Balearic Islands (11 per cent above), Catalonia, the Basque country and Madrid contrasting sharply with the lowest in Andalucia and Extramadura (50 per cent below). The dominance of the capital-city regions remains a constant feature of spatial inequality in France and the United Kingdom. For example, Southeast England lay 30 per cent above the EC average in

1988, with Greater London far outstripping all regions with a GDP per capita (PPS) 65 per cent in excess of it. Not surprisingly, Northern Ireland fell 20 per cent below this average with several other regions – Cleveland/Durham, Northumberland/Tyne/Wear, South Yorkshire, Lincolnshire, Devon/Cornwall, Lancashire, Merseyside, Salop/Staffordshire, and the whole of Wales – falling 10 per cent below the average score. In France, the Ile-de-France region with Paris at its centre generated a GDP per capita 64 per cent above the Community average in 1988, far ahead of the increasingly troubled island of Corsica (24 per cent below) where parallels with Northern Ireland become ever more appropriate. Many other regions around France's peripheries and southern rural centre had values 10 per cent or more below the Community average (Fig 7.1). Furthermore, the gap between the British and French capital regions and their provinces increased during the 1980s (Eurostat 1990a: 2).

Another major indicator of regional welfare used by Community and national policy-makers relates to employment, or rather the lack of it. Since the establishment of the ERDF in 1975, this index has assumed increasing importance in the regional debate as unemployment has soared. In 1975, the Community had 5 million unemployed which amounted then to 3.2 per cent of the active population (Eurostat 1975–90). By 1986, those out of work in the EC 12 amounted to 16.1 million, producing an unemployment rate of 10.8 per cent. By 1988, the situation had improved somewhat with 15.6 million jobless representing 10.3 per cent of the labour force, but the situation remains serious, particularly for the young and women. At the end of 1988 8.2 per cent of men in the Community were without work, whilst the rate for women stood at 13.3 per cent. Of the under-25s in the EC, an average of 17.3 per cent were without work at the same time, with the corresponding figure for young women rising to 22.7 per cent.

Obviously, the countries and regions of the Community are not affected evenly by unemployment. Furthermore, the employment problem tends to exacerbate GDP inequalities, although excessive generalization must be avoided (compare Fig 7.1 and 7.2 on regional GDP per capita and unemployment rates). At the geographical core of the Community wealthy Luxembourg continues to enjoy a very low rate of unemployment (2.5 per cent), whilst Denmark and West Germany succeeded in reducing

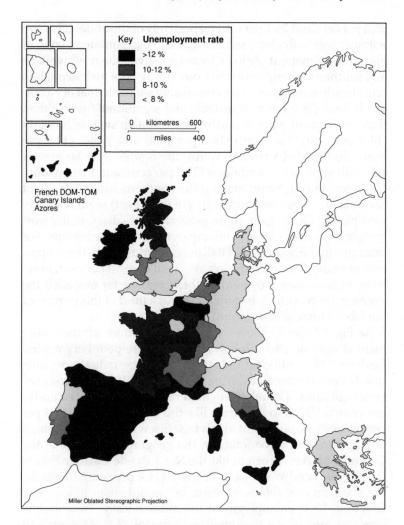

Figure 7.2 Regional variations in unemployment rates in the EC, 1989 (*Source:* Eurostat, 1990a; Commission, 1990b).

theirs to 5.9 per cent and 6.4 per cent respectively by 1988 after having always stayed below the EC average during the years of economic crisis. At the other end of the scale, the rates remain persistently high in Spain (19.8 per cent) and Ireland (17.6 per cent). The problem of youth unemployment has become exceptionally urgent in Spain, Italy and Ireland where 43.8 per cent,

35.4 per cent and 26.1 per cent respectively of the under-25s were without work. Regions recording the most persistent rates of high unemployment are to be found mostly in the northwestern and southern extremities of the Community. The Irish Republic's rate already noted above was remarkably similar to that of Northern Ireland (18.9 per cent in 1987) and significantly worse than those in hard-hit parts of northwestern Britain such as Scotland (14.8 per cent), the North (14.7 per cent) and Wales (12.9 per cent). To the Mediterranean south, the figures were far greater still with regions like Andalucia (31.3 per cent) and Extramadura (26.0 per cent) in Spain making the southern Italian islands of Sardinia (18.7 per cent) and Sicily (16.0 per cent) seem relatively well-placed! Once again, these general figures disguise the worryingly high rates of youth unemployment in these regions. For example, in the Spanish and Italian regions just cited, the proportion of under-25s without a job averaged over 50 per cent. Similarly, female unemployment in these regions far exceeded the average, representing, in general, about a third of this portion of the labour force seeking work.

As Fig 7.2 clearly shows, the regional pattern of unemployment is not one which follows a simple core-periphery model. Regions with traditional industries that were radically restructured or even eliminated during the 1970s and 1980s also endured very high rates. The relatively high rates recorded in the northern-central UK as well as areas like the West Midlands (12.4 per cent in 1987) are testament to this fact. Elsewhere, patches of high unemployment can be found in the geographical centre of the Common Market in regions like the Nord-Pas-de-Calais in France (14 per cent) and Wallonia in Belgium (14.4 per cent). Similarly, the statistics available warn us to be careful about linking low GDP and high unemployment too automatically. Notably low levels of jobless are registered in Portugal (7.1 per cent) and Greece (7.4 per cent). Doubtless, these figures conceal much underemployment in the large agrarian sectors of these two countries as well as much of their secondary and tertiary industries. Also, these statistics are a reminder that a simple, common definition of unemployment is not possible, given the large number of different cultural and economic concepts that bear on the question. For example, many of those in work of some sort in

Greece and Portugal would be regarded as economically inefficient, and therefore jobless, in the Member States with more
developed economies. Indeed, even between countries with
such economies there is ample room for dispute on the nature of
employment. To make the point starkly, it is difficult to imagine
any UK government defending the cause of very small farms
(seen by British eyes as hopelessly inefficient) with the vigour of
successive West German governments (which see them, not only
as important voters, but as valuable sources of rural
employment).

There is another increasingly serious dimension to Community
unemployment that underlines the scale of the regional problem:
namely, the long-term jobless. More than half (56 per cent) of
those out of work towards the end of the 1980s had been without
a job for more than a year (Eurostat 1990a). Belgium, following
the drastic decline of its traditional coal, steel and chemical industries in the Sambre-Meuse valley, headed this unhappy league
with some 74.6 per cent of its unemployed in this category in
1987. Countries with underdeveloped peripheral regions followed, namely: Italy (66.3 per cent), Ireland (66.1 per cent) and
Spain (65.7 per cent). Denmark was markedly better placed than
any other country in this respect, having 29.5 per cent of its
jobless in this long-term category. But again, this element intensifies in the regional unemployment problem in both core and
periphery areas. For example, when the analysis focuses on those
out of work for more than two years, the situation becomes worse
in the UK, Italy, the Netherlands and France.

Finally, the scale of the regional problem facing the Community can be appreciated by looking at the map on infrastructural
divergences across its territory (Fig 7.3). Much of the EC's regional development effort is directed at improving infrastructures in
order to allow lagging areas to attract investment, develop their
inherent potential and compete on more equal terms with the
dominant parts of the Community. Therefore, the Commission
devised an overall infrastructure index to measure regional disparities in this regard (Commission 1988h: 94). This index took
into account four major categories of infrastructure linked to
economic performance: the transport network (roads, railways,
ports, etc.); communication networks (telephone, telex, etc.);

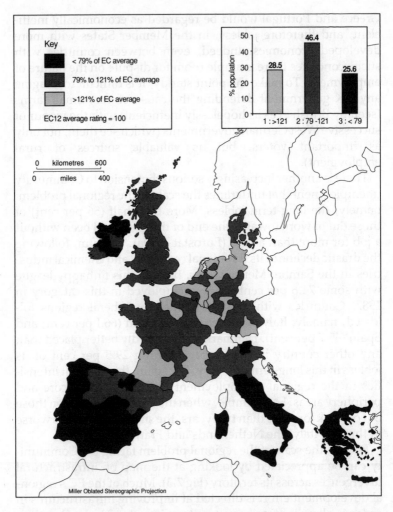

Figure 7.3 Regional variations in infrastructural quality in the EC (*Source*: Commission, 1988l).

energy availability (networks for the distribution of fuel, electricity, gas, etc.); and education facilities (numbers of students at university level, in professional and vocational training, etc.). The resultant map reveals once again the severe weaknesses of southern Mediterranean Europe and Ireland. Here, the spatial correlation with low GDP is clear, highlighting yet again where the problem of regional development is most acute.

CRITICISMS OF EC REGIONAL POLICY

Despite the Community's growing commitment to regional policy since 1975, doubts remain about the efficacy of its efforts confronted with the size of the task and the competitive forces unleashed by the internal market (Wise, Croxford 1988). Critics have argued that EC regional policy often appears to have a 'cosmetic' character which camouflages the lack of a really meaningful effort to reduce the very substantial regional inequalities existing across the Community. Such arguments have been largely based on the following contentions: first, that the available resources are too small; secondly, that often these limited funds do not provide genuinely additional investment to that already available from national governments; thirdly, that these restricted resources have not been concentrated enough on the least developed areas of the poorest Member States; and, fourthly, that expenditure has often been geographically scattered over a wide range of disparate projects to little real effect. These criticisms are examined in turn, before assessing whether the Community's reformed regional policy adopted in 1988 is likely to make much difference. Until this reform, the ERDF was the financial heart of EC regional policy so the analysis prior to 1988 concentrates upon this specifically regional fund although the regional impact of other EC policies should not be forgotten (Croxford, Wise 1988).

1. Does the EC allocate sufficient resources to regional development?

After years of hesitation, the European Regional Development Fund (ERDF) finally started operations in 1975. This Fund grew steadily both in absolute terms and as a proportion of the Community budget, rising from 4.8 per cent of total EC spending in 1975 to 9.6 per cent in 1989 (Fig 5.2). But despite this growth, the amount of Community aid for regional development has always been extremely limited, both in relation to other government spending and the scale of the problem. High inflation has also made the increased allocations to regional policy more apparent than real; for instance, the Fund's resources in 1985 were up 7 per cent on the previous year in nominal terms, but an average EC inflation rate of 5.1 per cent reduced this to a real increase of only 1.8 per cent. Furthermore, this augmented ERDF was still equivalent to a mere 0.1 per cent of the Community's GDP (Commission 1986b:9). Although the proportion of the EC budget devoted to agricultural price support diminished from 80.6 per cent in 1973 to 67.0 per cent in 1989, it still dwarfed EC spending on regional development. It is true that comparisons with CAP expenditure can be misleading in that the EC has overwhelming financial responsibility for agriculture, whereas other sectors – such as regional development and social policy – are dealt with at both EC and, more importantly, national level. Nevertheless, however one plays with the statistics, EC resources directed towards reducing regional inequalities look meagre in relation to the size of the problem. For example, national spending on regional development has always been much greater. In 1982, the Commission calculated that, on average, ERDF spending on infrastructure in areas eligible for regional aid was a mere 3 to 4 per cent of equivalent national investment. Similarly, ERDF funding for industrial projects in the private sector amounted to less than 5 per cent of comparable national aid (Commission 1986b: 9; Commission 1987e: 69). Obviously, such averages hide major variations in the ERDF's financial impact from country to country. For example, over much of the period of its operation the ERDF provided up to 20 per cent per annum of public infrastructural investment in small, relatively poor countries like Ireland, Greece and, more recently, Portugal. Similarly, in 1987 ERDF spending in Portugal was equivalent to 1.27 per cent of the country's GDP, whilst the comparative figure in Greece was 0.73 per cent and in Ireland 0.64 per cent (Commission 1986b, Commission 1989c: 4). But given that national assistance to problem regions – far in excess of what the EC as a whole has provided – has failed to forge any marked change in broad geographical patterns of well-being in western Europe (Wise, Chalkley 1990), it is clear that the relatively minute resources deployed by the ERDF up to the end of the 1980s did little to close the gap between the

Community's richest and poorest regions. In fact, the Commission concluded that these disparities had, if anything increased during the first decade of the ERDF's operation (Commission 1984). With the addition of Spain and Portugal to the Community in 1986, the gap was widened even further.

2. Has the EC provided truly additional resources for regional development?

In formulating Community regional policy it has always been the Commission's intention that ERDF monies should be additional to those allocated by national governments to development areas (Commission 1986b: 16). However, evidence accumulated to reveal that ERDF grants were, more often than not, being used to replace a slice of national public expenditure rather than add to it (Keating, Waters 1985: 74–5). Obviously, the labyrinthine processes of government spending make it hard to determine with certitude what a Member State's expenditure would have been had assistance from the EC not materialized. This has been particularly true over the last decade when public spending, not least on regional policy, has been progressively cut back in many EC countries (Wise, Chalkley 1990). Nevertheless, many analysts have reached the conclusion that several Member States have seen ERDF grants as a subsidy to national regional development budgets rather than as an addition to them. All EC countries kept a tight control on ERDF and other EC grants, significantly resisting the option – permitted in the ERDF regulation – of allowing a grant to be paid to the successful applicant directly from Brussels. Instead, such grants had to be channelled through national ministries where they could be used as a substitute for, not a supplement to, national regional investment (Wilson 1980: 15; Preston 1983: 25). In fact, some governments, notably in the UK and France, made little effort to disguise this fact. Bruce Millan, the current (1991) EC Commissioner for Regional Policy, was Secretary of State for Scotland in the late 1970s and a member of Cabinet in the Labour government of the time; he described the process thus:

Every quarter we drew up a list of projects or companies due to get national assistance. We knew roughly what the UK as a whole and Scotland would get from the EC each year. So we just picked out as many projects as we needed to make up the UK quota, and sent the list off to Brussels. Back came the EC money, and the Treasury simple lopped that amount off its expenditure. (*Financial Times* 1989)

A study in France reported the same phenomenon, noting that

the French government uses the ERDF as a compensation fund for expenditures it has already undertaken...(applying)...the infamous unwritten additionality rule, practised by all European governments, according to which European aids are treated as reimbursements of national subsidies. (Meny 1985: 196–8)

This practice was facilitated by the dominance of national quotas in the allocation of ERDF resources throughout the 1970s and 1980s. As Millan's confession above makes clear, governments already knew more-or-less what slice of the ERDF cake they would get each year, so there was no real difficulty in formulating a national budget to take into account what was seen, much to the irritation of the Commission, as the forthcoming 'ERDF contribution' to it.

Of course, it would be wrong to dismiss ERDF assistance as totally fictitious. Even in Britain, where there has been little pretence about trying to apply additionality, local authorities receiving ERDF support have enjoyed some real increase in the resources available to them in that the EC money comes as an interest-free grant. If ERDF assistance had not been forthcoming, the authority would often have been obliged to borrow money to complete a project and thus pay interest on the loan. However, even this tiny measure of real additionality must be kept in perspective, for the winning of an ERDF grant has not permitted a British local authority to carry out extra spending beyond existing capital expenditure limits laid down by central national government. It merely reduced the cost of borrowing the permitted amounts (Croxford 1988). A similar situation has persisted in France (Arlett 1990; Arlett, Wise 1991) and elsewhere (Keating,

Jones 1985). Thus, much of the publicity surrounding the winning of EC regional grants has conveyed as much illusion as substance over the years since 1975.

3. Have ERDF resources been sufficiently concentrated on the weakest regions?

The European Commission has long advocated that the meagre resources of the ERDF be geographically concentrated on the most deprived areas of the Community. Such targeting would allow 'grants from the Fund to achieve a critical mass and to have a significant impact on the economic development of regions' (Commission 1986b: 14). Table 7.2 and Fig 7.4 show that the Fund's resources have been channelled mainly to the poorest parts of the EC's least affluent states. For example, over the period 1975–85 Ireland obtained almost five times the average ERDF receipts per capita, while the other countries receiving in excess of the Community mean – Greece, Italy, the UK and, since

Table 7.2 ERDF allocations by country 1975–87.

Country	Million ECU	ECU per capita
Ireland	1153.95	326
Greece (since 1981)	2107.16	211
Italy	6947.95	121
UK	4539.95	80
Portugal (since 1986)	769.83	79
France	2504.98	45
Luxembourg	15.89	43
Spain (since 1986)	1301.56	33
Denmark (inc. Greenland)	169.60	33
Belgium	178.35	18
Netherlands	221.51	15
West Germany	814.15	13
EC 12	20726.19	64

Source: Commission 1989c.

1986, Spain and Portugal – all have serious regional problems. When the analytical focus is switched to a more precise regional level, it can be noted that those particularly depressed regions given priority status in the allocation of the Fund – namely, the Mezzogiorno, Greece, the whole of Ireland, the French Overseas

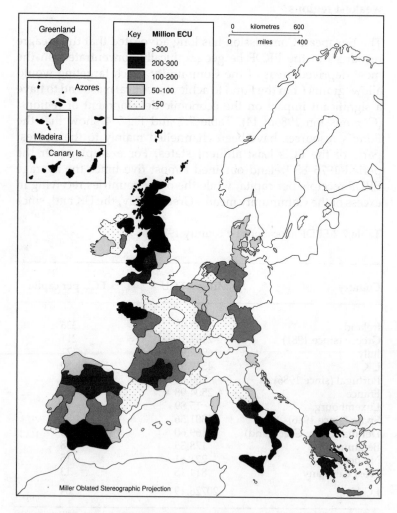

Figure 7.4 Regional distribution of ERDF grants, 1975–87 (*Source:* Commission, 1989c).

Departments and Greenland (until it left the EC in 1985) – obtained 57 per cent of the available aid over the period 1975–85 (Commission 1986b: 88). This meant that ERDF assistance in the priority zones amounted to ECU 240 per capita over that decade compared to ECU 130 in other areas eligible for regional grants. Since the accession of the Iberian countries in 1986, their poorest regions have benefited from a similar level of targeting.

However, despite this limited measure of success, the fact remains that over most of the period since 1975 a sizeable proportion of this relatively small Fund has been directed towards the wealthier Member States. For example, over the 10-year period prior to the entry of Spain and Portugal, nearly a quarter of ERDF spending (22 per cent) took place in countries with a GDP per capita above the EC average (Wise, Croxford 1988: 168). Certainly, these richer countries had regional problems, but they were in a better position to cope with them nationally without recourse to assistance from the ERDF's tiny coffers. The strength of this argument, championed by the Commission, intensified when the Iberian countries joined the Community. Thereafter, the proportion of the EC's population living in the seriously underdeveloped areas approximately doubled, greatly increasing demands on the Fund. However, in the late 1980s the states with above EC average GDP per capita were still insisting on getting at least 12 per cent of the Fund in a revised and, admittedly, more flexible system of national quotas. Whether they should get any at all in a Community where spatial disparities in socio-economic welfare are so great remains a valid question.

4. Has ERDF expenditure been sufficiently coordinated?

A final major criticism of ERDF spending is that it has tended to be too haphazard in nature, thus reducing its real socio-economic impact. Grants have gone to a multitude of separate, unconnected projects rather than to schemes forming part of a coherent strategy of regional development. Just as central governments have tended to use the ERDF as simply another source to subsidize the national budget, so local governments have often seen it as merely one more potential source of finance for a particular project. The Commission has long aired its frustration with the diffuse pattern of spending these attitudes have produced, and pressed for a much more coherent approach based on long-term programmes of investment aimed at specific objectives. The socio-economic impact of EC regional development policy would thus, it is hoped, be more measurable and give real substance to these efforts to build one element of a genuine European 'social dimension' (Martins, Mawson 1983).

THE ERDF AND UNEMPLOYMENT

The major weaknesses of the ERDF outlined above led critics to see it as a 'cosmetic' policy designed to give the impression that regional inequalities were being tackled, thus concealing the fact that little of real substance was being achieved, to deal with the root causes of spatial disparities. In other words, the ERDF was being used, not as a serious instrument to reduce the gap between rich and poor parts of the Community, but as a way in which Member States could: 1) obtain a 'fair' share of the overall EC budget; 2) subsidize their national spending on regional development; and 3) demonstrate to sceptical electorates that some social benefit was being gained from membership of a Common Market often associated in the public's mind with big business interests, high food prices and, increasingly, unemployment.

The association with unemployment grew following enormous oil price increases in the 1970s and the major industrial restructuring that ensued (Wise, Chalkley, 1990). Thus it is appropriate to illustrate the ERDF's lack of substance by contrasting efforts to publicize the Fund's activities with forecasts of the jobs it was supposed to save or create. The Commission has always attached 'very great importance to the publicizing of Fund operations' because they 'are a particularly apt advertisement for the direct benefit people derive from Community action' (Commission 1985c: 39). Thus, a plethora of press releases and roadside signboards 'convey to all Europeans the same image of the Community's presence' (Commission 1986b: 61). Yet what reality lies behind this image? What impact has the ERDF had on reducing the major problem of regional mass unemployment?

When submitting ERDF grant applications for investment projects in industry, craft industry and services, Member States must indicate the predicted effect on employment. Such forecasts are an important factor in whether a request is successful or not (Commission 1986b: 20). Thus it can safely be assumed that job-creation forecasts made by applicants for aid will err on the optimistic side! Using the hopeful predictions of such applicants over the period 1975–85, it can be calculated that the ERDF contributed to the creation or maintenance of 711,330 jobs over that critical decade when unemployment in what were to become the 12 EC states rose sharply from around 5 million to some 16 million. The minimal impact of the Fund on employment generation can best be appreciated if the figures for a particular year are analysed. In 1984, the successful grant applicants optimistically assessed that their projects would, overall, create or save some 68,950 jobs. Assuming these predictions proved correct (it is impossible to know), these jobs would have reduced EC 10 unemployment of 12,430,200 in that year by a tiny 0.5 per cent. Indeed, given that the average ERDF contribution to each assisted project was just below 20 per cent, it is more accurate to estimate that the Fund helped a mere 0.1 per cent of the Community's jobless or job-threatened in that typical year.

Admittedly, the above analysis is very crude and the Commission has always argued that for every job directly created, another is produced by the multiplier effect. Furthermore, jobs (it is impossible to specify how many) are created directly or indirectly due to infrastructural projects partially supported by the ERDF (the Fund can never finance a scheme alone). Such projects, according to some estimates, employed about 1.2 million people in the first decade of the ERDF's operations (Commission 1986b: 21). However, it has to be remembered that many of these schemes would have gone ahead with or without EC support (see additionality arguments above) and the Fund merely had a minority participation in the great majority of them.

THE EUROPEAN COMMUNITY'S POLITICAL SYSTEM AND A WEAK ERDF

To understand why the ERDF amounted to little more than a token gesture towards the stated aim of reducing regional inequalities in the EC, reference has to be made to the balance of decision-making forces in the Community's political system.

Contrary to popular myth based on images of all-powerful 'Eurocrats', Member State governments are firmly embedded into this system. Indeed, positioned in the Council of Ministers at the decision-making centre of the Community, they dominate it (Fig 1.1). The Commission has the influential role of formulating policy proposals while the European Parliament can suggest amendments to them, but it is the national ministers in the Council who finally decide what should be done. Moreover, these ministers make their decisions after detailed negotiations in bodies like the Committee of Permanent Representatives (COREPER) and numerous other committees where national representatives predominate in discussions with the Commission. Furthermore, in their European dealings, Member-State ministers remain very sensitive to the demands of their different national parliaments and electorates, which are thus drawn into the overall Community system. These realities of Member-State power in the EC's political structure explain why what amounts to a de facto 'national veto' has long persisted in the Council of Ministers (see Chapter 1). This power wielded by national governments helps to explain why the ERDF remained such an insubstantial 'social dimension' to the EC's activities despite the Commission's constant efforts to strengthen it.

THE RESTRICTION OF EFFORTS TO STRENGTHEN THE ERDF

The original ERDF introduced after much hesitation in 1975 was allocated far fewer resources than the Commission had first proposed. The West Germans, not wishing to increase their already large 'net contribution' to the EC budget led the opposition, while the Italians and Irish – potential net beneficiaries – supported the Commission's ambitions. Britain occupied an intermediate position, torn between its reticence to increase the scope of EC activities and the need to get policies of a social nature that would demonstrate to a hostile British public that the Community could deliver something more beneficial than ever more expensive butter! Eventually, a British decision to support an EC regional fund, plus Irish and Italian threats to block moves towards greater economic union, led to the setting up of the ERDF.

However, as we have seen, this Fund was very small and ineffectual. Thus, the Commission made persistent attempts following 1975 to increase the size of the Fund, to concentrate it more effectively on the most needy areas in the poorest countries, to ensure that the Fund was genuinely additional to national resources, to promote a coherent programme approach where EC funds could be spent to real effect, and to loosen the decision-making grip that the richer states held over the making and implementation of Community regional policy. Despite some success, the Commission constantly fell short of its ambitions to develop a policy which began to match the scale of the problem. The power wielded by the national governments of the richer and larger states in the EC's political system does much to explain this failure (Wise, Croxford, 1988).

Take, for example, the Commission's efforts to target resources on the most needy regions defined according to Community-wide criteria unhindered by national considerations. Initially, it resisted the idea that each Member State should automatically get a share of the Fund, arguing that a genuinely 'European' approach should be adopted in allocating this 'European' Fund; after all, separate national regional policies still persisted and collectively possessed far more resources than the ERDF. But its proposals to this effect were resisted in the Council where a system of fixed national quotas was eventually adopted permitting all countries, even the richest, to get a guaranteed annual share (Council 1975). Furthermore, the Commission's efforts to define problem regions according to Community-wide criteria were thwarted by national power; individual Member States were to decide what parts of their national territory would be eligible for ERDF help. Thus it was possible for a region in a richer state to receive EC assistance, while an area with much greater problems in a poorer country would not qualify. Over the years, the Commission fought to break the grip of national governmental power on the allocation of the Fund with some limited success. Reforms in 1979 (Council 1979) and 1984 (Council 1984) marked very limited shifts away from national quotas towards a more genuinely Community method of allocation. But even after the entry of Spain and Portugal into the Community in 1986, all states were still insisting on a guaranteed share, with the result that between 12 per cent and 16 per cent of what was still a relatively small

Fund was being directed towards states with GDPs per capita above the EC average.

Similar difficulties faced the Commission's efforts to prevent ERDF monies being scattered across a multitude of unrelated projects to limited effect and promote instead a more coherent approach based on the support of long-term integrated programmes of regional development with clearly defined aims. It was also hoped that such a strategy would make it easier for the Commission to enforce the oft-ignored additionality principle. However, the Member States, who often saw the ERDF simply as a means of clawing back money from the Community budget rather than a serious instrument of regional development, showed little enthusiasm for the Commission's proposals (Wise, Croxford 1988). For example, the 1984 ERDF reform left less than 12 per cent of the Fund available for the 'Community programmes' favoured by the Commission with the possibility that this figure might rise to 20 per cent after three years. The reticence of central governments was not the only factor hindering movement towards a less diffuse use of the Fund. Devising integrated programmes of development requires increased effort and costs. Those pursuing investment funds sometimes find such organizational expense a deterrent, especially if there is no guarantee of success in a more competitive environment freer of automatic national quotas. Furthermore, there is the danger that the programme approach favours the richer countries with the larger, more efficient governmental bureaucracies skilled in the art of devising development strategies.

A final example of the way in which powerful Member States prevented the ERDF developing into a really substantial agent for regional change relates to the aim of moving towards greater economic and monetary union. Richer countries like West Germany could see little national interest in a strong Community regional policy, but the prospect of a European Monetary System (EMS) which would facilitate their massive trade transactions with the rest of the Common Market was attractive. However, a reduction of national control over exchange rates poses problems for poorer countries on the Community's periphery. If competition within the Common Market creates problems for such states, they can try to protect their industries and increase their exports by devaluing their national currency. Such considerations led states like Italy and Ireland to demand a substantial enlargement of the ERDF as a price for their acceptance of an EMS in the late 1970s. Although an EMS would help control inflation, they insisted that

> to offset the burdens and dangers of association with countries that were both more advanced and geographically better placed, there would have to be a meaningful regional policy that would ensure a significant distribution of resources from the richer to the poorer countries. (Ludlow 1982: 117)

But another country with serious regional problems, Britain, which might have allied itself with the Italians and Irish, remained aloof, uncertain about both the EMS and the ERDF. The former it saw as a threat to national sovereignty, whereas the latter was part of an overall EC budget which the UK, as an aggrieved large 'net contributor' to it, was little inclined to augment. The French, the other major initiators of the EMS along with the Germans, also saw little advantage in an increased ERDF to cope with the potential regional costs of monetary union. Therefore, the balance of power in the vital decision-making chambers of the Council of Ministers was against linking the introduction of the EMS in 1978 (an economic dimension of European unity) with an enlargement of the ERDF (a social dimension).

THE SINGLE EUROPEAN ACT AND EC REGIONAL POLICY

The Single European Act (SEA) of 1986 was a major step in the Community's evolution, setting new objectives for the Community. Although its aim of creating a single internal market by the end of 1992 has dominated public debate, it is a comprehensive treaty which, as we have already seen, also calls for greater economic and social cohesion amongst the Twelve. Essentially, it reiterated the old aim of reducing the gap between well-developed regions or social groups and less favoured ones. We have seen that many Member States had traditionally resisted efforts to make a strong linkage between economic union and Community social policies (including regional), but now an EC 'social dimension' was widely accepted as 'an indispensable corollary of the large market' (Commission 1990b: 2). Although the specific role of the ERDF in promoting regional development was repeated, the SEA also required the Commission to submit comprehensive proposals on the role of all three Structural Funds (ERDF, European Social Fund and the Guidance section of EAGGF) in reducing socio-economic disparities. The Commission quickly responded to the task and by February 1988 the Council of Ministers had adopted a reform package which meant that Community Funds available for regional development and other social measures were to be doubled in real terms (ie, taking inflation into account) between 1988 and 1993 when the single market was due for completion. In 1987 the three Structural Funds had some ECU 7,000 million to spend; that is, about 19 per cent of the Community budget. Between 1988 and the end of 1992, the equivalent expenditure will amount to around ECU 60,000 million and should account for more than 25 per cent of an enlarged EC spending programme (Commission 1990b; Commission 1989d; Shackleton 1989).

The concern of all three Structural Funds – not just the ERDF – with spatial inequalities was underlined by the setting of 5 Objectives, all of which are concerned with regional problems in some form or other. Priority was given to 'Objective 1', designed to help those areas lagging seriously behind in terms of overall

Table 7.3 Structural Funds appropriations for the period 1989–93.

Objective	Million ECU (1989 prices)	
1. Regions lagging behind in development	38,300	(63%)
2. Regions in industrial decline	7,205	(12%)
3. Long-term unemployment }	7,450	(12%)
4. Youth training/employment }		
5a. Adaption of agricultural structures	3,415	(6%)
5b. Development of rural areas	2,795	(5%)
Transitional measures and innovation	1,150	(2%)
TOTAL	60,315	(100%)

Source: Commission 1990b.

economic development. Two-thirds of the increased resources of the combined Structural Funds were allocated to this aim (Table 7.3). Furthermore, this money was to be directed mainly at the poorest parts of the Community in a deliberate effort to define regional problems in a Community rather than a national context

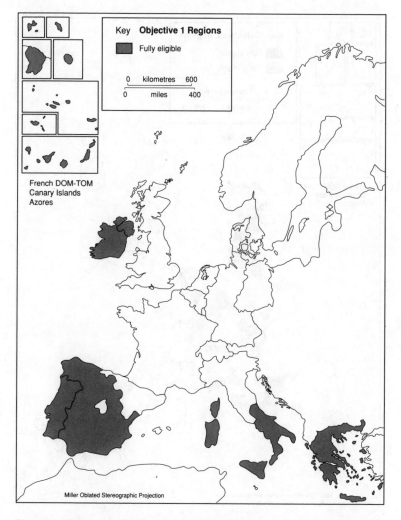

Figure 7.5 Regional distribution of EC assistance under 'Objective 1' of the reformed Structural Funds, 1988–93 (*Source:* Commission, 1990b).

(Fig 7.5). For example, up to 80 per cent of the ERDF was to be geographically targeted on these least developed zones, namely, all of Portugal, Greece, Ireland (including the North) and the French overseas departments, as well as much of Spain (excluding Madrid and the northeast) and all of the Italian Mezzogiorno.

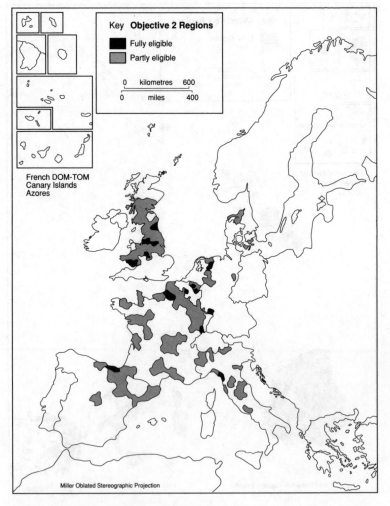

Figure 7.6 Regions eligible for EC assistance under 'Objective 2' of the reformed Structural Funds, 1988-93

'Objective 2' was concerned with selected areas especially hard-hit by industrial decline (Fig 7.6), but given that many of these areas were to be found in the richer Member States, the proportion of the Structural Funds (12 per cent) directed to them was markedly less than for 'Objective 1' regions (Table 7.3). The

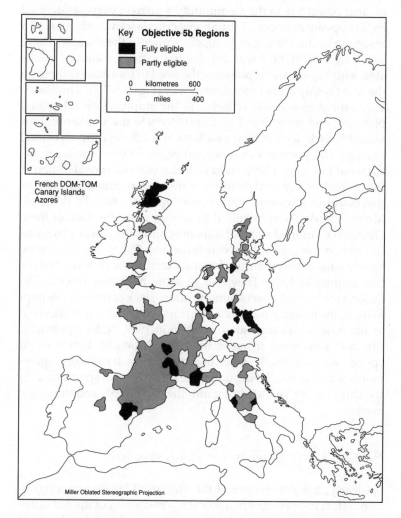

Figure 7.7 Regions eligible for EC assistance under 'Objective 5b' of the reformed Structural Funds, 1988–93 (*Source:* Commission, 1990b).

remainder of the money is directed towards the acute problems of long-term and youth unemployment (Objectives 3 & 4), and the challenges of rural development, including the adaptation of agricultural structures to modern demands (Objectives 5a and 5b) (Fig 7.7).

This combining of the reformed Structural Funds in the pursuit of clear objectives in the Community's poorest parts, as defined by 'European' as opposed to national criteria, obviously marked a response to the criticisms discussed earlier in the chapter. There was now a substantial real increase in financial resources associated with a general acceptance of the need to concentrate them on the most needy areas in a coherent way (Figs 7.5-7.7). This insistence on coherence was reflected in the emphasis on integrated planning and programming. Efforts to help the weaker regions would have to look at their problems as a whole, form an overall strategy and pursue it over several years. In theory at least, EC aid would no longer help build factories without consideration of the infrastructure and workforce training required to make it successful in a comprehensive development plan. To this end, Member States were required to submit plans for each of the 5 Objectives outlined above. To ensure continuity, these plans had to refer to periods of between three and five years, indicating clearly where their priorities lay and exactly how they wanted the Community to help. They had to show how they intended to tackle problems of poor communications, lack of training, depopulation, industrial job losses and so on. These plans were devised as the new rules came into operation in 1989. Not surprisingly, the bids amounted to more than the Structural Funds could spend, but eventually a set of Community framework agreements were agreed, laying down the broad lines of spending over the three or five years leading into the early 1990s and the single market.

How adequate is structural funds reform?

Clearly, the 1988 reform of the Structural Funds was a significant effort to overcome many of the weaknesses of the old ERDF and place more meaningful instruments of regional development in the hands of Community policy-makers aware of the need to assist potential losers in an increasingly competitive single European market. However, doubts still remain as to how substantial this particular aspect of social Europe will really prove to be. Analysis of the findings of a report undertaken at the request of the Commission by the Deputy Director of the Banca d'Italia reinforces such scepticism (Padoa-Schioppa 1987). Whereas the Cecchini report on the anticipated benefits of the single market (see Chapter 2) suggested vaguely that 'the redistributive effects in the wake of freer trade need not be excessive' (Cecchini 1988: 105), the so-called Padoa-Schioppa Report argued that 'there are serious risks of aggravated regional imbalance in the course of market liberalization' (Padoa-Schioppa 1987: 5). Placing less emphasis on the forecasts of abstract free-market theory and more on the experiences of economic history, the Report called for a much reinforced Community regional policy to effect a significant redistribution of development resources from richer to poorer areas.

In line with the traditional EC approach, the Padoa-Schioppa Report assumed that deficiencies in basic infrastructure were the root cause of most regional problems. In other words, a lack of such things as transport links, energy provision, educational facilities, telecommunications, and services in general hold back the weaker regions (Padoa-Schioppa 1987: 163–8). Therefore, the Community should increase its efforts to make up these shortcomings, thus equipping these regions to compete with the strong in the single market. Put simply, in accordance with the liberal economic theory underpinning the Community's general approach to development, the poorer regions should be helped to help themselves! In order to assess the needs of these regions, Padoa-Schioppa estimated the level of 'infrastructural endowment' in the five poorest EC countries expressed as a percentage of the average (100) for the EC 12 in 1985. Portugal had an endowment only 40 per cent of the EC average and Greece 50 per cent, while Spain, Ireland and Italy (whose problem is clearly concentrated in the Mezzogiorno) stood at 60 per cent. The report then estimated what levels of investment would be needed to bring these countries up to 80 per cent of the EC mean over a ten-year period. The total cost of such an investment programme was put at ECU 153 billion; in per capita terms, this amounted to

ECU 4000 for each person in Portugal, ECU 3000 for Greeks and ECU 2000 for Italians, Spaniards and the Irish.

Such figures far exceed the capacities of even the enlarged Structural Funds which are destined to double in the run-up to 1993. As we have already seen, the total appropriations for these Funds for all purposes for all countries over the period 1989–93 is only ECU 60.3 billion, far short of the ECU 153.2 billion need in the poorest regions calculated by Padoa-Schioppa. The old criticism about the small size of EC funds not matching the scale of the regional problem cannot be buried yet. Of course, the EC would not be the sole provider of such investment. Indeed, Community grants are 'matching grants' which can only be made if national governments also commit funds to an assisted project (in fact, the EC usually has a minority participation in infrastructural schemes). What all this would mean for Greece, in the highly unlikely eventuality of the Padoa-Schioppa plan being applied, has been assessed and produced gloomy conclusions (Cutler 1989: 100–5). The plan for Greece would require nearly ECU 3 billion per annum over ten years. Assuming that the current upper limits on EC Structural Fund assistance for Greece are maintained at late 1989 levels, the Greek government would have to find some ECU 2.1 billion a year from its own resources. This would be equivalent to some 12 per cent of total annual national public expenditure and a mighty burden on the Greek economy. Furthermore, if Greece were to make such a commitment and thus increase its borrowing, it would almost certainly run foul of other Community policies which deplore large public-sector deficits. The poorer countries such as Greece, Portugal, Italy, and Ireland have long had such deficits way above the Community average and far in excess of richer states like West Germany, France and the UK.

In the moves towards Economic and Monetary Union (EMU), which have been paralleling the development of a single market, these large deficits are increasingly criticized. In the Commission's strategy for EMU, laid down in the so-called Delors Plan, a single currency was proposed which would, amongst other things, require all Member States to accept 'binding rules governing the size and the financing of national budget deficits' (Delors 1990: 19). The Padoa-Schioppa Report also reflects this growing monetary orthodoxy by pointing to an 'urgent need' to reduce government deficits to 'sustainable levels' and suggests that Structural Fund grants might be made conditional on cutting them back:

> It would be hard to justify the Community extending much increased budgetary assistance to these (poorer) countries unless their macroeconomic strategies were simultaneously directed towards financial stability in the medium-term. (Padoa-Schioppa 1987: 101)

One reason for the growth of Greece's deficit was the adoption, by successive governments, of policies to cope with unemployment by creating jobs in the public sector (it will be remembered that Greece has one of the lowest jobless rates in the EC – see Fig 7.2). These measures were accompanied by other improvements which should, in theory at least, win applause from the advocates of a social Europe (see Chapters 5 and 6). For example, the social security system was extended to include farmers and returning emigrant workers, whilst expenditure on pensions increased from 7.3 per cent of GNP in 1979 to 13.3 per cent in 1985. This meant that by 1985 public expenditure in Greece was approaching the equivalent of 60 per cent of its GNP!

To reduce public-sector deficits and adopt the financial strategies now current in the EC, governments can seek to increase their revenues by increasing taxes and/or cut national expenditure on such things as infrastructure, defence, education, health and social policies in general. A reduction of 'social' expenditure by the Greek government would not only entail the risk of political disruption, but retard the country's efforts to align its social security system more closely to those found in its richer Community partners in a common European 'social space'. On the other hand, the scope to increase taxes in order to reduce government borrowing also runs a severe risk of promoting public disorder. For example, farmers in Greece are largely exempt from direct taxation and would appear to offer an obvious opportunity to increase government revenues. But they make up over a quarter of the workforce and any government proposing to increase their tax burden is likely to face unrest and electoral defeat. Furthermore, any increase would certainly push many of these small, marginal farms into bankruptcy and increase the unemployment rate. Where would be the sense of a European 'social dimension' in all this?

So Greece and other peripheral countries with severe regional problems might find themselves in a 'Catch 22' situation as they move into the 1990s and the challenges of the single market and EMU. To obtain relatively modest sums from the Structural Funds, they will have to match them with substantial national resources if the gap between richest and poorest regions is to start closing. But to provide this matching finance on an adequate scale, they will face unpleasant choices concerning public expenditure cuts, higher taxation and other measures undermining social policies! An acceptable balance between the economic and social dimensions of the Community's development is not easy to find and the strength of the axiom 'to him that hath shall be given' appears to be demonstrated yet again, even in the field of regional policy.

CAN EC COMPETITION POLICY AND REGIONAL POLICY BE RECONCILED?

The aims of Community regional policy also come into potential conflict with other EC objectives in the field of competition policy. A belief in the benefits of free-market competition has always occupied an important place in Community policy. It is seen as the best stimulant of economic activity, the most efficient way of producing an ever greater flow of goods and services to ever larger numbers. Hence, one of the Guiding Principles (Article 3) of the Rome Treaty in 1957 states the EEC shall establish 'a system ensuring that competition in the common market is not distorted' (Treaties 1987). Furthermore, the EEC Treaty also required the establishment of a common competition policy (Articles 85 and 86) aimed at ensuring that a healthy competitive environment exists throughout the Community. A major Directorate-General of the Commission (DG IV) has the task of proposing and enforcing EC competition policy (Swann 1983).

The development of common rules of competition has given rise to one of the most complex areas of Community law. Nearly two decades of discussions about the principles and enforcement mechanisms of the Treaty's anti-trust provisions produced little consensus. The Council of Ministers wanted to preserve substantial national controls over competition law, whilst the Commission sought to produce a strong European policy. Fears of market control generated by a period of merger mania in the late 1980s as the single market project took shape, led to compromise and a new competition policy which came into force on 21 September 1990 (Economist 1990c).

Underpinning this new policy was a belief that the predicted economic benefits of the '1992' programme would not materialize without genuine internal-market competition. The economic rationale behind the SEM is often perceived in quite narrow terms with a stress on the benefits emanating from the removal of non-tariff barriers to trade. However, as the analysis in Chapter 3 illustrated, the direct economic benefits arising from the removal of barriers is restricted to reducing the costs of trade and production. This impact will be felt only in the short term, leading to once-and-for-all savings estimated to be in the order of 1.8 per cent of the total value of goods in the Community. The substantial economic benefits predicted to arise from the internal market are associated with the creation of a new and competitive environment resulting from the removal of the non-tariff barriers. The Cecchini Report (Cecchini 1988) predicts that the removal of impediments to the free flow of trade will promote a growth in demand as the cost of goods and services is reduced. This new demand, taking place within a genuinely free market, will strengthen competitive pressures which in turn will lead to the restructuring of industry based upon enhanced economies of scale and more efficient production units. Competition is the key to unlocking the substantial economic benefits to be derived from the internal market. As Cecchini states:

> Ever present competition will ensure the completion of a self-sustaining virtuous circle. (Cecchini 1988: XIX)

However, there are serious concerns regarding the employment ramifications of this 'ever present' competition, particularly in the problem regions. Cecchini accepts that competition will inevitably produce redundancies as a result of industrial restructuring in those parts of the economy that are at present protected by non-tariff barriers. However, he makes the simple assumption that these released resources will be redeployed productively in areas of the economy experiencing high demand. Nonetheless, official estimates predict an initial unemployment figure of 500,000 jobs as the economy adjusts to new competitive pressures (Emerson 1988). The positive employment benefits arising from the SEM will only become evident when the positive feedback of competition becomes fully operational. It is this initial negative impact on employment, together with an undetermined time-lag, that causes serious concerns over the issue of wealth distribution, not least in spatial terms. It reinforces the belief that single-market integration will lead to an increasing divergence of living standards between EC Member States and that the gap between the richest and poorest regions will widen. The fear is that the SEM will further intensify the centre/periphery dichotomy. In other words, the predicted restructuring and plant closures will be greatest in the marginal areas whilst the primary place for the released excess resources to be effectively redeployed will be in the core. It is this prospect that led to the Single European Act's provisions requiring action to reinforce Community regional and social policy (see above) in order to mitigate the costs of open competition.

Clearly, the potential for conflict between the forces for increasingly open competition in the single market and those advocating government intervention to assist the weaker regions in the Community is considerable. There is no neat formula to determine an acceptable balance between these different Community objectives. When does national or Community aid to a problem region become a financial interference which 'distorts' the free play of market forces? At what point does a subsidy cease to be a 'sound public investment' and become a source of 'unfair competition' in a common market? Is it reasonable to protect or generate employment in a weaker region by protective measures of one sort or another? Obviously, the responses will vary according to the political ideology of the observer or the particular interests involved. Recipients of assistance obviously tend to view economic interventionism with a more favourable eye than their unassisted competitors!

Within the Commission, this conflict between the 'economic' aim of open market competition and 'social' aims associated with intervention and market management can lead to tension. On one hand, the Directorate-General responsible for the internal market (DG III) together with the Competition Directorate (DG IV) strive to eliminate protective barriers and subsidies which prevent free competition in a single market. On the other hand, DG XVI, concerned with regional policy, casts a more sympathetic eye on public assistance to struggling regions. True, the broad Community philosophy on regional development is the economically liberal one of 'helping regions to help themselves' by improving their infrastructure rather than subsidizing uncompetitive industries or compelling companies to invest in certain areas. Nonetheless, the potential for conflict is present, not least because most expenditure on regional assistance is still made by national governments (see above) which are very tempted to provide direct subsidies or adopt protective measures if national companies, jobs and votes are at stake. Consequently, rules on the permitted levels of subsidy for different regions have been drawn up in order to produce acceptable compromises between the two camps.

Over the last decade the aim of encouraging transnational industrial cooperation within the EC, in order to achieve scale economies and thus compete more effectively in the global market, has entered this policy-making arena to render the task of balancing regional-social and competitive-economic demands yet more delicate. Fears of being ever less able to match the industrial might of Japan and the USA, with their large domestic common markets, underlie the '1992' venture (Chapter 2). Confronted with these economic challenges, governments became more concerned with the generation of wealth rather than its redistribution (Wise, Chalkley 1990: 185). Thus, the advantages of the central areas were to be exploited more intensively rather than restrained in a ruthless global economic battle. As one French geographer put it: 'Paris no longer carries the responsibility for the economic backwardness of the provinces, but is seen as an asset' (Kahn 1987: 19). Similar sentiments were expressed throughout western Europe, not least in the UK where traditional regional policy was severely cut back as Britain sought to compete in world markets. The hope was that the success of unfettered richer core areas would spread or 'trickle down' to the poorer regions in the new competitive environment.

ACTION TO ENFORCE COMPETITION

Articles 85 and 86 of the Treaty of Rome are the traditional tools for enforcing a common competition policy. Article 85 prohibits agreements 'which have as their object or effect the prevention, restriction or distortion of competition within the common market'. Similarly, Article 86 states that 'any abuse by one or more undertakings of a dominant position within the common market or in a substantial part of it shall be prohibited as incompatible with the common market in so far as it may affect trade between Member States'. However, these Articles are subject to a variety of exceptions, not least for the sort of regional and social reasons already discussed. For example, Article 92, dealing with the issue of government subsidies to industry, first lays down the general provision that 'any aid granted by a Member State...which distorts...competition by favouring certain undertakings or the production of certain goods shall...be incompatible with the common market'. However, it then lists several circumstances where this need not apply. In particular, 'aid to promote the economic development of areas where the standard of living is abnormally low or where there is serious underemployment' (Article 92.3a) may be acceptable, revealing again the classic conundrum of reconciling free competition with regional policy. The problems of particular industries in particular areas (coal-mining, steel-making, ship-building, etc.) are also not forgotten in Article 92.3c which envisages the continuation of 'aid to facilitate the development of certain economic activities or of certain economic areas where such aid does not adversely affect trading conditions to an extent contrary to the common interest'! Beyond the scope of regional policy there are other broad exceptions such as: 'aid having a social character, granted to individual consumers'; 'aid to make good damage caused by natural disasters or exceptional occurrences'; 'aid to promote the execution of an important project of common European interest or to remedy a serious disturbance in the economy of a Member State'; and, most all-encompassing, 'such other categories of aid as may be specified by decision of the Council acting by a qualified majority on a proposal from the Commission' (Article 92.2a–d). Clearly, such provisions, especially the last, provide ample scope for political negotiation about the precise balance between the 'economic' demands of competition policy and 'social' demands emanating from problem regions and elsewhere.

Thus it is extremely difficult to develop and apply a coherent and consistent competition policy. To what extent should the restructuring engendered by the SEM be based upon ruthless competition, transnational cooperation or government intervention aimed at a more equitable regional distribution of wealth? These potentially contradictory goals have resulted in European policy decisions which have been very unpopular with national governments concerned with more than simple common-market competition. For example, the British Conservative ministers – champions of free enterprise – were very unhappy that the Commission required British Aerospace to repay some £253 million to the UK Treasury in 1990. This followed the UK government's decision to write off £800 million of debt in the sale of the Rover Group to British Aerospace in March 1988 and the ensuing accusations of unfair competition. In 1990, the French state-owned car manufacturer Renault were similarly required to repay some some FFr 6 billion to the national exchequer. Like its British counterpart, the French government was a very reluctant recipient of this repayment because, in this case, it was more concerned with protecting a vital national industry, preserving employment and maintaining social peace in a politically sensitive sector than promoting open competition in a single European market (Economist 1990d). The Commission is also investigating Fiat's purchase of Alfa Romeo in 1986, another reflection of the way in which a whole series of conflicting pressures bear on the EC's car industry. A Member-State determination to maintain production of national models confronts a European need to meet the challenge of Japanese manufacturers. The fact that motor manufacture has sometimes been used to stimulate regional development adds a further complication to the simple pursuit of 'open competition' (note Nissan in northeast England, Volkswagen in Spain, Citroën in Brittany and Alfa-Romeo in southern Italy).

A new EC competition law came into force in September 1990 giving considerable new powers to the Commission in its efforts to reconcile such conflicting economic and social pressures. Within a week of announcing a bid, takeover or merger, the companies involved must send the Commission a completed notification form. The Commission must then decide, within a month, whether or not the deal threatens competition. If it has doubts, an investigation has to be completed within four months to provide a reasoned basis for decision. Although the new competition policy gives the Commission new powers and is designed to speed up the decision-making process, the old political questions inevitably remain. No amount of bureaucratic streamlining can conceal them. The confusing compromises of the real political world will still have to be made between opposing pulls of the 'free-market' and the social demands arising from, amongst other things, weaker regions and localities, as well as the threat of unemployment anywhere in the Community. It remains to be seen whether the Community's 'social' commitment to regional development will match its 'economic' demand for fair competition in the Single European Market. The somewhat ineffectual regional policy produced by the Community in the past offers little comfort to those who fear that the need to compete in European and world markets will continue to dominate geographical patterns of socio-economic well-being.

8. The external economic impact of 1992

The creation of a truly integrated Community market has a number of profound implications for both the global economy as a whole and the EC's established trading partners (Fig 8.1). The removal of most impediments to the free movement of goods, people, capital and services will create the largest single market in the industrialized world, comprising approximately 340 million inhabitants in 1990. The restrictions imposed upon overseas access to this market are therefore critical to the economic well-being of both developed and developing countries. Despite the Community's important influence in affecting world trade patterns and the conditions within which that trade is enacted, little attention has been paid to the external economic and social effects of '1992'. EC documentation and the vast majority of academic publications focus on the consequences of the internal market programme for the Community economy. The Cecchini Report (1988) and the Commission (1988a) notably ignored the external effects of '1992'. At the beginning of the 1990s, the uncertainty concerning Community market accessibility was enhanced by four parallel and independent changes taking place in the international trading environment: the GATT Uruguay Round, the new EC Lome Convention IV, the end of the fourth Multifibre Agreement (MFA) and the reform of the Generalized System of Preferences (GSP). In negotiating these new trading agreements, the Community represents the collective voice of the twelve Member States. Whilst in theory the changes to the international trading environment are independent of the internal economic

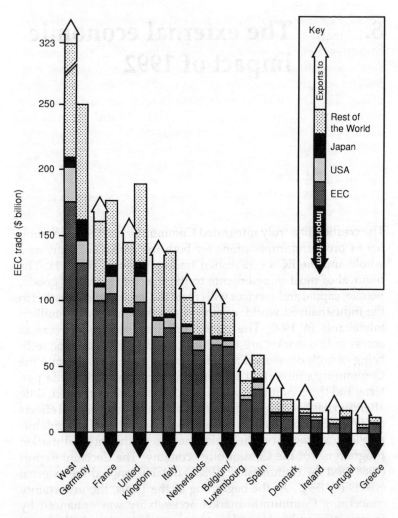

Figure 8.1 European Community trade, 1988 (*Source:* Eurostat, 1975–90).

reforms associated with the internal market programme, they are in practice interlinked and have often been evaluated as an integral part of the integration process (Langhammer 1990). Changes in internal market prices brought about by the SEM will affect the relative competitiveness between imports and domestic substitutes. Simply put, the internal economic impact of '1992' will have a direct external impact on third countries. Consequently

GATT, Lome, the GSP, MFA and SEM will have a direct influence on EC market accessibility for third countries. To most non-EC countries '1992' represents a threat to free trade. The Commission's commitment to eliminate Europe's internal frontier controls inescapably implies the creation of a common external trade policy. The Treaty of Rome created a European customs union with a level of protection from overseas competing markets. Clearly protectionism has an important social dimension. A common justification used for the imposition of tariffs is the objective of reducing the social problems arising from free trade. Tariffs and quantitative restrictions on iron, coal and steel from non-EC countries have been imposed to safeguard communities threatened by cheaper imports. Equally, vigorous agricultural levies are applied to non-EC produce on the grounds of safeguarding the agricultural industry and associated rural communities.

The internal market programme may well accentuate calls for a more protectionist external trade policy. Anxiety over the internal economic consequences of a more competitive 'domestic' market have already led business leaders and governments to demand higher levels of protection for those industries adversely affected. 'Sensitive areas' that experience difficulty in adjusting to the enhanced internal competition within the Community may call for more restrictive common external barriers so as to delay the necessary adjustment. The call for enhanced protection will be particularly acute if unemployment rises as a consequence of the short-term adjustment brought about by the internal market. Under such a scenario, the Community would be under severe pressure to readjust the burden of internal adjustment towards third countries. The European car industry, the textile and clothing sector, together with steel and agriculture, are all attempting to put at least some of the internal adjustment burden stemming from internal liberalization on non-EC countries. As the internal market reforms start to bite, with greater competition, specialization, innovation and economies of scale, European businesses will face the task of closing plants, axing jobs and cutting costs. '1992' will in fact cause problems for thousands of weak European firms that have previously hidden behind the non-tariff barriers erected by Member States. Consequently there is likely to be resistance to the SEM reform programme from the very people who were supposed to be the markets firmest friends: the captain's of European industry. Calls will be made for higher tariffs, more exacting technical and safety standards, bigger state subsidies and other protectionist measures designed to lessen the internal consequences of adjustment. Furthermore, if the EC is actively going to pursue a 'social dimension' which adds costs to production, then it may be perceived as necessary to protect European industries burdened with these extra costs against non-EC industries unhampered by such legislation. Consequently, the debate over the desirability of creating a European social space to accompany the internal market has ramifications that stretch beyond the Community's geographic boundaries. Paradoxically, an enhanced European social policy may lead to some form of protectionism detrimental to the economic well-being of developing countries. A primary objective of 'social harmonization' is to reduce the threat of social dumping and worker-exploitation. If social legislation therefore creates a convergence in the costs of Community labour, reducing the disparity between the core and the periphery, the relatively labour intensive production in the periphery could lose its competitive advantage. If this production is in turn lost to areas outside the EC, with lower social and therefore labour costs, calls for protectionism will be enhanced. A bizarre situation may well therefore arise where the internal adjustment costs stemming from social harmonization are pushed on to third countries. As far as business leaders are concerned, social legislation could be advantageous in blunting the competitive edge of countries able to excel in labour-intensive industries.

In addition to these protectionist concerns, the internal market programme is perceived to be creating a new and pervasive competitive threat. Removing non-tariff barriers and adopting the principle of mutual recognition will reduce the costs of intra-EC trade, lowering the relative costs of both Community 'imports' and 'exports'. As a result, Community goods will become more competitive and it is predicted that a trade diversion from third countries to EC Member States will take place (Emerson 1988). The enhanced competitiveness of the EC economy will result in immediate price and cost reductions which should in turn enable Community producers to displace third country imports. Cecchini (1988) considers the 'trade diverting' impact of the SEM programme to be an important factor contributing to the predicted economic benefits of the internal market. It is therefore not surprising that since the signing of the SEA in July 1987, the USA, Japan, the EFTA countries, the Third World and Eastern Europe have all expressed broadly similar fears that the Community is becoming inward-looking and protectionist, a so called 'Fortress Europe' (Heitger, Stehn 1990). The current chapter outlines the background to the EC's Common External Tariff (CET) and examines the views of the Community's largest trading partners on the creation of an SEM. An analysis of how overseas markets have reacted to the SEA of July 1987 is then undertaken through a case-study of Japanese Foreign Direct Investments (FDI) in the EC.

However, the external economic impact of '1992' is by no means restricted to the issue of market access. The success of the internal market programme forced a number of European states outside the Community to re-evaluate their relationship with the EC. Member States of EFTA, fearing that improved Community competitiveness would result in adverse effects on their trade and welfare, have been eager to either sign a joint EC-EFTA agreement to establish a European Economic Space (EES) or, as in the case of Austria and Sweden, apply for Community membership. There is no doubt that '1992' caused a number of EFTA states to re-evaluate the benefits of Community membership, and enlargement is now firmly on the Commission's agenda for the 1990s. This move was precipitated not only by the threat of protectionism but by the predicted economic benefits arising from the internal market programme. However, the policy of the EC Commission has been to postpone the Community's enlargement agenda until a significant deepening of the Community has been achieved. The Commission clearly consider enlargement before the internal market programme is completed to be a threat to the economic and social objectives held within that programme. The final section of the current chapter therefore examines the economic and social ramifications associated with EFTA's desire to either establish a common economic space with the EC or apply for Community membership.

THE COMMON EXTERNAL TARIFF

The CET, sometimes referred to as the Common Customs Tariff (CCT), represents the duty paid on goods entering the Community customs union from third countries. As the name suggests, the tariff should in theory be a common levy applied uniformly throughout the Member States of the Community. This is of critical importance to exporting countries as the level of EC protection should be the same wherever a product enters the Community market. As a consequence, once an imported product enters the customs union and has paid the levy imposed by the CET, it is often able to move freely between Member States without having to pay any further duties whatever the distinction of the good. The CET differentiates the EC from other free-trade areas, such as EFTA. EFTA operates a system whereby there are no internal barriers to the free movement of goods which have been manufactured in the trade area and, critically, no common external tariff is applied to third countries. A free-trade area allows Member States to impose an independent customs policy tailored to fit their own specific economic policies and conditions. Consequently when a product enters the free trade area it cannot, unlike a customs union, move freely between member states without paying further duties (see Chapter 1).

Article 113 of the Treaty of Rome explicitly states that after a 'transitional period', the CCT should have matured to the point where it can replace the separate commercial policies of Member States. It argues that a Common Commercial Policy should be based on:

> uniformly established principles, particularly in regard to tariff amendments, to the conclusion of tariff and trade agreements, to the establishing of uniform practice as regards measures of liberalisation, to export policy and to commercial protective measures including measures to be taken in cases of dumping and subsidies. (HMSO 1967: 42)

However, under Article 115 of the Treaty, Member States have the right to impose quantitative restrictions against other Community states on imports from third countries. Discriminatory barriers levied on non-EC imports can be enforced with or without the approval of the Commission. The purpose of this legislation is to prevent non-EC exporters gaining access to a protected Community market through a Member State who adopts a more liberal trading policy. Nonetheless, in selecting such measures Article 115 makes it clear that:

> priority shall be given to those which cause the least disturbance to the operation of the common market and which take into account the necessity for expediting, as far as possible, the introduction of the Common Customs Tariff. (HMSO 1967: 43)

The trade restrictions imposed via Article 115 are dependent on the barrier functions performed at the Community's internal frontiers. When these barriers have been removed to create the internal market, all the restrictions currently imposed on intra-EC trade will also have to be eliminated. Article 115 should therefore be phased out and replaced by a truly common Common External Tariff. There are at present two principal forms of quantitative restrictions imposed by Member States against each other on imports from third countries. The most common practice is to establish bilateral trading agreements with the exporting third country based upon 'Voluntary Export Restraints' (VERs), 'Gentlemen's Agreements' or 'Orderly Marketing Agreements' (OMAs). These unofficial and discriminatory bilateral barriers have no legal basis and are not part of the CCT. Secondly, Member States can apply for EC authorization to deviate from the common commercial policy and apply restrictions that prevent the free circulation of goods which enter the Community from third countries. Finally there have also been illegal actions designed to protect markets, such as the 'Poitiers' incident in France in, 1982. To prevent the rapid increase in video recorder imports, the French state declared that all such imports had to be cleared at a single, and incidentally very small, customs post at Poitiers. The result of this action was to restrict temporarily the import of video recorders until the measure was withdrawn.

The automobile industry is a fine example of how official and voluntary quantitative restrictions are used to prevent imports from non-EC countries being deflected from open to protected Community markets. In 1988 bilateral import controls, officially sanctioned by the Commission, kept the sales of Japanese cars to 0.7 per cent of the Italian car market compared to around 15 per cent in free-trading West Germany. In addition both the UK and France negotiated OMAs with Japanese automobile manufacturers that restricted import penetration to 10 and 2.9 per cent of their respective markets. Most ominously, these agreements also referred to a pricing structure that 'respects' existing markets. Both the unofficial and bilateral export restraints, such as the OMAs and officially approved deviations from Article 113, prevent the free circulation of goods and protects Member States from receiving non-EC imports deflected from elsewhere in the Community. However it is interesting to note that Japan was the only developed country to have Article 115 exclusions imposed upon its exports (O'Cleireacain 1990).

If the internal market programme is faithful to the 1985 White Paper, nationally orientated import controls of any nature will become meaningless as barriers between EC countries disappear. In a truly integrated market, any import control has to be imposed on a Community-wide basis. The main worry for non-Community countries is that '1992' will introduce EC-wide import restrictions at a level above the existing EC average. The nature and magnitude of such import restrictions will depend, in part, on the evolution and development of a European social dimension to accompany the internal market. In order to protect the competitive advantage of Community producers burdened with extra production costs directly attributable to social welfare programmes, it may well be necessary to impose considerable import tariffs on goods being produced in countries with minimal labour and welfare provisions. This argument has a parallel with the debate going on within the Community over the need to prevent 'social dumping'. Chapter 6 outlined the current fears in the Community that investment and jobs will naturally gravitate towards countries where income expectations and social provisions are less restrictive. If international companies have access to the Community market and freedom to move capital investment, the threat of social dumping at the global scale, in both developing and developed countries, is considerable.

FORTRESS EUROPE

One of the most important but least understood aspects of the '1992' programme is its impact on the EC's trading partners. The Commission, eager to stress its free-trading philosophy, points out that the Community economy is heavily reliant on the maintenance of a worldwide liberal trading system. The Community is already the world's largest trading partner; its exports of manufactured goods represent 26 per cent of those of the OECD countries, compared with 14 per cent for the USA and 17 per cent for Japan. Nonetheless, third countries remain suspicious of the protectionist instincts of Member States and a Commission headed by a French socialist who does not naturally side with the free-market philosophy. But as Colchester and Buchan (1990) point out:

> He [Jacques Delors] has not yet tried to quash the new Commission's free-market tendencies. Instead, he has sought to compensate for them by championing Europe's 'social dimension' and by projecting with great vigour a vision of Europe that stretches way beyond the completion of an open market. (Colchester, Buchan 1990: 198)

The Commission recognize that national protectionist measures will in certain circumstances have to be replaced by Community-wide measures. Third countries fear that the overall level of protectionism will be raised. These fears, particularly expressed by the USA and Japan, are focused on three aspects of the '1992' programme.

1. Standards

There is considerable concern outside the Community that as the internal barriers come down, new external non-tariff barriers will be erected to take their place. There is a particular worry that the new technical regulations and standards, necessary to enforce the mutual recognition of certain goods, are being drafted in obscurity and without consultation with the Community's trading partners. America is concerned that the EC's new approach to regulations is not only being undertaken behind closed doors, but in a way that will damage US exports. The USA has therefore requested, but subsequently been denied, a 'seat at the table' during the drafting of EC technical standards by CEN and CENELEC. The USA considers this to be discriminatory as the Europeans have 'observer status' at the American National Standards Institute. The setting of new EC standards also represents a threat to the export potential of EFTA countries. In 1989 approximately 50 per cent of all EFTA exports were destined for the EC. Responding to EFTA complaints of protectionism, the Commission launched a plan in January 1989 proposing the creation of a European Economic Space (EES) to link the EC formally with the six states of EFTA. Members of EFTA were then allowed to participate in formulating new regulations and technical standards but were excluded from the decision-making process taking place in the Council of Ministers.

2. Reciprocity

In 1988 the Commissioner responsible for external relations, Willy de Clercq, firmly established the reciprocity principle in formulating the Community's external trade relations. In the area of services, de Clercq commented:

> we see no reason why the benefits of our internal liberalization should be extended unilaterally to third countries. We shall be ready and willing to negotiate reciprocal concessions with third countries, preferably in a multilateral context, but also bilaterally. We want to open our borders, but on the basis of a mutual balance of advantages in the spirit of GATT. (de Clercq 1988)

The reciprocity principle implies that a company located outside the EC will be permitted free and unhindered access to the internal market if Community businesses are, in turn, permitted the same levels of access to that company's domestic market. The United States in particular regards such a stance as effectively forcing the USA to import Community practice. The issue is a highly sensitive one to a country such as America where some companies, for example banks, are not allowed to trade freely throughout the union. As such, the reciprocity principle implies making changes to US state and federal laws which would allow European banks greater privileges than are presently enjoyed by indigenous US banks. A more protectionist interpretation of the reciprocity principle is outlined by Curzon Price (1988). This is where bilateral negotiations, such as the EC-Japanese discussions on automobiles, consider reciprocity in the context of a bilateral balancing of trade flows. This form of reciprocity would be both protectionist and interventionist, and in the long term pose a serious threat to the worldwide liberal trading system.

3. Rules of origin

Another non-tariff barrier that concerns third countries is the Community's attempt to restrict the level of imported components destined for overseas manufacturing facilities established in the EC. By establishing 'rules of origin' or 'local content regulations', the Community hopes to persuade non-European manufacturers to locate within Europe and, furthermore, for those manufacturers to purchase Community components. In order to enforce OMAs, VERs or straightforward quota restrictions, it is necessary to define the nationality of a particular product. In other words, the Commission has to be able to distinguish between a Japanese photocopier made in Japan, the EC, EFTA or America. As each one of these locations will have varying levels of access to the Community market, it is essential to decide which product is liable to tariff barriers. At present EC local content regulations are enormously complex, depending on the type of product and the country of origin. However, there is a worry amongst third countries that the rules of origin regulations are being abused to prevent legitimate access to the Community market.

AN OPEN COMMUNITY MARKET

The Community institutions and members of the Commission have sought on numerous occasions to allay fears of a protectionist SEM. In 1988 the British Foreign Secretary directly addressed the Japanese business community through the pages of the Anglo-Japanese Journal, stating that:

I reject the idea that as internal barriers come down, external barriers should go up.... An inward-looking Community would do itself – and the world economy – no good. (Howe 1988)

In 1988 the prospect of a 'fortress Europe' forced the Commission to establish the principles and philosophy that would support the Community's common policy towards third countries. The Commission, supported by the UK, West Germany and Denmark, proposed free-market policies and an opening of the EC's market to overseas competition. At the Hannover meeting of the European Council in June 1988 it was declared that: 'The internal market should not close in on itself'. However, as well as reaffirming its commitment to free international trade, the Council also reiterated its commitment to the reciprocity principle when it went on to say that,

In conformity with the provisions of GATT, the Community should be open to third countries, and must negotiate with those countries where necessary to ensure access to their markets for Community exports. (European Council 1988)

For once the British Government wholeheartedly supported the Commission's policies. In what was otherwise perceived to be an anti-European speech, Mrs Thatcher, then Prime Minister of the UK, commented at Bruges:

My fourth guiding principle is that Europe should not be protectionist.... It would be a betrayal if, while breaking down constraints on trade to create the single market, the Community were to erect greater external protection. We must make sure that our approach to world trade is consistent with the liberalisation we preach at home. (Thatcher 1988)

At the end of 1988, the Commission prepared its own detailed statement on trading relations. In it, the Commission restated the importance of the EC as an international trading partner and its commitment to free international trade and to the provisions of GATT. While the EC has on a number of occasions asserted that the removal of internal non-tariff barriers will not be accompanied by the creation of a fortress Europe to the rest of the world, the actions of the Community and the strong protectionist instincts of Member States still leave considerable doubt that this will in fact be the case. Japanese fears of discrimination have been reinforced by the Community's continued use of aggressive 'anti-dumping' legislation including, for example, a 33 per cent tax on Japanese-made computer printers, and by France's initial refusal to accept Nissan cars produced in the UK as 'European' and not therefore subject to France's quota restriction on imports of Japanese vehicles. Similar fears of being denied access to EC markets resurfaced in the USA when the Community refused to allow access into the EC of hormone-treated meat; in effect, not accepting that US standards met with European ones. Clearly, the principle of mutual recognition does not extend to third countries.

The '1992' programme can therefore be interpreted to be both market oriented and protectionist. By allowing overseas companies access to a truly integrated European market of 340 million people, without the cost penalties of nationally oriented non-tariff barriers, the SEM could well enhance the export potential of third countries (Henderson 1988). In a speech written to reassure a suspicious world audience, de Clercq commented:

> The removal of internal barriers will make the Community more – not less – accessible. Once a product has crossed our external border it will be able to circulate freely throughout the 12 member States. (de Clercq 1988)

In agreement with this perspective, Henderson (1988) interprets '1992' as assisting free market principles and promoting liberal trade policies. This has led to the fear expressed by many European companies that the major beneficiaries of '1992' will be the large American and Japanese multinationals. At the same time, however, the removal of internal barriers will reinforce the external identity of the EC, necessitating a definition of 'European' goods. More importantly, a more robust CET, with fewer deviations aimed at preventing trade deflection, will be needed to accompany the removal of non-tariff barriers. The uncertainties raised by these issues have persuaded a growing number of businesses from outside the EC to establish a base within the Community ahead of '1992' and in anticipation of a fortress Europe. The following case-study highlights the scale of Japanese direct investment into the EC and the importance of that investment to the UK economy.

JAPANESE FOREIGN DIRECT INVESTMENT IN THE EUROPEAN COMMUNITY

Japanese anxieties over the nature and evolution of Europe's single market programme have increased since the early 1980s. When the Commission (1988e) produced a document entitled *European Economy: Creation of a European Financial Area* that clearly established the principle of reciprocity in the financial services sector, there was a genuine fear that this principle would be applied to all trading transactions. In other words, any sector of the European market would in future be accessible to non-EC states on a reciprocal basis only. The Japanese clearly perceive the EC's movement towards internal free-trading will result in increased protection against third countries. The evolution and extent of Japanese fears is clearly illustrated by the increasing levels of direct Japanese investment in the EC (Figure 8.2). More than any other measure, the level of Japanese foreign direct investment (FDI) provides an accurate barometer of the perception of a fortress Europe.

Direct investments in the EC by Japanese manufacturing interests is a recent phenomenon. Compared to the FDI activities undertaken by the USA, Japanese interests have been limited in both relative and absolute terms. As the EC's customs union began to emerge in the 1960s, there was a considerable movement of FDI into the Community from the USA. By 1964 the value of American FDI in the original six Member States has more than trebled its value compared to the 1957 total, the year of the EEC's establishment (Yannopoulos 1990). The extent to which European economic integration and its associated threat of protectionism contributed to this upward trend is debatable. Wallis (1968) argues that whilst the level of US FDI showed an almost continuous increase in the 1960s, the establishment of the EEC decisively contributed to an upwards deflection in the overall trend. On the other hand Mikesell (1967) forwards evidence to the contrary: that the 1957 customs union was not the only, or the most decisive, factor in attracting investments from America. There has

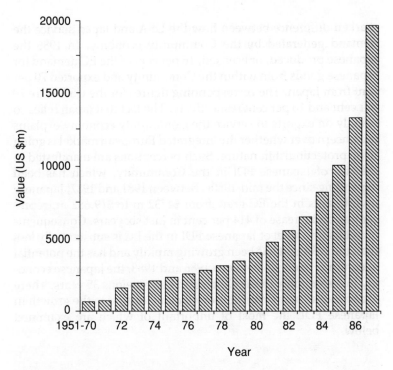

Figure 8.2 The growth of Japanese Foreign Direct Investment stock in the EC, 1970–87 (*Source:* Europe 2000, 1989).

been a great deal of empirically oriented research into the importance of the first stage of European economic cooperation (1957–67) and FDI, much of which is contradictory. However whether the Treaty of Rome exclusively initiated this American FDI is not really the issue. Much of the evidence supports the contention that the 1957 customs union did act as a catalyst, amongst many other factors, in an upwards trend in US FDI destined for the Community.

Between 1951 and 1988, the value of Japanese FDI in manufacturing industries located within the Community was approximately $6bn, representing 9 per cent of all Japanese FDI. When compared to the corresponding levels of investment undertaken by manufacturing interests from the USA, Japanese investments are of limited importance. In the corresponding time period, USA multinationals invested $64.9 bn which accounted for 51 per cent of all USA direct investment. This discrepancy has resulted in a marked difference between how the USA and Japan service the demand generated by the Community economy. In 1986 the Japanese produced, or licensed, 16 per cent of the EC demand for Japanese goods from within the Community and exported 70 per cent from Japan. The corresponding figures for the USA were 79 per cent and 16 per cent respectively. The fact that Japan relies so heavily on exports to service the Community economy explains its concern over whether the integrated European market is going to be protectionist in nature. Such perceptions are manifested in the rise of Japanese FDI in the Community, which has been expanding since the mid-1980s. Between 1981 and 1987, Japanese investments in the EC grew from $4732 m to $19,682 m, representing an increase of 414 per cent in just six years. Consequently, whilst the level of Japanese FDI in the EC is substantially less than the USA's, it has been growing rapidly and has the potential to continue to do so. Between 1986 and 1988, the Japanese economy invested more in the EC than in the previous 35 years. There are of course many contributory factors leading to the growth in Japanese FDI, the most of important of which are examined below.

1. An expanding Community economy

Apart from Japanese FDI taking place as an insurance policy against fortress Europe, it is also based upon the anticipated benefits likely to be derived from a genuine internal market as predicted by the Cecchini Report (1988) into the 'costs of non-Europe'. Japanese industry has increasingly adopted the attitude that in order to exploit its competitive advantage a European manufacturing facility, owned and managed by Japanese multinationals, is necessary. As the costs of production are reduced following the elimination of non-tariff barriers, European companies should become more competitive following the introduction of larger scale-economies. This increased Community competitiveness will have a detrimental impact on the EC's trading partners. Smith and Venables (1988) examined the impact of '1992' on extra-EC trade. They conclude that the level of Community imports is set to decline, and the extent of this decline depends on the level of market segmentation remaining after

1992. They estimate that extra-EC imports could fall by up to 68 per cent in office machinery, 64 per cent in motor vehicles and 58 per cent in artificial fibres. These figures are confirmed by Cecchini's macroeconomic estimates of a single market which predict a long-term improvement in the Community's external balance of trade, amounting to one per cent of the EC GDP. By locating manufacturing plants in Europe, Japan hopes to retain its competitive strength in both the EC and world economies.

2. The exchange rate

The attractions of investing in Europe have been reinforced by exchange rate fluctuations which have resulted in the overall appreciation of the yen and a corresponding reduction in Japanese industrial competitiveness. The yen appreciation has increased Japanese unit labour costs and made the weaker currency countries in the Community, such as the UK, a favoured location. Exchange rate fluctuations partly explain the redirection of Japanese FDI away from America toward the EC. Since 1987 the profitability of exports to the US has declined sharply as the Japanese yen appreciated against the US dollar.

3. Protecting the internal market

The degree of protectionism arising from the SEM programme is at present an unknown factor. With the details of the Community import policy yet to be decided, the uncertainties surrounding this issue have led to an surge in Japanese investments. In fact the uncertainty surrounding the future of the Community's CET may have encouraged unnecessarily high levels of Japanese FDI. Nonetheless, over the past decade as Japan's trade surplus with the EC has grown there has been a corresponding increase in the calls for some form of protectionism. Japan's trade surplus with the Community stood at a staggering $30 billion in 1988 (Fig 8.3). European protectionism, although seemingly having little impact, materialized in the form of quota restrictions, tariff barriers, anti-dumping levies or 'gentlemen's agreements' based on 'voluntary' export restraints.

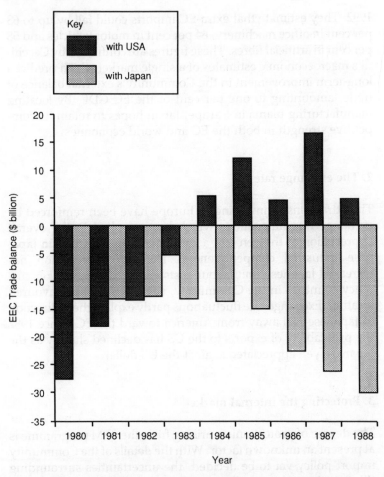

Figure 8.3 Trade balance with Japan and the USA, 1980–88 (*Source:* Eurostat, 1975–90).

The European car industry is a good example of how Community governments have introduced protectionist policies that have precipitated Japanese FDIs in to EC manufacturing units. Four Community states have negotiated 'voluntary' agreements with Japan that limit the number of vehicle imports allowed to enter their domestic markets: France (2.9 per cent), Britain (10 per cent), Spain (2,000 cars a year) and Portugal (10,000 cars a year). Italy has an EC-sanctioned quota restriction limiting the sales of Japanese cars to 3,200 per annum. These restrictions have been

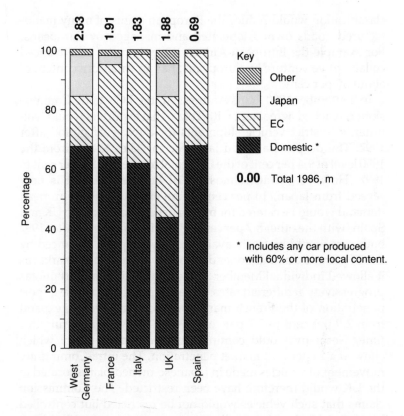

Figure 8.4 New car registration by area of manufacture, 1986 (*Source:* Economist, 1988a).

successful in reducing the level of Japanese automobile imports (Fig 8.4). According to the Nomura Institute (Europe 2000 1989), these protective measures cost the Japanese motor industry approximately 1.2 billion in lost sales during 1987. Consequently, Toyota, Nissan and Honda have all invested in manufacturing plants within the Community in order to avoid such protectionist policies. This has raised the critical issue of how 'European' these transplant factories have to be in order to gain access to the SEM. Initially France refused to recognize the Nissan 'Bluebird', produced in northeast England, as being a European car on the grounds that it did not have an 80 per cent European content. However as many observers pointed out at the time, such a rigid classification would reduce the European status of many manufactured goods owned, operated and managed by Europeans. For example the European Airbus, the epitome of an advanced collaborative venture by Europeans, has an American content of about 30 per cent.

In September 1990 Frans Andriessen, the EC's trade Commissioner, reached agreement with Tokyo that exporters would 'voluntarily' restrict vehicle shipments for a five-year period after 1992. The proposal allowed Japanese car sales to rise from the 1990 level of 9.4 per cent of the EC's total market to 18.7 per cent in 1997. However, whilst almost all of Europe's market is now served from Japan, 10 per cent of the expected 1997 European demand would be catered for by Japanese factories in the UK and Spain, with the other 8.7 per cent being direct imports. After 1997 both cars would be freely available. The proposal advanced by the EC's trade Commissioner did not envisage a single market as it allowed individual Member States to raise their import quotas progressively at different rates. For example, the Japanese import penetration of the French market was to be allowed to expand from 2.9 per cent to 5.7 per cent in 1997. However, during this time, Germany would continue its free-trading policy which allowed a 15 per cent market penetration. The intra-Community movement of vehicles made in Japanese-owned plants located in the UK would therefore have been restricted. The Commission claims that such vehicles would not be restricted but controlled by an 'informal understanding' not to target sensitive markets. That the European manufacturers should complain and call for protectionism is hardly surprising. Having successfully restricted direct competition from Japanese motor manufacturers for so long, Community companies felt vulnerable. Although Frans Andriessen's proposal did not envisage a single market for motor vehicles, it was nevertheless met with considerable opposition from the French and Italian governments. In September 1990, France's minister for Europe, Edith Cresson, opposed the ultimate objective of an open and single car market for the Community.

The trade talks surrounding the level of Japanese automobiles allowed to penetrate the European market highlight three important issues concerning the future external relations of the Community. Firstly, there is a widespread suspicion amongst the EC's trading partners that '1992' will result in more protectionism. This perception is reinforced by Commission efforts to establish common Community policies towards imports in areas previously the preserve of Member States. Secondly, such perceptions have led to a surge in FDI in an attempt to establish 'European' manufacturing plants. The rights of these transplant factories to access the Community market have yet to be defined. Thirdly, it highlights the desire amongst many Member States to protect their own national, and therefore European, companies from competition emanating from third countries. Whilst having a straightforward economic objective, protectionism has an important social dimension. This is particularly the case in the European automobile industry which has traditionally been used by governments to further social and regional policies. Motor manufacturing has been a favoured recipient of aid to stimulate regional development because of the labour intensive, high value added and large multiplier characteristics of the industry. Many European motor manufacturers, and many non-EC ones such as Ford in South Wales and Nissan in northeast England, have developed plants in underdeveloped areas with the explicit aim of attracting government regional assistance. European governments that have invested heavily in such projects, and who also have the aim to seek greater social justice and promote economic and social cohesion, will be very reticent to see such projects undermined by competition emanating from non-EC countries that have perhaps not followed such policies of market intervention.

THE UNITED KINGDOM AS A FAVOURED LOCATION

Although a marked feature of previous Japanese FDI has been its orientation to the EC market as a whole as opposed to any particular Member State, there has been an unequal geographic distribution of inward investment. There has also been marked spatial variations in the geographical patterns of Japanese inward investments over time. The United Kingdom has consistently received the largest share of Japan's EC investments. In 1970, three years before Britain's membership of the EC, the UK played host to 88 per cent of Japan's outward FDI in the EC (calculated on the basis of the existing EC of 12 Member States). France, the

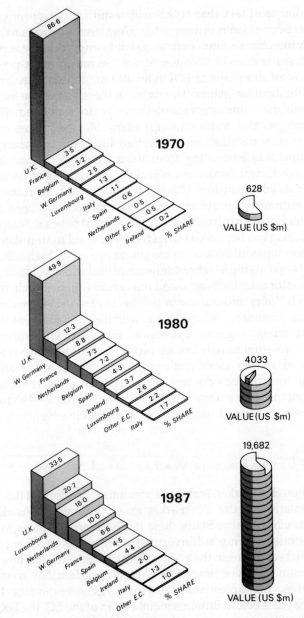

Figure 8.5 Japanese Foreign Direct Investment in the EC 12, 1970, 1980, 1987 (*Source:* Europe 2000, 1989).

second most favoured recipient, played host to just 3.5 per cent (Fig 8.5). Whilst Britain's relative share of Japanese inward investments has been declining, falling to 50 per cent in 1980 and 33.5 per cent in 1987, it still receives more Japanese investment than any other Community state. In 1987 Luxembourg, primarily due to the financial services sector, and the Netherlands were the second and third most favoured EC countries for Japanese investments, with 21 per cent and 16 per cent respectively. Furthermore, although the UK's relative share of Japanese FDI has been declining, in absolute terms it has grown in an exponential way. Between 1980 and 1987, the value of Japanese FDI in the UK grew from $2010 m to $6598 m. This has resulted in an increasing number of Japanese manufacturing units in the UK, rising from 28 in 1986 to over 100 in 1988. In 1989 Japanese investment accounted for approximately one-third of all total foreign direct investment in the UK.

This raises the issue of why Japanese companies favour the UK for their European location. Recent literature identifies four possible reasons for this phenomenon. Firstly, the UK is a relatively cheap economy within which to invest. Unit labour costs are approximately 20 per cent below other major Community economies. Furthermore, high local levels of unemployment have resulted in large pools of un-unionized workers willing to accept 'no-strike' agreements or single union representation. Secondly, the political environment in the United Kingdom is attractive to overseas multinational manufacturing concerns. The policy on overseas predators, cross-border takeovers and transnational mergers, has been notably pragmatic, based almost entirely on free-market principles. The 20 per cent stake taken by Honda in the Rover Group and the incentives given to other Japanese multinationals are testament to the British government's tolerant attitude to takeovers and its enthusiasm towards FDI. Thirdly, the UK has a unique cultural and language advantage. Japanese multinational corporations have in the past concentrated their investments on North America, with approximately 46 per cent of Japan's FDI going to the USA. Given the similarities between the UK and USA in business attitudes, Anglo-Saxon culture, working practices and, perhaps most importantly, language, much of the experienced gained by Japanese multinationals in the USA is directly relevant to the UK. Finally, Japanese manufacturing plants are attracted to the UK because of the already existing base of Japanese establishments in Britain. The concentration of foreign manufacturing plants in a host country can be attributed to the effects of psychological agglomeration (De Smidt 1966). Psychological agglomeration differs from agglomeration economics as the latter refers to significant external economies of scale in production, whereas the former refers to selected information from an already established manufacturer on the desirability of a particular location in the host country. This in turn leads to a positive feedback situation, attracting more foreign manufacturing establishments to invest in the host country.

The first and perhaps most important explanation behind Japanese FDI favouring the UK, concerned with labour costs and working agreements, highlights the direct links between economic and social policies. It could be argued that a degree of 'social dumping' has already taken place, with Japanese multinationals exploiting the favourable labour costs and 'no-strike' agreements available in the UK. This favouritism has, however, taken place at the direct expense of other Community countries unable to attract such large levels of Japanese FDI as a result, in part, of high social costs. Multinational companies are already developing European trade and investment strategies that exploit the potential for 'social dumping'. It is therefore not surprising that there have been calls for a social space to accompany an economic space as well as protectionist measures to be imposed upon manufacturing units locating in the EC from third countries.

FUTURE TRENDS AND PROSPECTS

The most influential factor persuading overseas firms to invest in the Community is the present system of protection and the prospect of increased external tariff barriers. As Community businesses will be faced with enhanced competition as the internal barriers are removed, there is likely to be an increasing call for external barriers to take their place. In a genuinely internal market, trade barriers are the exclusive preserve of external tariffs. In addition, if an active European social policy is developed to accompany the internal market, demands for greater protectionism are likely to develop as EC businesses are faced with higher costs. Another contributory factor explaining the recent increase in FDI is the expected trade diversion resulting from a further step towards European economic integration. The under-representation of Japanese multinational manufacturing plants located outside Japan, contributing only 4 per cent to Japanese manufacturing output compared to 20 per cent in the USA, indicates an enormous growth potential. Japan's Ministry of Industry and Technology predict that Japanese overseas manufacturing investments will grow by 14 per cent per annum over the period to 1995 and that the EC will be a favoured location (Europe 2000 1989). In all probability, the expansion of Japanese EC production units will not substantially reduce the absolute size of Japan's exports to the Community. Following the experience of US multinationals, it is expected that both Japanese EC production and Japanese exports are likely to rise.

This leaves the Commission with the difficult task of regulating the overseas manufacturing facilities now being built in the Community. Apart from the 'rule of origin' regulations, the Commission has been making use of 'anti-dumping' laws as a sanction against successful importers. This perhaps more than any other piece of legislation has heightened fears about 'fortress Europe'. Since 1987 the Commission has been able and willing to impose 'anti-dumping' duties on the completed products of overseas manufacturing plants established in the EC by taxing the parts sent to such factories from the home country. These so-called 'screwdriver plants' are accused of importing all their products from the home country whilst at the same time expecting access to the Community market as a 'European'. Electric typewriters, photocopiers, dot matrix printers and silicon chips have all been subject to anti-dumping levies. In addition, the Commission successfully applied anti-dumping duties on the Ricoh manufacturing plant in the USA, a maker of photocopiers. Whilst American firms had access to the EC market, Ricoh was forced to pay extra duties. In effect, the Community refused to recognize the American nationality of a manufacturing plant located in America. The issue of anti-dumping levies in immensely complicated but serves to illustrate the critically important issue of defining what is European. The uncertainties surrounding the future trade and investment relations between the EC and third countries is bound to be both continuing and fiercely contested: testament to the increasing economic importance of the EC and the economic benefits of European integration. For Community businesses the issue of restricting access to the European economy becomes ever more important as the level of welfare provision expands and imposes extra costs on Community production. Conversely, for third countries gaining access to the Community market becomes more important as the level of economic integration expands the Community economy. These legitimate concerns over the future character of the EC's external trade policy forced a number of European states outside the Community to re-evaluate the costs of non-membership.

FURTHER ENLARGEMENT OF THE COMMUNITY

On 1st January 1986, Spain and Portugal became members of the EC and the Ten became Twelve. This third enlargement will almost certainly not be the final one. Five years after the signing of the SEA, Member States had received applications from Austria and Sweden for EC admission. Both of these EFTA countries seem certain to become members sometime in the 1990s. The Community's attractiveness to the economically backward Mediterranean countries (Greece, Spain and Portugal) has long been recognized, but has only lately begun to attract more prosperous north European countries as well. In addition, the newly democratized states of Czechoslovakia, Hungary and Poland are also eager to establish EC negotiations leading to full membership (see Chapter 9). The causes and consequences of these applications for the internal market programme are significant.

Under Article 237 of the 1957 Rome Treaty,

> any European state may apply to become a member of the Community.... The conditions of admission and the adjustments to this treaty necessitated thereby shall be the subject of an agreement between Member States and the applicant state.

Before 1989, every non-Communist country in Europe, with the exception of Finland and Iceland, had applied for EC admission or association. In 1978, the European Council, faced with a series of new applicants, agreed on a 'Declaration of Democracy' which all new members of the Community had to endorse as part of their treaties of accession. From then on, if any Member State ceased to be democratic, the EC would be legally entitled, and perhaps even obliged, to expel them from the Community. The desire of Greece, Spain and Portugal to join the EC was partially based on their desire to secure their fragile democracies emerging from years of dictatorship. For the existing Member States, the economic and social consequences of Community enlargement were as important as the strategic implications.

Iberia's 1977 application for EC admission received a less than positive welcome by the Ten Member States. In fact, Spain and Portugal's entry negotiations proved exceptionally difficult and dragged on for over nine years. The accession of Iberia posed problems in agriculture, fishing, manufacturing and social policy. Spanish agricultural output is similar to that in southern France and Italy, with a concentration on wine, olives, fruit and vegetables, produce in which the EC already had substantial over-production. The 1978 French general election reflected this unease over enlargement, with both the Gaullists (RPR) and the Communists (PCF) standing against Iberian entry. In addition, the Iberian economy threatened to add to the problems of over-capacity in the shipbuilding, oil refining, footwear, steel and textile industries. For the wealthier north European Member States, there was also a genuine fear that Iberia's accession would have a damaging effect on employment and social security systems as large numbers of workers moved to the more prosperous north to find jobs (Perry 1984). As a result of these problems, the initial target date set for Iberia's entry, that of the 1st January 1983, was abandoned and negotiations dragged on over specific economic and social policy safeguards. Spain and Portugal's accession was finally made possible by a series of policy initiatives designed to lessen the impact of enlargement. Notable amongst them was a seven-year transitional period restricting the free movement of labour from Spain and Portugal to other Community economies. The creation of an Integrated Mediterranean Programme (IMPs) was also a direct response to the social and economic threats posed by Spain and Portugal. The IMPs directed payments to existing EC members likely to suffer as a result of the third enlargement.

The accession of Iberia highlights a number of issues central to the theme of the present text. First and foremost, enlargement has important economic and social impacts on the existing Member States. Secondly, by accepting the inevitability of further enlargement, the Community has demonstrated the acceptance of its own political nature and its concern for the social and economic stability of Europe (Daltrop 1982). Finally, developments within the EC can have a significant external impact in securing political stability and promoting the democratization of Europe. Previous enlargement negotiations have, however, been dominated by the economic and social problems posed for the existing Member States by the applicant state.

The Community is now faced with an unprecedented number of states wanting EC admission or association. Whilst the desire of the wealthy EFTA countries to join the EC stems in part from the '1992' programme, the consequences of further expansion could threaten the very objectives of that very same programme. The policies of the EC Commission towards new membership can be reviewed against the background of the three competing objectives guiding the development of the Community outlined in Chapter 2: widening into new policy areas not explicitly mentioned in the Rome Treaty, enlarging to incorporate new Member States, and deepening to further the economic and social cohesion of the Community. It is the argument over the economic and social consequences of enlarging Community membership and its perceived negative influence on the policies of deepening which is at the centre of the EC's debate over EFTA. The EC has in the past been unable simultaneously to pursue vigorously all three trends of widening, deepening and enlarging. The Community has therefore had to establish priorities which necessarily exclude major developments in other areas. At the time of the 1973 enlargement, it was agreed that British entry would be accompanied by a 'deepening' of the Community through the adoption of a policy designed to introduce monetary integration. However, the decade that followed that first enlargement supported the view that enlarging and deepening are incompatible processes. The deepening process got bogged down in rising unemployment, inflation and arguments over the British budgetary contributions to the EC. The period was characterized by stagflation and Eurosclerosis as opposed to developments in deepening. Each subsequent enlargement has involved complex, detailed and time-consuming negotiations designed to resolve the minutiae of economic and social problems. The EC's desire to establish an appropriate policy for the 1990s has again focused attention on the conflict that exists between deepening the Community, based on the SEA and progressive moves towards economic and monetary union (EMU), and enlarging the Community to incorporate new member states.

EFTA AND THE INTERNAL MARKET

The negative economic consequences associated with over 15 years of enlarging provided the principal stimulus for the reforms embodied in the SEA. Paradoxically, the success of the internal market programme resulted in a spate of new applications as the Community's neighbours realized the major prospective implications of a European single market. The seven member states of EFTA were perceived to be the most vulnerable to the '1992' changes. The internal market integration process will have significant implications for the EFTA countries, regardless of how they react or adjust to the process. The EC and EFTA are based on two very different philosophies of integration and cooperation. EFTA is less ambitious than the EC, being concerned to retain the national sovereignty of member states by adopting intergovernmental decision-making methods. EFTA has none of the supranationalism and sovereignty-pooling characteristics of the EC. It also has a very small secretariat based in Geneva. Despite initial rivalry and suspicion between these two European trading blocs, EFTA-EC trade exceeds EC-US and EC-Japanese trade. Economically, the EC has always been the more powerful of the two organizations. However, successive enlargements of the Community have enhanced its relative economic strength compared with EFTA. In 1988, approximately 85 per cent of western Europe's GDP was produced by the EC (Table 8.1). The Community is therefore the dominant partner in trade talks and matters concerned with European integration. Nevertheless, the seven small but highly industrialized EFTA states – Austria, Finland, Iceland, Liechtenstein, Norway, Sweden and Switzerland (Fig 8.6) – collectively represent the EC's major trading partner.

Throughout the latter part of the 1980s, 25 to 30 per cent of EC exports went to EFTA countries. EFTA's dependence on the EC is even greater, with approximately 65 per cent of its non-mutual trade going to the EC, representing about 14 per cent

Table 8.1 West European GDP.

	EC of Six 1958	EC of Nine 1973	EC of Twelve 1988
EC	54.1%	78.5%	85.3%
EFTA	31.7%	12.2%	12.4%
Others	14.2%	9.3%	2.3%
Total	100	100	100

Source: Wijkman 1990.

of EFTA GDP. This cosy relationship arose from a series of free-trade agreements between the two European trading blocs. The original aim of EFTA was to establish free trade in industrial products among its member states and western Europe more generally. By 1966 it had successfully completed the former objective. However it was only when the UK and Denmark left EFTA at the time of the first EC enlargement that the remaining members succeeded in negotiating free-trade agreements with the EC. A number of bilateral free-trade agreements secured the free movement of industrial products between EFTA countries and the EC by 1st July 1977. Both the EC and EFTA gained, in both economic and political terms, from the free-trade negotiations of the 1970s. For the seven member states of EFTA, the organization had the attraction of safeguarding sovereignty, enabling geopolitically neutral states (Sweden, Austria, Finland and Switzerland) to join a pan-European organization and, through the group of 'EFTA old boys' (Denmark and the UK), access to the Community market without having to pay the cost-penalties and tension caused by common EC policies.

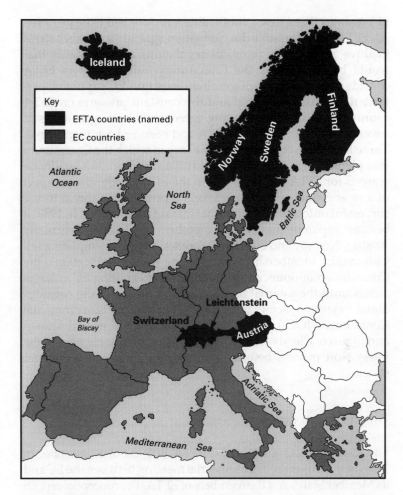

Figure 8.6 The European Free Trade Area, 1991.

This mutually beneficial relationship that EFTA had established with the Community was threatened by the programme for
the completion of the EC's internal market. The threat took the
form of Community protectionism and the projected economic
benefits arising from the SEM. With the prediction that intra-EC
trade would rise by 10 per cent and be accompanied by a comparable increase in exports, EFTA states began to feel vulnerable. In
addition, fears over a fortress Europe, based on exactly the same
worries as expressed by the USA and Japan, persuaded the seven

EFTA states that a new joint EC-EFTA regime had to be negotiated. EFTA feared relative discrimination against its member states in three main areas: technical regulations and standards that would be adopted by the Community independent of EFTA considerations, relative discrimination of non-EC suppliers, particularly in manufacturing, and the constant pressure on EFTA countries to reciprocate trading agreements leading to a loss of sovereignty, the very thing EFTA had been so keen to preserve. These legitimate concerns over the way in which the Community was planning to oversee external trade also represent legitimate reasons for EFTA countries to join the EC. Equally, the prospect of a new round of EC applications represented a threat to the successful outcome of the internal market programme. In 1989, it became apparent that several members of EFTA – particularly Austria, Norway and Sweden – were seriously contemplating full Community membership. Anticipating formal applications, the Commission announced its objective of preventing EC enlargements until the internal market and the results of the constitutional revisions being undertaken by the Intergovernmental Conferences (IGCs) on political and economic union were known and in place. Clearly, the EC was attracted by a deepening of the integration process before attempting to absorb new member states.

THE EUROPEAN ECONOMIC SPACE

The idea of creating a joint EC-EFTA EES is not a new one. In 1984, at the Luxembourg ministerial meeting between the EC and its Member States and the members of EFTA, the concept of an EES was proposed for the first time by Claude Cheysson, the French foreign minister. In order to pursue this matter further, a group comprising the high officials of the two trading blocs was established. This 'High Level Contact group' has met twice a year since its foundation in September 1984. The group, which was keen to establish an EC-EFTA free market in industrial goods, reflected a concern to deepen and strengthen the cooperative procedures between the EC and EFTA states. In the late 1980s, the idea of an EES relaunched itself as a way of safeguarding EFTA's accessibility to the Community market whilst at the same time allowing

Community internal development priority over enlargement. However, the new EES was to expand its jurisdiction beyond industrial products to include the free movement of capital, services and people, reflecting the Commission's 1985 White Paper on completing the internal market. The Commission, and particularly its President, Jacques Delors, saw the EES as a way of postponing EC admissions until after the internal programme had been implemented. The Community was anxious to avoid getting into a new set of enlargement negotiations in a period of such intense deepening. In addition, the Member States of the Community, supported by the Commission, were determined to impose strict limits on the benefits EFTA states could reap from their creation of the internal market. In 1987, the EC's Commissioner for external affairs, Willy de Clercq, formulated three principles to govern the Community's relations with EFTA:

1.   priority for internal EC integration over EFTA relations;
2.   preservation of the EC's autonomous powers of decision; and
3.   the need to achieve a balance of costs and benefits between the two European trading blocs in any future agreement.

This set of guidelines clearly spelt out the supremacy of the Community's internal agenda over external matters dealing with EFTA. The Community specifically stated that its supranational sovereignty to make decisions for the Twelve would not be influenced by any EFTA agreement, that EFTA negotiations would not be the priority concern and, most importantly, if the EC was to open its market it wanted something in return. The EC therefore rejected any form of co-decision-making and made it abundantly clear that it was determined to push ahead with the internal market legislation. For the EFTA states, the attractiveness of the EES was seriously reduced. EFTA was being asked to accept the Community's laws governing the free movement of the factors of production – and to accept them as taking preference over their individual national laws. The laws and regulations designed to remove the non-tariff barriers fragmenting the EC Twelve would under the EES be applicable to the EFTA Seven. Mutual recognition, selective harmonization and the codes of essential requirements would all have to be adopted by the seven sovereign states of EFTA. In addition, the Community demanded an EC-EFTA court, including EFTA judges, to ensure compliance with EC Directives. In other words, the EES would be imposing some form of supranationalism on EFTA. These EES proposals presented a real dilemma to EFTA, causing a split between those countries willing to cede sovereignty (headed by Austria) and those opposed to supranationalism (Switzerland). The raison d'être of the EFTA organization is to promote free trade whilst at the same time safeguarding the sovereignty of its member states. The proposed EES would not only reduce the sovereign powers of the seven, it would also prohibit them from taking part in the working parties and ministerial meetings that actually create the legislation. In so doing, the EES would represent a loss of sovereignty far greater than anything sustained by the EC Twelve who at least take part in the decision-making process and, in matters other than those relating to the SEA, have the automatic right of veto. Under this scenario, Switzerland, like the other six EFTA states, would have to accept 30 years of Community economic legislation and align its policies on economic and social affairs – without being able to veto or regulate future decisions on any of these matters. The Commission had been keen to stress the distinction between 'decision-shaping' and 'decision-making', arguing that EFTA would have significant influence in the drawing-up of legislation. The loss of sovereignty implied by this decision-making process was originally perceived to be unacceptable by the majority of EFTA states who called for a 'genuine joint decision-making mechanism in substance and form' with 'direct participation of the EFTA countries in the Community's decision-making processes'.

The equilibrium between the advantages and obligations referred to in the third of de Clercq's guidelines highlights both another obstacle in the way of the proposed EES and a major focus of the present text. Within the Community, those states that fear enhanced peripheralization as a result of the internal market have been successful in securing a resource-transfer through various Community common policies, particulary the ERDF (as outlined in Chapter 7). The decision to double the EC's Structural Funds as part of the SEA package to promote the 'economic and social cohesion' of Community space was the price paid by the richer northern states to secure the support of the poorer southern members. The Structural Funds allow resource transfers or side-payments to be made to the Community's poorest regions in order to compensate for the expected benefits likely to arise in core regions. If the seven highly industrialized EFTA states gained access to the internal market and reaped the benefits of that market, should they not be expected to support an equivalent resource transfer to the Community's more depressed regions? A number of southern states, particularly Portugal, Spain and Greece, argued that their economies would not be able to compete with the high-technology advanced economies of EFTA. Whilst both the EC and EFTA have gained from the trade creation that followed the widening of the European market through the free-trading agreements, the benefits have not been evenly spread. The southern members of the EC resent the Community giving preferential trading arrangements to rich non-members at the expense of the EC's own peripheral regions, posing the question why should EFTA be given open market access while remaining free of the financial burdens imposed by the common social policies of the EC, such as the ERDF and parts of the CAP? Reflecting the EC's desire to promote social cohesion alongside economic integration, EFTA states were accused of seeking a free ride on the back of the poor southern states. In order to overcome this accusation, serious consideration was given to the possibility of EFTA states making financial contributions to aid the economic and social cohesion of the EC. Simply put, EFTA states would be paying compensation to the southern states of the EC in exchange for the privileges of preferential market access. This would be an unprecedented situation, with developed sovereign states in one trading bloc paying for the social and economic policies designed to promote cohesion in a competing trading bloc, comprised of equally developed states. In 1991, the EFTA countries offered ECU 1 billion a year of loans and ECU 500 million of interest-rate subsidies for the Community's poorest regions. However, if the EFTA states contributed to the structural funds they quite rightly argued that they were entitled to a say in how those funds were managed, arguing 'no taxation without representation'. Supporting Willy de Clercq's guideline of preserving the EC's autonomous powers of decision-making, the Commission refused to permit EFTA states any influence over any Community policy, preserving the EC's sovereignty over decision-making. For the EFTA states this would represent more than a supranational dilution of sovereignty, it would represent a fundamental loss of sovereignty to an organization it was prohibitively excluded from influencing.

Given these problems in the areas of decision-making and supporting Community common policies, which question the very sovereignty EFTA states were so keen to preserve, an increasing number of these states began to regard the EES as a staging post on the way to full Community membership. The overriding paradox of the EES is that it was conceived as a way of sidestepping any immediate enlargement of the EC, but has in fact spurred countries to join the Community club.

EFTA APPLICATIONS

The present text is thick with examples of the spillover concept, the way in which the seemingly simple objective of creating a free trading area inescapably leads to policies in the social, economic and political sphere. The EFTA-EC search to promote some form of joint economic space is an example of the internal market programme promoting an external spillover effect, with the prospect of many defections from EFTA to the EC. The inability of the EFTA-EC negotiations to create rules and policies without compromising sovereignty persuaded a number of hitherto neutral and independent states to accept some level of supranationalism. Having however accepted this point of principle, a number of EFTA states took the argument one stage further and applied for Community membership. Austria was the first state to break ranks with the EES and apply for EC admission in July 1989. The Commission was cautiously favourable to Austrian membership, foreseeing few economic and social problems. There were however two political reservations. The first concerns Austria's neutrality and its compatibility with the Community's desire to promote some elements of a common foreign and security policy. Secondly, if Austria was admitted, it would create an avalanche of applications that would be difficult to turn down.

In 1991, Austria's conclusion that nothing short of full Community membership would do was supported by Sweden's application for membership. Sweden's application completely undermined the original purpose of the EES, which was to allow EFTA states to join the internal market but not the Community. EFTA states perceived the EES as a way of promoting EC economic obligations without EFTA political rights. Consequently, the EC-EFTA joint regime became regarded as a staging post to Community membership and not as a viable alternative to joining. On 22 October 1991, an agreement was reached between the EC and EFTA to establish a 19-state 'European Economic Area' (EEA) stretching from the Arctic Circle to the Mediterranean. The term 'area' had replaced the original 'space' (Espace Economique Européen) at the insistence of the British, who considered that there was something too abstract and intangible about the concept of an 'economic space'. The EEA will create a market of 380 million consumers, representing more than 40 per cent of world trade. The 800-page EEA agreement reflected the guiding principles outlined by Willy de Clercq in 1988. The key points of the EC-EFTA treaty were:

* free movement of products in the EEA from 1993
* EFTA countries accepting all EC regulations on company law, consumer protection, education, the environment, research and development and social policy
* EFTA being exempted from the CAP and having special arrangements to cover fish, energy, coal and steel
* free movement of capital throughout the EEA
* free movement of labour with the mutual recognition of professional qualifications
* an independent 'supranational' court to make judgements over EEA-related disputes and on appeals on competition policy
* Switzerland to be given a five-year transitional period in order to remove its strict limits on immigration
* EFTA countries not allowed to vote on EC legislation
* an EEA council of ministers to decide on whether to extend new EC legislation to EFTA

The EEA treaty was based on the desire to secure the free movement of the factors of production throughout the EC and EFTA. In addition, it also secured a resource transfer from the wealthier

EFTA states to the poorer southern states of the EC. The EFTA nations committed themselves to supplying ECU 2 billion in soft loans and ECU 425 million in grants as a contribution to the EC structural funds. In addition, Spain and Portugal received what is referred to as 6000 tonnes of 'cohesion cod' from EFTA waters. Overall, the EEA treaty reflects the economic powers of the EC, with a population of 344 million, compared to the much smaller EFTA, with a population of 32 million. EFTA states were obliged to introduce existing EC legislation which they have no say on and, in addition, commit themselves to taking on future EC legislation which they will have a limited say in shaping but no direct input in decision-making. The EEA will not, however, be a full common market, since only goods produced in the EEA and not imports from outside will circulate freely. The new EC-EFTA agreement therefore creates a free trade area, not a customs union with common external tariffs. EFTA members will therefore maintain border controls with the EC.

If the sole reason of the EES/EEA was to forestall a string of applications for full membership from EFTA countries, then it was an unmitigated disaster. However, if the Community's aim in negotiating an EEA was to enable the small and prosperous EFTA countries that had hitherto hung back from EC membership to resolve most of the economic and social issues which could be seen as stumbling blocks to EC membership, whilst at the same time highlighting the reasons why it is better to be in than out, then it was an unbridled success. The member states of EFTA realized that the only way they were going to be allowed to share in the internal market economic benefits was if they adjusted their own rules, standards, regulations and specifications to those already agreed on by the EC. Although there will be a joint EC-EFTA committee in which the seven will be able to express their views on draft EC laws, the actual decisions on law-making will be made solely by the Community's Council of Ministers. Formally transforming Community law into EEA law will be the responsibility of a joint EC-EFTA committee. Collectively, EFTA states can veto the imposition of such laws; but in such circumstances the Community has the right to re-balance the agreement by removing whole sectors from the EEA. For example, if the EFTA countries refused to adopt a new technical specification on lawnmower noise, the Community could refuse the mutual recognition of all EFTA technical standards. At the apex of the EEA structure is the joint EC-EFTA court which will judge EEA matters, while leaving the Community's Court of Justice as the sole interpreter of EC law. The EEA has therefore forced the EFTA states into a second-class European tier, governed by laws that they did not make and obliged to contribute to the costs of policies designed to enhance the economic and social cohesion of a Community of which they are not yet members. However, the EFTA states agreed to the EEA Treaty because of its transitional nature. As soon as the Treaty had been signed, Switzerland announced its decision to apply for full membership of the Community. Austria, Norway, Sweden, Switzerland and Finland support the EES but only as a 'half-way house' to full EC membership. These five states are unwilling to pay the price of long-term non-membership. None of the EFTA countries can be inside the Community before 1995 and all want the economic benefits of an interim agreement. However, the EEA was successful in settling the vast majority of economic issues that the EFTA countries have to negotiate with Brussels. In many ways the EEA represents an end to the 32-year-old economic battle for Europe; the member states of EFTA, by agreeing to join the EC in an EEA leading to full Community membership, have signed the death warrant of EFTA.

There is little doubt that the spillover effect associated with the external economic implications of the internal market programme forced many EFTA states to re-evaluate their relationship with the Community. The net result of this re-evaluation was a series of membership applications. Deepening therefore led to enlargement pressures. Clearly, the internal market programme was perceived to be a threat to free trade. EFTA, Japanese and American fears over being denied access to the Community market resulted in policy decisions based upon the predicted external economic impacts of '1992'. The debate and search for a joint EC-EFTA regime and Japanese FDI in the Community helps reinforce two central and interconnected themes of the present text: the spillover theory and the linkage that exists between the economic and social policies of the internal market in influencing both the EC's internal developments and its external affairs.

9.   The Community in the 1990s: growing unity or continuation of competing visions?

The '1992' programme to build an SEM, along with other moves to enhance unity amongst EC states, has been motivated by a variety of interests and ideas, sometimes contradictory. These different aspirations are at the core of the present debate concerning the desirability of building a common 'social space' within the European Community to accompany the fast developing 'economic space' represented by the single market. In this debate, as we have seen, there are those who want to restrict Community action to a relatively limited economic field, whilst others see the creation of common social policies as an essential complement to a genuine common market. Some analysts might conclude that this debate is of somewhat secondary importance in that it overlies an apparently unstoppable process whereby the '1992' single market programme inevitably spills over into demands for a social Europe and even wider political action in fields such as foreign policy and security. Those who take a limited view of integration – sometimes described as 'Euro-pragmatists' in Britain – are eager to impose a liberal market philosophy on the process of European integration and little else. Based upon the premise that the EC is a sophisticated free-trade area (Chapter 1, Fig 1.2), these self-styled 'pragmatists' want open transnational trade of a competitive nature without recourse to regulation or policies that infringe upon the sovereignty of Member States. It is the uneasy relationship between nationalism and a liberal economic market that is the root cause of the conflict within the Euro-pragmatist camp.

This so-called pragmatic approach to European integration is based upon cooperation between independent sovereign states rather that an integrationist approach which accepts some loss of national sovereignty. It allowed the British Conservative government of the 1980s to support '1992' free-trade policies in the Community as vociferously as any other Member State. However, when the open-market philosophy encroaches upon the issue of sovereignty or appears to unleash demands for common social action, then it is deemed unacceptable to concede more power to the Community. For example, when Lord Cockfield proposed the harmonization of excise duties in order to negate distorting impacts on trade and competition, thereby allowing the market to operate more freely, the British government rejected the concept on the grounds of diminishing sovereign control. Paradoxically, although Britain fought hard to ensure that single market legislation created a free internal market unleashing competitive forces, it is these very same forces that lead to demands for a single currency based upon a European central bank, the so-called 'Eurofed', and the adoption of a common macroeconomic policy. Put simply, a free market in the factors of production cannot coexist with 11 separate currencies (Belgium and Luxembourg share their franc) and an equal number of differing macroeconomic policies. A genuine common market requires a 'level playing field' within which social, economic and monetary policies do not unduly distort competition and trade. It is therefore ironic that whilst Britain's self-styled Euro-pragmatists vigorously pursue competition and free trade, what many would see as the ultimate common market project, that of creating a single European currency, is considered by many to be an unacceptable infringement of sovereign control. The irony of this situation is further reinforced by the de facto domination of global financial and monetary markets over the macroeconomic policies adopted by apparently sovereign Member States which find their powers of decision in this domain seriously curtailed.

INEXORABLE STEPS FROM SINGLE MARKET TO SOCIAL EUROPE AND BEYOND?

As we have already said, Lord Cockfield's *Completing the Internal Market* was a technical and pragmatic document focusing on a specific, limited aim. It was originally perceived by many, somewhat mistakenly, to be a rather technical issue where Member States could be persuaded to cooperate in order to ensure a genuine common market within which economies of scale could be achieved and the economic challenge of Europe's global competitors met to the benefit of all Member States. Importantly, the parts of the SEA dealing with the internal market broadly followed the common market principles and philosophy of the 1957 Treaty of Rome. How could Member States object to pursuing policies that were already agreed upon and in existence for 35 years? As we outlined in Chapter 3, it seems fair to assume that some Member States signed the SEA without fully realizing the full economic and political consequences of so doing. As we have shown, the 'technical issue' of removing non-tariff barriers and allowing jurisdictions to compete with one another has increased pressure for an overall harmonization of Community law, be it on social policy (Chapters 5 to 7), the environment or health and welfare. By requiring the elimination of economic barriers, the SEM programme inevitably unleashes forces to merge national jurisdictions into common European regimes, thus illustrating well the spillover workings of neo-functionalist integration processes.

More particularly in the context of this book's central theme, it illuminates the link between the drive to create an SEM by 1993 and the demands to create a European 'social space' to accompany it. Clearly, it is naive to think that the SEM programme will suddenly produce a genuinely internal market in a 'Europe without frontiers' overnight on 31 December 1992! It is very much an on-going process in a larger picture of European integration. As Franklin notes:

> Perhaps one should regard the internal market programme as being rather like painting the Forth Bridge: initial moves at liberalization will be seen not to have gone far enough or to require modification in one way or another. (Franklin 1990:43)

There is no doubt that as the Community evolves, the interplay between economic policy, social policy and politics in general is becoming greater all the time. As we have shown in Chapters 5 to 8, it is incorrect to perceive the SEA as a purely economic document. But even if the SEA had made no mention of 'economic and social cohesion' (Article 130A), 'cooperation in economic and monetary policy' (Article 102A) and 'Treaty provisions of European cooperation in the sphere of foreign policy' (Article 30), the objective of progressively establishing a single market that 'comprises an area without internal frontiers' inevitably entails joint action and collaboration in the aforementioned areas. The spillover theory therefore identifies a simple but forceful logic pushing the Community towards greater unity without political leaders having to pull overtly in that direction. In fact, some political leaders have found themselves Canute-like trying to stem a growing flow towards integration that they have unwittingly unleashed. There is no doubt that if the '1992' internal market programme had to be judged by its ability to further the cause of wider European unification, it has been an unbridled success. As we have shown, there is a very real sense in which the drive to create a single market has overflowed into pressures for a stronger 'social dimension' to the Community.

Running through our discussion of the single market and social Europe projects has been this implication that both are part of a larger process of integration where European action in one sphere leads inexorably into action elsewhere, so that Community integration intensifies and national sovereignty merges almost imperceptibly into a common pool. But is there a danger that the analyst becomes too convinced by the seemingly inevitable logic of this process and underestimates the ability of sovereign states to resist these centripetal forces and maintain their national independence? After all, although the restricted 'economic' vision of British 'free-traders' can be criticized by those who point to the ever widening competence of the Community in fields from foreign policy to education, it remains a fact that EC policies are still more prominent in the economic area than elsewhere. Indeed, our chapter on regional policy revealed that Community action in the social domain often has a 'cosmetic' character about it, with proposals often proving more impressive than action. The Community's Social Charter on the Fundamental Rights of

Workers may have been heralded in with high expectations in 1989, but converting the Commission's proposals to put a solid 'social market' stamp on the single market into concrete European legislation is proving a tough task in the face of opposition from supporters of a simpler 'free-market' ideology. That there has already been an element of 'spillover' from single market realities to proposals for a wider social Europe is undeniable. But the degree to which that vision turns into solid social action to counterbalance a dominantly 'businessman's Europe' remains to be seen. Will there be overflow from the single market into more and more policy domains and how substantial is such a broadening of EC activities likely to be?

THE BALANCE BETWEEN THE EC'S ECONOMIC AND SOCIAL DIMENSIONS

We saw in Chapter 6 how the programme to implement a single market is progressing far faster than counterbalancing efforts designed to strengthen the EC's social policy. By the end of 1991, over two-thirds of the almost 300 measures proposed to establish the SEM by the end of 1992 had been adopted by the Council of Ministers; in sharp contrast, hardly any of the proposed measures in the Commission's social action programme to implement the Social Charter had been agreed.

The speed with which the economic dimension of the SEA has been implemented, coupled with the slow progress on its social dimension, suggests that the criticisms formulated by Holland and others on the Left (see Chapter 1) remain valid. Their models of the western state would lead them to expect such an outcome, given the dominance of big business interests in political life. We saw evidence in Chapter 6 that this economic-social imbalance has indeed resulted from the ability of business interests to influence the Community's political process more effectively than other groups. The way in which the UK Conservative government from 1979 onwards blocked EC social initiatives, favoured by the TUC but resisted by British employers, has been particularly open to public view. But we have also shown how this opposition often reflected the attitudes of European business leaders in general, who frequently sided with their UK colleagues in the more discreet discussions amongst the Community's so-called social partners, and the less visible pressures put on Member State governments, the Commission and the European Parliament. Even employers from Member States which had a commitment to a social-market ideology have proved reluctant to accept European legislation on such matters as employee representation within companies (Chapters 5 and 6).

In the 'corporate state' structures set up by the Commission to promote employer-employee dialogue at EC level, European business organizations have undoubtedly been more successful in defending their interests than European unions. This is partly because they possess financial resources and lobbying skills superior to those of the other social partners. But it is also arguable that business had an easier 'status quo' position to defend. Essentially, they were on the side of the 'negative' integrationists (Chapter 1) who simply had to say no to the more 'positive' social integration proposals coming from the Commission. It is easier – especially in a political structure like that of the Community where progress often depends on unanimity amongst the Member States – to resist change than to promote it.

Of course, forces for a more positive interventionist approach to integration do exist, not least in the Commission. It is an erroneous caricature to represent this institution as a servile instrument of capitalist interests. As we have shown, it has multiplied social initiatives over the years in a manner not appreciated on the British Right suspicious that 'Brussels' was trying to open a 'backdoor to socialism' (Chapter 5). The greatest problem faced by the Commission and others in trying to forge a social dimension is the lack of effective political support for such initiatives. When the Commission proposed the single market programme, it obtained overwhelming support from the Member States in the Council. Even the UK government, renowned for its 'reluctant Europeanism', lent enthusiastic support to a project which conformed to its 'free-market' ideology and perception of what was good for business. However, when the Commission promotes Community social policy it does not receive such unanimous approval. Certainly, it has proved able to win the support of most Member States for general and non-binding 'statements of intent' like the Social Charter (Chapter 5). However, when it tries to convert these declarations into concrete legislative measures, it encounters stiff opposition from Member States in the

Council, and not only from Britain. Clearly, many Member States are under no great electoral or interest-group pressure to respond positively to proposals for a more social Europe. Trades unions, keen advocates of a more social Europe, have been tending to lose rather than gain strength in recent years as traditional industries of mass unionized employment (eg, coal and steel) have declined throughout the Community. To sections of the general public which might have some sympathy for a stronger EC social dimension, the Community remains a remote and largely incomprehensible organization subjected to much misrepresentation of an antagonistic kind in the popular press, especially in Britain. Therefore, the potential to mobilize mass political support for the notion of social Europe remains limited. Members of the European Parliament might well hold impassioned debates on the need for a single social market (Chapter 6) and castigate the Council and Commission for lack of progress in this direction, but hardly anyone beyond an initiated intelligentsia wants to listen or even knows where to lend their ears! Speeches by unknown MEPs in Strasbourg are not going to put much pressure on Member State ministers in the Council. The single market project went ahead without much reference to largely indifferent and unaware electorates because Member State governments and many big business interests favoured it. If a social dimension is to be built to match it, it will be necessary to win larger public support to provide electoral backing for the wishes of trades unions and the aims of the Commission. In the 1990s it will be a major challenge for the Community to see whether it can attract the mass allegiance it needs to make populist notions of a 'people's Europe' meaningful. The role of democratic forums like national parliaments and, of course, the European Parliament will be particularly important in this regard. If the latter body had more power, there is much to suggest (Chapter 6) that the EC's social side would not, at present, be so obviously overshadowed by its economic face.

In reaching this general conclusion about the imbalance between the Community's economic and social dimensions, some qualifying notes of caution must be added. Opposition to the competitive philosophy of the SEM emerged from both Member State governments and the very people who were supposed to be

the single market's firmest allies: the barons of European industry (see Chapter 8). European business leaders had an influential
role in shaping the economic character of the SEA. Indeed Wisse
Dekker, the chairman of Philips, even helped draft the Commission's 1985 White Paper on *Completing the Internal Market*. However, resistance to the economic character of the internal market
began to emerge as European business faced the prospect of
deregulation and rationalization, involving forced redundancies,
plant closures and cost-cutting programmes (Chapter 4). As
Chapter 8 outlined, project '1992' spelled disaster for the many
weak European firms that had been protected by the non-tariff
barriers erected by Member State governments. Reacting to the
threat of unfettered competition associated with the SEM, European business during the late 1980s entered into a bout of
mergers and alliances. This resulted in some of the biggest private sector cross-border dealings ever seen, Italy's Fiat and Alca-
tel-Alsthom of France swapped shares and some businesses;
Siemens of Germany and Britain's GEC acquired Plessey; and
France's Carnaud and Metal Box of the UK merged to form CMB
Packaging. By circumventing the competitive edge of the internal
market programme by a series of alliances and mergers, the very
foundation of competitive advantage and therefore project '1992'
were threatened (Chapter 4). Whilst therefore accepting that the
single market programme has proceeded faster than that of social
Europe, not all European business leaders have been over-enthu-
siastic about unfettered EC competition. After all, non-tariff barriers were erected by Member State governments to protect
national industries threatened by competition. It is therefore not
surprising that the legislation designed to remove these barriers
provoked resistance from some Member States and some business leaders. Indeed many European companies perceive project
'1992' to be too market-oriented, especially in the drawing up of
protectionist measures against non-EC countries (Chapter 8).
The competitive threat posed by Japanese and American multinationals prompted European business leaders to call for EC protectionism to replace the national measures eliminated by the single
market. The European business community fought hard to stop
the EC becoming a truly open and competitive trading group,
what Roger Fauroux, then the French minister for industry,
called 'a land that is open to all winds'. It is therefore too easy to

get carried away with the argument that the internal market programme represents a manifesto drawn up by the barons of European industry to promote capital accumulation. Project '1992' created strong resistance from European industries concerned that the internal market remedy for Eurosclerosis would in the long term be more painful than the disease. This resulted in many industries calling for higher tariffs on imports (Chapter 8), larger state subsidies (Chapter 7) and other interventionist and protectionist painkillers designed to lessen the free-market competitive forces of the internal market.

Furthermore, for all the disappointment experienced by the EC's social architects, some foundations have been laid down for a European house which is more than purely economic in character. We have seen how a variety of interventionist Community policies and funds have been operating from the early 1950s onwards to cope with problems of unemployment, regional development and so on (Chapters 5 to 7). They may be inadequate in relation to the scale of the problems at hand, but they are steadily growing. We have also shown how common EC policies in areas like agriculture and fisheries are full (too full, some would say) of provisions concerned with social objectives which thwart free-market forces. To dismiss such policies as products of a simple capitalist blueprint for production is absurd; farmers and fishermen have been able to exert enormous pressures on EC policy-making over the years to fix prices, provide subsidies and protect producers in ways that incense proponents of open competitive economies. Similarly, the growing impact of the EC's common environmental policies can be seen as a success for those wanting to give the Community a more human face. There has also been a trend for national environmental groups to use the Commission and EC legislation as means whereby they can exert pressure on industries, states or local governments to improve the quality of life in a more managed economy.

Less obvious than these publicized 'social' policies for the environment, agriculture, regional development or whatever, a maze of transnational European organizations has been evolving to encourage cooperation on a multitude of matters from social security harmonization to youth training and education (Chapter 5). The possession of an E 111 form giving EC citizens rights to medical treatment in all Member States may seem a trivial achievement, but it is one of many minor EC measures facilitating geographical mobility within the Community. In 1991, its fifth year of operation, the Community's ERASMUS programme was helping nearly 75,000 EC students in higher eduction to carry out part of their studies in another Member State institution. Other examples could be cited to demonstrate that structures are already in place around which more solid Community social policies could be constructed if a will to do so existed on an adequate political power base. Whether a variety of disparate forces in a pluralistic Community can be channelled to achieve such social ends will be one of the Community's many challenges in the 1990s.

THE STREAM OF EUROPEAN UNITY: EVER WIDER AND DEEPER?

In thinking about the possible development of the EC's economic and social dimensions during the 1990s in some deeper European union, it is instructive to remind ourselves of the comprehensive political ambitions of early architects of the Community (Wise 1991). The aim of uniting the peoples of Europe in a political-economic union going beyond a mere common market arrangement was clearly articulated in 1950 when the apparently limited European Coal and Steel Community was proposed by the French Foreign Minister, Robert Schuman, in the following terms:

> The French government proposes to place the whole of Franco-German coal and steel production under a common High Authority, in an organization open to the participation of other European countries. The pooling of coal and steel production will immediately ensure the establishment of a common basis for economic development – first step towards a European Federation – and change the destiny of those regions for so long dedicated to the making of weapons for war of which they have been the most constant victims. The interdependence of production thus established will make all war between France and Germany not only unthinkable, but physically impossible. (Schuman 1950)

This 'Schuman Plan' highlights several points that contemporary students of Community affairs should not ignore. First, it is undeniable that the Plan had a very 'economic' character in that it required the creation of a common market within which internal national barriers to the movement of raw materials, products, people and capital related to the coal and steel industries were to be abolished. Furthermore, a common external tariff was to replace national tariffs placed on coal and steel imports from third countries (see Fig 1.4). But, despite the apparently limited economic nature of this first European Community (albeit concerned with interlocking what were in those days two fundamental industries), it is important to note the highly political character of Schuman's declaration. Without equivocation he saw the ECSC as the 'first concrete foundation of a European federation indispensable to the preservation of peace' (Schuman 1950). These larger federal objectives explain why a set of distinctive supranational institutions were set up to manage the common market for coal and steel. Such political management involved the making of genuinely European policies and laws to be enforced throughout all Member States. This was no simple common market arrangement, but clearly a basis for further integration (see Fig 1.4–1.6) which could involve all areas of human endeavour, be they economic, social or, of course, political. The key point being made here is that the EC has never had limited economic objectives, even though certain Member State governments, not only in Britain, have at times made great efforts to restrict its ambitions to the making of a common market alone. This is useful historical context when tackling the contemporary debates about whether there should be a Community 'social area' to match the 'economic space' of its would-be single market by the end of 1992.

The potential scope of the EEC to act in a multitude of policy areas is apparent to anyone who reads the Treaties carefully. Indeed it was this potential for ever deepening integration that led Britain to promote its own much looser form of European unity by setting up the European Free Trade Association (EFTA) in 1959. This organization had none of the supranational institutional structure so strongly embedded in the European Communities and was strictly concerned only with free trade among its members (Fig 1.2). This attracted the smaller, more peripheral states of western Europe, also wary of being sucked into a supranational system.

Despite this attempt to follow an alternative and more limited route, history has shown that the path leading from the Schuman Declaration has proved more successful. Indeed, there has been a steady evolution of the European Community towards greater integration of ever increasing political-economic scope and ever widening geographical extent. In fact, less than eighteen months after setting up EFTA, the UK, at last coming to terms with its loss of world power status, applied to join the Community. After a decade of tortuous diplomacy, Britain eventually joined the EC in 1973 along with the Irish Republic and Denmark, to be followed in the 1980s by Greece (1981), Spain and Portugal (1986). At present other countries are seeking to join while many more (see Chapter 8) are seeking associate status of some kind. What is more, this growing number of Member States have been pooling their sovereignty in ever more fields. As we enter the 1990s, the Community is not just dealing with the single market and social Europe proposals of primary concern in this book, but overtly striving to create a common currency and reinforce its existing common foreign policy procedures. Furthermore, the highly charged issue of a common EC defence policy is back on the agenda after the collapse of the European Defence Community scheme in 1954.

Does all this suggest that a process of 'spillover' or 'engrenage' has been inexorably leading towards the contemporary realities of the single market project and the programme of EC legislation stemming from the Social Charter? There is strong evidence to support the case. For a start, we can note how Britain's efforts, first to stay out of the Communities and then create a much looser free-trade alternative, failed; despite their fears about sovereignty, the British, in general, have come to accept that national interest is best served inside the Community. Present outsiders such as Sweden, Switzerland and Norway are currently tussling with the ever stronger tugs towards EC membership in much the same way. What influence can an independent sovereign state exercise on the economic, social and security future of Europe outside of the Community's supranational institutions?

Having reluctantly succumbed to integrative logic by entering the Community in 1973, the UK then tried to restrain the pace of integration by stressing the more limited trading objectives of the Community and clinging firmly to the idea of a national veto in

EC affairs. Often, this was not difficult to do, given the reluctance of other national governments to decide many matters at European level. But 'spillover' pressures have always been present. For example, the basic idea of free and fair trade in the common market became increasingly dubious as conflicts erupted due to the distorting effects of national currency fluctuations. When the pound was high, the cross-Channel ferries were even fuller with British trippers seeking bargains in continental supermarkets; when the opposite was true, bilingual signs sprouted in shops along Britain's south coast! Retailers on different sides of the border (as elsewhere in Europe) were elated or depressed accordingly, but certainly not convinced by the simple slogans of free and fair trade in a common market (Gibb 1985). Thus in 1978 the majority of Member States decided to establish a stabilizing Exchange Rate Mechanism (ERM) within a European Monetary System (EMS). Once again Britain decided to resist these integrating pressures by allowing the pound sterling to float outside of the ERM. For the next decade, the UK government resisted all pressures to join, despite the fact that these fluctuations contributed significantly to certain 'free trade' frictions, not least those associated with the notorious 'Lamb Wars' between Britain and France. The monetary debate surrounding this issue can become very sophisticated and this is not the place to discuss the conflicting arguments. However, in the context of 'spillover' theory it is noteworthy that in 1990 the UK government eventually found the pressures to join ERM, not least from the leaders of British big business, irresistible.

As we have seen in Chapters 2 to 5, it was 'spillover' processes, at least in part, which led to the proposal for a single internal market. Following the successful abolition of customs duties between Member States and the creation of a CET (Fig 1.2), trade between the Community countries grew. However, this increase in trade in a so-called common market revealed how many non-tariff barriers remained to impede genuinely free and fair trade (Chapter 2). In other words, the initial aim of creating a common market triggered off processes which created problems that required further, more integrative steps to be taken. The Commission's crucial *White Paper on Completing the Internal Market* was thus published in 1985, in turn leading to the much publicized

'1992' deadline for the establishment of a Single European Market. As we saw in Chapters 5 to 8, similar processes of 'one thing leading to another' can be detected in calls for a social Europe to complement the genuine Common Market that is now being built.

So we can see that the contemporary issues of economic and social integration under scrutiny in this book flow out of a lengthy and comprehensive process of Community development. It is tempting to assume that, for all the difficulties that will be encountered along the way, a genuine 'Europe without frontiers' will eventually be constructed, based on a genuine common market humanized by appropriate common social policies. But nationalism is still a vibrant force in Europe, always prone to resurrection, especially if the promised economic and social rewards of an integrated Europe do not materialize. If a sufficient number of people feel 'losers' in a uniting Europe, there will certainly be those who have national alternatives to offer. This thought should prevent the reader being too overwhelmed by a sense of inevitability. Our final thoughts on an agenda for the 1990s should carry this cautionary rider with them.

THE AGENDA FOR THE 1990s

The SEM programme has been successful in reviving the drive towards European unification and making the notion of a third economic superpower alongside the United States of America and Japan seem less fanciful. Given the stagnant and acrimonious nature of Community relations throughout most of the 1970s and early 1980s, reference to such a prospect is remarkable. However, as soon as the SEA had been ratified and legislation began to emerge to enforce the free movement of goods, people, capital and services, east-central Europe collapsed following 18 months of revolution against one-party communist rule. This refuelled the drive towards European economic and political union which supplemented the impetus to unification created by the '1992' project. These events serve to reinforce a central theme of this book: that the SEM is part of a well-established process rather than an isolated project on the Community's internal agenda.

POLITICAL, ECONOMIC AND MONETARY UNION

More than any other proposal put forward by the Commission, EMU illustrates both the spillover effects of '1992' and the difficulties of reducing the sovereign powers, real or imagined, of Member States. As such it will be a major touchstone of Community integration in the 1990s. The link between '1992' and EMU was neatly illustrated by the former Chancellor of West Germany, Helmut Schmidt, when he observed:

> Who ever heard of a single market with eleven different currencies? (Colchester, Buchan 1990: 164)

The dissatisfaction with the dependence of the European Monetary System (EMS) on the German Deutschmark, which meant the Bundesbank had become an unofficial EC central bank, further convinced the majority of Member States of the need to renew their pursuit of monetary union, long simmering as an idea on the Community's back-burners. In 1988, at the Hannover meeting of the Council of Ministers, it was decided (with support from the UK) to establish a Committee with the objective of 'studying and proposing concrete stages leading towards economic and monetary union'. The Committee was a powerful one. Headed by Jacques Delors, it also included the governors of the 12 national banks. On 17 April 1989, the Committee produced the so-called 'three-stage plan for economic and monetary union'. The first stage was relatively easy. Starting July 1990, all currencies would be brought into the existing EMS whilst, at the same time, the Twelve would strengthen the coordination of their economic and monetary policies. Stage two, for which no date was set, would be seen as a transitional phase between stages one and three. It would begin with the creation of a new European system of central banks (the 'Eurofed') which would encourage more collective decision-making and collaboration amongst the Twelve. However, economic and monetary policy would continue to be the sole preserve of national banks and governments. The final stage three would permanently fix exchange rates and create, de facto, a single European currency. An independent European central bank would be established to promote price stability and set interest rates for the European

Currency Unit, the single currency. Importantly, the final stage proposed that the Community would have the power to force Member State governments to apply certain budgetary policies 'to the extent necessary to prevent imbalances that might threaten monetary stability'.

Characteristically, the British government under Mrs Thatcher described Delors' three stage plan as 'the biggest transfer of sovereignty we've ever had' (Colchester, Buchan 1990: 173). Nothing better encapsulates the tension between the liberal market commitment to free trade and fears over losing sovereignty. The tension created by this conflict in philosophies was felt most acutely in the UK and, to a lesser extent, Denmark. Britain's predictably negative response to the Delors' plan had nothing to do with pure economics; it was the loss of political sovereign control that the UK found so objectionable. However, it was two years later, at the Council of Ministers' Rome summit in October 1990, that the conflict between the UK and the other 11 Member States of the EC erupted into a full-blown political crisis. Mr Andreotti, Italy's Prime Minister, was acting President at the Rome summit and persuaded all States, with the exception of the UK, to agree on January 1994 as the starting date for stage two of the Delors' plan. Britain's strident opposition to EMU and political union left the United Kingdom totally isolated at the Rome summit and caused a devastating split in the British Cabinet, which eventually led to Mr Major succeeding Mrs Thatcher as Prime Minister. However, despite this turmoil, the October 1990 Rome summit of EC leaders was able to decide upon stage two of the Delors' plan starting in January 1994 with a new bank to oversee the development of the ECU.

At the second Rome summit held in December 1990, two Intergovernmental Conferences (IGCs) were established to explore further the issues of both EMU and European Political Union (EPU). IGCs can be established by a majority vote amongst heads of government and, whilst any proposed constitutional change requires unanimity, recommendations emanating from IGCs carry a great deal of moral authority. The conference on EMU adopted the Delors' three-stage plan as a model upon which to base proposals. However, the United Kingdom declared that there was no need to surrender any more sovereignty to Europe and categorically rejected 'an imposed' single currency (Economist

1988a). In March 1991, the Commission called for stage three to begin once it had the backing of at least eight countries, allowing other Member States to hold back and remain in stage two for as long as they want. Significantly, the British government had not ruled out such a formula at the time of writing.

After the SEA had been ratified, the Commission became eager to ensure that the impetus to unification created by the SEM programme was not lost. The obvious success associated with the 1992 deadline as well as the problems it revealed spurred European integrationists to plan or resurrect other ambitious projects. In addition, the desire to further the cause of European union was stimulated by the rapidly changing conditions in east-central Europe and in particular, the unification of Germany. In order to anchor a united and economically powerful Germany to the EC, most European leaders recognized the need for further integrative measures. As we have seen above, the spillover effect from the '1992' programme, together with the revolutions in east-central Europe, spurred on a series of proposals aimed at furthering the cause of European Political and Economic Union. Clearly, the Commission and a majority of Member States were determined to build on the considerable achievements gained throughout the late 1980s and early 90s. The principal objective of the 'political' IGC was to examine the Community's decision-making processes with the aim of improving legislative procedures and filling a so-called 'democratic deficit' in EC affairs. It had the task of paying 'particular attention' to a list of possible constitutional reforms, with emphasis upon increasing the powers of the European Parliament, increased use of majority voting in the Council of Ministers, and so on. As the 1990s progress into a changing, less stable, world, so the calls for a more common EC foreign policy (required by the SEA) grow more frequent, as do demands that the vital issue of common defence and security be dealt with at Community level. Indeed, it is now hard to think of an area of government where the Community does not act in some way, or has not been called upon to do so. Such talk of extending the Community's competence into the most sensitive areas of governance, such as defence, is often dismissed as 'Euro-rhetoric', particularly in a Britain jealous of its national sovereignty and proud of its pragmatism. But in rejecting the 'rhetoric' of the Schuman Declaration in 1950, and then struggling belatedly into the Community some 23 years afterwards, one might question how pragmatic the British really are in comparison to their more visionary neighbours!

THE RE-BIRTH OF EAST-CENTRAL EUROPE: A DILEMMA FOR THE COMMUNITY

The magnitude and speed of the events in east-central Europe (Fig 9.1) which transformed the region at the end of the 1980s took almost everybody by surprise. The collapse of the communist regimes in east-central Europe represented a start to the end of the division of Europe and the industrialized world into two distinct and hostile political economies. The dismantling of the last European empire – the USSR – will have a profound impact on numerous spheres of economic, social and political activities in the west, including the future development of the EC. However, whilst the consequences of the east-central European revolutions on the internal market programme are potentially great, the revolutions in themselves were not directly related to developments in the EC, such as the internal market programme. The reasons behind the events of 1989/90 are extremely complex and varied. They were also primarily of an internal character which had existed for a considerable length of time. At the end of the 1960s, the countries of east-central Europe experienced considerable political and social unrest culminating in the Soviet invasion of Czechoslovakia in 1968 and the leadership crisis in Poland in 1968 and 1970. These events were the long-term consequences of over four decades of forced transformation, re-shaping the political and economic structures of east-central Europe in accordance with the classic Stalinist model based on the one-party state and the centrally planned economy. The systemic inability of the command economies to absorb innovation and new technologies, deteriorating terms of trade with the west, the continuation of the one-party state and ever-increasing hard-currency debts led to the peaceful revolutions that swept across east-central Europe in 1989/90.

The internal market reforms of '1992', together with associated spillover effects, and the external economic impact of the SEM programme had little influence on the east-central European

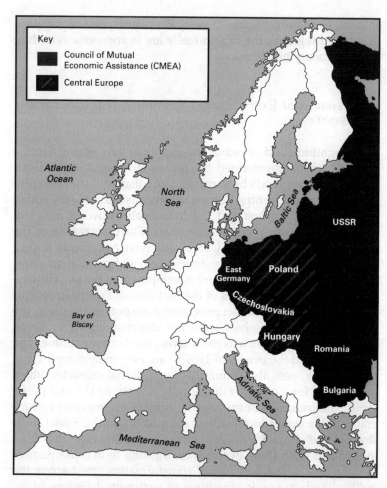

Figure 9.1 The countries of East-Central Europe.

revolutions. However, these revolutions have raised the possibility of reintegrating parts of east-central Europe, particularly Poland, Czechoslovakia and Hungary, into the rest of Europe, an issue that was formally addressed for the first time since the Second World War during the Conference on Security and Cooperation in Europe in November 1990. The states of central Europe perceive membership of the EC as essential not only to the successful transition from Soviet-style command economy to free market, but also as a guarantee of long-term political stability. There is also the option that EFTA, which appears likely to lose members again to the EC (see Chapter 8), may be able to survive as a European organization by providing a long-term home for the east-central European countries eager to adopt market economics and keen to forge closer links with the west. These various scenarios raise a whole host of complex issues affecting the way in which European economic integration has until quite recently been analysed. Some western academics view the SEM as a rather parochial western concern, given the momentous changes taking place in east-central Europe. This perception is misconceived as the outcome of the internal market programme will influence east-central Europe's case for joining the EC. In addition, if the former communist regimes gained early membership, the deepening process associated with the internal market reforms, both economic and social, would in all likelihood falter. The entry of east-central European states into the EC and the SEM are not unconnected. In line with the EC's policy on EFTA states applying for membership, the Community has been keen to postpone the enlargement agenda until a significant deepening has been achieved through the SEA reforms. Despite calls for the Community to slow down its plans for economic and social integration as a result of the revolutions in east-central Europe, the EC has in fact tried to speed up moves towards economic and political union, not least because of the fear of a united and potentially more powerful Germany.

By 1991, the old eastern European systems had been replaced by a pluralistic collection of countries and a maze of conflicting political, ethnic and economic interests. Hungary, Czechoslovakia and Poland (referred to as central Europe) have a number of distinguishing characteristics that separate them from the rest of east-cental Europe and make them the most likely candidates for early Community membership. First and foremost, they have all embraced the radical approach to transforming their command economies. A commitment to extensive price liberalization, wage control and currency convertibility distinguished these three countries from either Romania or Bulgaria, where the pace of economic and political reform has been much more sedate, or Yugoslavia, which has been savaged by civil war. The division between those countries committed to a radical transformation of their command economies and those taking a more cautious approach has been reflected in the policies and plans emanating from the west. The EC, the European Bank for Reconstruction and Development (EBRD), the International Monetary Fund (IMF) and the European Investment Bank (EIB) have all favoured Poland, Czechoslovakia and Hungary.

CENTRAL EUROPE AND EC MEMBERSHIP

Despite the west's officially declared support for the political democratization and economic liberalization of central Europe, the EC has been extremely cautious in developing a coherent policy towards this region. Before 1991, the EC had few contacts with the Council of Mutual Economic Assistance (CMEA), the Soviet equivalent of the EC. Although CMEA was from the start territorially much larger than the Community, it was never intended to be an evolving organization with its own political institutions and supranational powers. It was an intergovernmental committee of states whose official purpose was to stimulate intra-CMEA trade. CMEA did not make the progress in economic integration experienced by the EC. The economic collapse of the Soviet economy in 1989 wholly discredited the Soviet model of economic management and dealt a terminal blow to the process of economic integration supported by CMEA. For almost its entire existence, CMEA, supported by the Soviet Union, refused to grant diplomatic recognition to the EC, frequently attacking the Community concept. Under President Mikhail Gorbachev, the USSR finally recognized the EC in 1990. However, trade between the EC and CMEA was relatively small, reflecting the very real difficulties of trading between socialist states committed to controlled central planning and the essentially free-market economies of the EC. In 1991, the member states of CMEA decided to dismantle the organization.

In the early 1990s both the USSR and the central Europe experienced sharply deteriorating economic conditions. Those countries most committed to reform have experienced a decline in aggregate output and real incomes. Poland experienced a dramatic fall in economic activity during 1990, with industrial output falling by over 25 per cent and GDP by almost 15 per cent (OECD, 1991). Hungary and Czechoslovakia experienced similar structural difficulties. The negative economic consequences that accompany the initial stages of systemic reform make it politically difficult for the reforming governments to persist with the stabilization and market-oriented policies. It is therefore not surprising that membership of the Community is regarded in central Europe as essential not only to the successful transition from Soviet-style economy to free market, but also as a guarantee of long term political stability. However, the enormous social consequences associated with this systemic transformation would seriously threaten the deepening programme of the internal market if the central European states gained early membership. The Community again adopted the policy of internal development taking priority over enlargement. But if the Community expects the central European states to wait until their economies reach western standards of sophistication before joining the EC, whilst at the same time the Community continues to deepen its political and economic integration, the region would be faced with impossibly tough criteria for membership. The EC is firmly committed to a deepening of the integration process before attempting to absorb new member states, particularly states that by virtue of their underdeveloped nature would seriously retard further integrative moves. The idea of enlarging the Community to include the poor central European states affronted many whose priority was the deepening of the existing Community.

The EC's response to the political democratization and economic liberalization of central Europe has been to coordinate ad hoc economic aid and advice. The most tangible symbol of this action was the establishment of the European Bank for Reconstruction and Development (EBRD) in 1990. The broad objective of this London-based institution is to help finance the rebuilding of ex-Communist Europe. Another example of the EC's involvement in central Europe is the PHARE programme, ironically instigated by the USA administration rather than the Commission. In 1990, the PHARE or G24 programme of aid to central Europe produced ECU 300 million for Poland and Hungary, and ECU 200 million for the rest of central Europe. On the negative side, however, the EC and other western countries have significantly increased travel and immigration restrictions between the two parts of Europe.

Yet it is the establishment of trading agreements that will in large measure determine the nature of the EC's relations with central Europe. Here, the central Europeans argue that in order for the Community to secure the economic liberalization of the region it should give less attention to the supply of aid and credit and put more emphasis on the opening up of the EC market to central European goods. As a consequence, a number of association agreements have been established between the EC and central Europe in order to make the Community market more accessible. For the EC, such association agreements produce considerable economic and social costs as the protected Community market is forced to compete with the steel, textile and farming products of central Europe. Although EC membership for these central European countries is regarded as a necessary step towards the long-term political stability of this region, the economic and social consequences for the existing Member States will be the determining factor influencing entry negotiations. Even though the majority of western commentators agree that the ultimate membership of these three central European countries is almost inevitable, the obstacles in the way of integration remain formidable.

The revolutions in east-central Europe and the desire of some of those states to join the EC throws some interesting light on those theories of the state advanced in the introductory chapter of this book. Despite its much hailed 'new approach' to social and political theory, human geography failed to develop a coherent framework for the analysis of the former socialist states and appears seemingly uninterested in examining the geographical dimensions of the 1989/90 revolutions within east-central Europe (Bradshaw 1990). Theories of the state advanced in Anglo-Saxon geography are almost entirely concerned with western capitalism and are thus ill-equipped to deal with the transformation of east-central Europe and the phenomenon of the totalitarian state. During the 1980s, the most influential works in geography focused on the theory of the state and economy incorporating elements of the Marxist political economy and historical materialism (Johnston 1982, 1984, 1989; Taylor 1985, 1989). When examining east-central Europe, such work has tended to argue that the developments in this region were deviant forms of 'true' socialist principles which reproduced the logic of the capitalist mode of production at the national or world scale. However, there is much evidence to support the view that the Soviet-style Leninist interpretation of not only what socialism is supposed to be but how it was to be achieved was a perfectly legitimate interpretation of Marxist theory (Kolakowski 1978; Dahrendorf 1990). Thus there was nothing inherently deviant or even incorrect in the despotic form of the one-party system (dictatorship of the proletariat) as a technique to achieve the Communist society. As Dahrendorf states:

> We have a considerable number of theories predicting the imminent downfall of capitalism and the inevitable rise of socialism...but today we know they are all wrong....intellectuals have explained events which never took place, and shied away from those which lie behind the revolution of 89 in Europe. (Dahrendorf 1990: 72)

It would appear likely, therefore, that a more pluralistic interpretation of the political economy within eastern Europe, which is now dominated by a collection of countries with a maze of conflicting interests, is a more useful tool of analysis in understanding the events in the region and the movement from socialism to capitalism and eventually the Community club.

Towards a United States of Europe?

The founders of the first European Community in 1950 – the ECSC – tended to merge elements of both federalist and functionalist thought. Most notably, Jean Monnet, the original architect of Community structures, designed the 'supranational' institutions of the ECSC with a federalist vision of a United States of Europe in view. However, unlike some more impatient federalists, he did not believe that European unity could be achieved by imposing some great federal constitution on European states protective of their national sovereignty. Thus, he was more like the functionalists in believing that unity had to be built up 'step-by-step' in ways which satisfied national self-interest and entailed a gradual pooling of national sovereignty by willing states. Therefore, specific areas had to be chosen where states could see a mutual advantage in working together in supranational institutions. Hence the proposal for the ECSC. Thus, although the Schuman Declaration calling for an ECSC was unambiguously aimed at the creation of a 'European federation' in the long term, it just as clearly expressed the 'functionalist' dimension of the strategy which underlay it:

> Europe will not be made all at once, or according to a single plan. It will be built through concrete achievements which first create a de facto solidarity. (Schuman 1950)

By 'functionalist' means aimed at economic and social ends, the European Community might well find itself achieving a genuinely 'federal' end as Monnet, Schuman and others envisaged. If so, the '1992' single market project and the demands for a stronger social Europe that were triggered off by its success will have been very important steps on the way to some kind of a United States of Europe.

Postscript:

The Maastricht meeting of the European Council in December 1991 marked another major step along the road to greater European unity. Concluding the work of two intergovernmental conferences (IGCs) on Political Union and Economic and Monetary Union, it agreed to a new Treaty on European Union (Commission 1991c). Old goals were more clearly defined with deadlines attached to them and some new aims were set with the clear intention of reinforcing the unity of the Community. Although the British government insisted that the word 'federal' be removed from the preamble to the Treaty Union, a further step towards the 'European Federation' envisaged by Robert Schuman in his call for the ECSC in 1950 was clearly made. In requiring 'an ever closer Union among the peoples of Europe, where decisions are taken as closely as possible to the citizens', the word 'federal' was avoided, but European federalist ideals permeated many of the Treaty's provisions.

It is best to think of Maastricht as a further step on the road to European unity rather than some final destination or revolutionary break from the past. Sweep away the emotions surrounding the semantic debate over 'federalism' (a concept particularly alien to British political culture with its attachment to highly centralized forms of 'national' government), and it is hard to resist the argument that there have always been elements of federal, or at least confederal, behaviour within the EC even before Maastricht. When representatives of Member States, including ministers, parliamentarians and civil servants, meet constantly in permanent supranational institutions in order to formulate common laws which take precedence over national legislation, a political process with strong federal elements is clearly present, even though nationalists might like to disguise this reality under other terms. Obviously, the Community is not a federation with the degree of centralization observable in the USA, Australia or Germany, nor is it ever likely to take the form of these established federal countries created in very different political-geographical circumstances. But it already contains confederal elements (see Chapter 1) which, with the aid of the Maastricht Treaty, is developing into something uniquely appropriate to European realities. Thus it is likely to remain a very decentralized organization with member states reluctant to relinquish powers to the centre. As such, it may be closer to original federal ideals than many existing federations where central governments have, according to some, become too strong.

In taking 'the peoples of Europe' down a road to 'an ever closer Union', the new Treaty contained significant implications for the single market and social Europe themes at the heart of this book. First, the logic that a genuine single market could not be fully created without a single currency passed another milestone in the commitment to create EMU by January 1999. The route to this would-be single currency was carefully mapped out in distinct stages. In 1996 the European Council will decide whether a majority of Member States (7 out of 12 if the UK chooses to participate, 6 if not) have attained a set of 'convergence' criteria, namely: a low inflation rate less than 1.5 per cent above the average of the three best performing states, low long-term interest rates not more than 2 per cent above the three best performing states, budget deficits less than 3 per cent of national GDP, a public debt ratio not exceeding 60 per cent of national GDP, and national currency stability. On the last point, a national currency must have remained in the narrower 2.25 per cent fluctuation margins of the EC's Exchange Rate Mechanism and not have been devalued during the previous two years. Clearly, this reflected the aim of basing 'the whole system... on strict economic disciplines' inspired by the example of the German Bundesbank and the Deutschmark. Once a 'critical mass' of countries has attained these conditions, then the European Council will finally decide by qualified majority which countries are ready to move into EMU and adopt the ECU as their single currency at the beginning of 1999. En route a European Central Bank and European System of Central Banks would have been created by July 1998 at the latest.

The setting of stages and deadlines to reach the single currency objective reflected the desire of certain countries, notably France and Italy, to make the progress towards EMU 'irreversible' (Economist 1991c: 55). However, doubts remained about whether a single currency in 1999 could be achieved, even among a limited number of 'core' states. Although Chancellor Kohl of Germany, the key state on currency matters, accepted the plan with some enthusiasm and stressed his country's positive role in building European Union, many of his fellow citizens were sceptical about, or indeed frankly opposed to, a scheme which would eliminate the Deutschmark, that symbol of post-war German stability and success. Public opinion polls showed that a substantial majority of Germans did not want to abandon their national currency. Even more important, the Bundesbank seriously called into question the Maastricht agreement to adopt a single currency by 1999 (Guardian Weekly 1992: 8). Amid reports of dissension on its central council, it declared its fear that political pressures would force some countries with lax fiscal policies into EMU before they were able to meet the Treaty's strict convergence criteria (see above), thus promoting price instability throughout the EC. This could threaten the financial disciplines which had underpinned German economic success along with social and political stability.

The tensions between the German government's lofty 'political' aim to promote European Union and the more prosaic concern of its federal bankers to protect the monetary bedrock of the German economy were obvious. In the view of the Bundesbank, the German government should not be trapped by the planned timetable towards a single currency in 1999. If countries did not meet the strict criteria laid down then the introduction of a single European money would have to be postponed until an ECU as strongly managed as the Deutschmark could be produced. One reason why German leaders wanted stronger European political structures to be developed in parallel to economic and monetary union was to protect the would-be single currency; national governments could not be allowed to insist on laxer financial management in order to achieve short-term political gains.

The reluctance of the UK Conservative government to relinquish national sovereignty to European institutions managing a European money explains why Britain insisted on attaching a protocol to the Maastricht treaty which gave it alone the right to opt out of moves towards a single currency. The UK was allowed to retain all its powers for monetary and exchange policy and was not subject to the relevant EC disciplines, although it did agree to the commitment not to run an excessive public deficit. Mr Major may have succeeded Mrs Thatcher as Prime Minister and given a more diplomatic tone to British dealings with the EC, but he continued the cautious, sceptical approach to European Union which had characterized his predecessor and those before her. Let the others sketch out the grand designs and set the big objectives! Britain would 'wait and see' and choose to opt in or out of these developments as seemed fit to its national interests.

The British government also succeeded in extricating itself from the efforts to reinforce the Community's social dimension at Maastricht. Again the much vaunted change of style in Mr Major's dealings with the UK's partners did not translate itself into any real change of substance. Just as Mrs Thatcher had refused to sign the Social Charter in 1989, so her successor, strongly backed by his party and British industrial leaders, refused to accept its transformation into a 'social chapter' of the treaty on Political Union. In addition to their general antipathy towards governmental intervention in social matters affecting business, they were particularly opposed to the proposal that qualified majority voting should be extended to areas covering health and safety at work, consultation with employees, sexual equality in the workplace, and the integration of unemployed into the labour market. Despite a substantial dilution of the original 'social chapter' proposals and the great stress laid upon the principle of subsidiarity in formulating these social provisions, UK ministers refused to budge. Faced with this absolute ideological intransigence of the British government, the eleven other member states eventually agreed to extract the social chapter from the treaty. Instead, a protocol attached to the Political Union treaty states that all members except Britain will continue to make Community social policy according to the provisions of this omitted social section. Thus, the European Commission, Parliament and Court of Justice will go on playing their normal roles in the preparation of policy and legislation. However, Britain will be absent from the relevant Council meetings of national ministers and the system of qualified majority voting will be amended accordingly (44 out of 66 votes will be required as opposed to the normal 54 out of 76 when the UK is present). Nevertheless, Britain cannot opt out entirely from the Community's social dimension. The existing social provisions in the Treaty of Rome as amended by the Single European Act to which Britain is still a signatory remain unchanged. Moreover, even under the new arrangements, Britain will be asked whether it wants to participate in any new social initiative. If it does, then the Commission would propose a 'normal' EC law in the usual way; if not, then the eleven would proceed without the UK under the terms of the special protocol.

There is no doubt that Britain's partners were frustrated by this reluctance to help construct a European 'social area' to match its single 'economic space'. Serious misgivings were expressed about the way Britain's ability to opt out of Community social policy would undermine the efforts to construct 'a level playing field' for competition in the single market (see Chapter 6). Would, for example, Britain gain an unfair advantage in the single market by being able to pull in Japanese and US capital attracted by very liberal employment legislation? Other governments obviously had reservations about the social chapter as well. But, on balance, they thought that there would be public condemnation of treaties which appeared to be concerned solely with markets and business at the expense of the working rights of employees and ordinary citizens. The British government clearly felt no such similar pressure from its electorate; in fact, the UK Prime Minister met criticism of his stance by arguing that he was not only protecting British employment potential from the stifling costs of social policy, but 'defending European jobs and competitiveness' as well (Guardian Weekly 1991b: 4). But this position won no public support from any significant quarter and the hope was that Britain would eventually become a full partner in the development of the EC's social dimension; Mr Lubbers, the Dutch prime minister, concluded the affair by saying that 'history teaches us that if one or two members lag behind, they always follow in the end' (Economist 1991c: 55). A Labour Party in power in the

UK would almost certainly mean that such a wait would not be long, given its enthusiastic support for the EC's social dimension.

The Maastricht treaties were by no means solely concerned with the Community's single market and social policy development. They reinforced processes whereby the Community extended its competence to have a greater or lesser influence on virtually all major areas of national policy. For example, at the insistence of the poorer countries led by the Spanish, policies to reduce the gaps between the EC's richest and poorest regions were to be strengthened. In particular, a Cohesion Fund was to be set up by the end of 1993 in order to finance projects in the fields of the environment and 'trans-European networks' (ie, infrastructures for telecommunications, transport and energy). In addition, the Council may decide, by unanimous vote, whether additional actions are required beyond the scope of the existing Structural Funds to promote economic and social cohesion within the Community. This increased funding would be aimed at Member States whose GDP per head is less than 90 per cent of the EC average. In the same spirit of transferring resources from the richer to poorer parts of the Community, there was a legally binding protocol laying down the principle that the poorer countries should pay into the EC budget according to their relative prosperity. The broader social dimension of the Community was also bolstered by several new chapters in the treaty dealing with matters including the environment, consumer protection, health, culture and education. Qualified majority voting would be common on many of these matters, although unanimity was still required on sensitive issues. Also the Community's concern in these areas would always have to be limited by the very federalist subsidiarity principle. The Treaty insisted that the EC should act only if 'the objectives of the proposed action cannot be sufficiently achieved by the Member States ...by reason of (its) scale or effects' (Commission 1991c: 4). For example, although a large range of common educational and training objectives were restated in the Treaty, there was also an insistence that the Member States' responsibility for the content of teaching and organization of educational systems, as well as their cultural and linguistic diversity, be respected. On these matters there was to be no harmonization of national laws and regulations. However, in areas where EC law was applicable, steps were to be taken to ensure that they were properly implemented. For example, the European Court of Justice will be able, on the basis of a reasoned opinion from the Commission, to fine a Member State for failing to respect its Judgements.

Further on the institutional front, the European Parliament increased its powers, largely thanks to German pressure. In certain major sectors covering single market measures, consumer affairs, environmental programmes, health, education, research and development, it gained powers of joint decision with the Council of Ministers. If agreement between the two bodies cannot be reached in a joint Conciliation Committee, an overall majority of MEPs may reject a proposal from the Commission. Furthermore, the Commission and its President will be subject to Parliamentary approval at the start of their mandate. Also, a majority within the EP can request the Commission to submit new legislative proposals when thought necessary. Communications between national parliaments and Community institutions were also to be improved, with EC proposals reaching the former bodies in time to allow proper scrutiny. In a further attempt to stop excessive centralization, a Committee of the Regions was to be set up consisting of representatives of regional and local authorities. It will be consulted by the Council or the Commission and may submit an opinion on matters of specific regional interest. Its 189 members will be made up of 24 each for the larger Member States ranging down to 6 for little Luxembourg. This persistent over-representation of some 375,000 Luxembourgers and the failure to meet the German request for an increase (81 to 99 seats) in their MEPs to take account of their enlarged reunified population was a reminder that many 'constitutional issues' remained unsolved. As already stated, Maastricht was a major milestone on an evolving road with no definite end in sight.

Efforts to reduce the so-called 'democratic deficit' within the Community spilt over into the efforts to develop the concept of a 'Community citizen'. A new chapter in the European Union Treaty declares that 'every person holding the nationality of a Member State shall be a citizen of the Union'. This can be seen as another part of the strategy to counterbalance the EC's more obvious economic character and construct a social Europe more directly relevant to individuals. These provisions gave every EC citizen: the right to move and reside freely within the territory of Member states, the right, by the end of 1994, to vote and stand as a candidate in local elections for EC citizens living outside their own country, a similar right to vote and stand as a candidate for the European Parliament, the right to diplomatic protection from any Member State when outside the EC, the right to petition the European Parliament or apply to an EC Ombudsman to be appointed by the Parliament. This developing concept of a common Community citizenship, already apparent in the standard issuing of national/EC passports is further indication of the essentially confederal structures (which do not mean that all power has to be transferred to Community institutions!) that most Member States, Britain notwithstanding, were overtly constructing.

These same essentially confederal ambitions were apparent in the agreement on foreign affairs and defence. The opening provisions of the Treaty state that the European Union should assert its identity on the international scene

through the implementation of a common foreign and security policy which shall include the eventual framing of a common defence policy. (Commission 1991c: 7)

However, these aims were to be pursued through 'intergovernmental' procedures in the European Council and Council of Ministers; in other words, outside of the institutional policy-making mechanisms laid down in the Treaties. Thus, although the European Commission would be associated with these developments and the European Parliament kept informed, they would play no determining role. The British government insisted on the elimination of a clause declaring that these two institutions should eventually be drawn fully into the process.

Decisions would have to be taken unanimously (although there could be unanimous agreement to permit qualified majority voting on implementation of agreed policy). Where the Council had not taken a decision on a foreign policy issue, a Member State would be free to act on its own. In fact, despite this renewed effort to forge common foreign and security policies, there was no way a powerful Member State could be prevented from unilateral action.

This was even more obvious in the extremely sensitive area of defence. Here, the impossibility of having an EC common defence policy involving such states as neutral Ireland, Britain (with its strong commitment to NATO and USA links), France (with its independent nuclear deterrent) and Germany (with the burden of its military past) was resolved by further resurrection of the Western European Union (WEU). This body, to which all EC states except Ireland, Greece and Denmark belonged, became the 'defence component of the European Union' (Commission 1991c: 7). As such it should not prejudice national defence policies and NATO obligations. Nevertheless, its aims were: to strengthen the European pillar of the Atlantic Alliance and to formulate a common European defence policy, to elaborate and implement decisions and actions of the Union which have defence implications, and to facilitate closer military cooperation, regular meetings of Chiefs of Defence Staff and more cooperation in the armaments field. Despite the care taken to keep defence outside of the established EC institutions, the sense that this strand of European Union might ultimately merge more fully into the Community was reinforced by inviting other EC countries to join and by the decision to move the WEU headquarters from London to Brussels.

Foreign policy and defence were not the only areas to be dealt with by 'intergovernmental pillars' running alongside, but not fully within, all the Community institutions. Justice and home affairs were also to be coordinated in these looser structures where national sovereignty was notably less 'pooled' than in the full EC political system. The Commission and the Parliament will be 'associated' and 'informed' on such matters, but decision would remain firmly in the Council where Member States would, in effect, retain a national veto. Joint positions and actions could be taken by the Council in a number of areas of 'common interest' including: asylum policy, crossing of the Community's external borders, immigration policy, drug trafficking, transnational fraud, judicial cooperation on civil and criminal matters, customs controls, and police cooperation. On the last point, it was decided to create a Union-wide system (EUROPOL) for exchanging information between European police forces. Although the Member States, some more than others, were determined to maintain strong national powers on these judicial matters, immigration policy was put under fuller Community control and subjected to procedures established in the Treaty of Rome. Thus, the Council will decide by unanimity on the basis of a Commission proposal which non-member state citizens will require a visa to enter the EC. From 1996 onwards, qualified majority voting will apply. This more integrated approach to the sensitive problem of immigration was in part a logical progression from the removal of internal boundary controls in the single market; what the individual Member States did not check at internal EC frontiers, the Community as a whole would have to control at the external boundaries. This concern to act together – despite the reservations felt by national governments, especially Britain – also reflected the growing fear about masses of would-be migrants pressing towards the Community, both from the third world and eastern Europe following the collapse of its communist regimes.

The Treaty on European Union agreed at Maastricht was a major event. In addition to some precise provisions, it laid down a framework within which further integration could take place to produce a Community of confederal character which, however much some national leaders might try to hide the fact, was already more than a single market married to some accompanying common social measures. What precise shape future developments take remains to be seen; a great many powerful forces are at work in Europe. In fact at the time of writing, the Treaty still has to be ratified by all the twelve national Parliaments of the Member States, a reminder that visions of a centralized 'superstate' trampling freely on traditional national institutions are misleading. A Community with overwhelming power concentrated at the centre is highly unlikely to take shape in a Europe still characterized by sharp differences of national identity, language, and political culture. A complex interplay of Community, national and regional power is certain to continue. Indeed, whether the present process of confederalization will continue on a continent which has such a bloody history of national conflict must always be open to question. For all the efforts to foster language learning, educational exchanges and mutual understanding, the peoples of Europe still largely live their political lives in distinct linguistic communities. As such their attitudes are determined largely by national forces operating within national mass media. European issues are translated into the various national arenas by national politicians and journalists who carry with them, consciously or unconsciously, their own national prejudices and interests. Thus, the French public gets an interpretation of Anglo-French disputes which tends to place France in a favourable light, while the reverse is true in Britain. Similar transnational distortions, born of ignorance and half-understandings, occur right across the Community. Indeed, there are sometimes signs that a dangerous gulf is opening up between political leaders who have adopted a European vision and their general publics which are still largely operating within purely national frames of thought. The gap between the German government and the German public over European monetary union (see above) is but one example among many. So, although the Maastricht summit was another step forward to the goal laid down by Robert Schuman and others in 1950, there is no guarantee that the process is 'irreversible' despite the clear desire of many continental leaders to make it so. This observation may give heart to those in Britain and elsewhere who have always been sceptical of schemes for some kind of United States of Europe. But if those with federalist ambitions fail, what alternative future can the peoples of Europe expect? All the old centrifugal forces in Europe, which have caused such massive destruction in this century, might easily be rekindled.

Bibliography

ALBERT M BALL R 1983 *Vers le redressement de l'économie européenne dans les années 80*. Report presented to the European Parliament, July 1983, Luxembourg, Office for Official Publications of the EC

ARLETT S 1990 *The implementation of the European Regional Development Fund in France*. Unpublished M.Phil thesis, Department of Geographical Sciences, Polytechnic South West, Plymouth

ARLETT S, WISE M 1991 Prospects for Brittany and the Far South West in the European Community. In: Havinden M (ed) *Centre and Periphery* Exeter, University of Exeter

ATKINS MANAGEMENT CONSULTANTS 1988 *The cost of non-Europe in public-sector procurement, Research on the cost of non-Europe*. Vol.5, Part 13, Luxembourg, Office for Official Publications of the EC

BLANPAIN R 1985 *Comparative Labour Law and Industrial Relations*. Deventer, Kluwer

BOSSON B 1987 *L'Express* 27 février, Paris

BOYER R 1988 *In Search of Labour Market Flexibility: European Economies in Transition*. Oxford, Clarendon Press

BRADSHAW M J 1990 New regional geography, Foreign-area Studies and Perestroyka, *Area* 22 (4): 315-22

BREALEY, M QUIGLEY C 1989 *1992 Handbook*. London, Graham and Trotman

BREWSTER C, TEAGUE P 1989 *European Community Social Policy: its impact on the UK*. London, Institute of Personnel Management

BURKITT B, BAINBRIDGE M 1989 *What 1992 really means: single market or double cross?* London, College Hill Press

BUTT-PHILIP A 1988 *Implementing the European internal market: problems and prospects*. London, The Royal Institute of International Affairs

CALINGAERT M 1988 *The 1992 Challenge from Europe*. Washington, National Planning Association

CATINAT M 1988 *Macroeconomic consequences of the completion of the internal market: the modelling evidence; Research on the cost of non-Europe*. Vol.2, Luxembourg, Office for Official Publications of the EC

CECCHINI P 1988 *The European challenge: 1992 The benefits of a single market*. Aldershot, Wildwood House

DE CLERCQ W 1988 *The European Community in a Changing World*. Speech by de Clercq given at the Fundación Jorge, Esteban Roulet, Buenos Aires, 2 August, 1988

COLCHESTER N, BUCHAN D 1990 *Europe relaunched: Truths and illusions on the way to 1992*. Somerset, *The Economist* Books, Butler and Tanner

COMMISSION OF THE EC 1974 Social Action Programme of the Community. *EC Bulletin*, 2, Luxembourg, Office for Official Publications of the EC

COMMISSION OF THE EC 1984 *The regions of Europe: second periodic report on the social and economic situation of the regions*. Luxembourg, Office for Official Publications of the EC

COMMISSION OF THE EC 1985a *Completing the internal market*. White Paper from the Commission to the European Council, CB-43-85-894-EN-C. Luxembourg, Office for Official Publications of the EC

COMMISSION OF THE EC 1985b The Thrust of Commission Policy. *Bulletin of the European Communities*, Supplement 1/85. Luxembourg, Office for Official Publications of the EC

COMMISSION OF THE EC 1985c *ERDF: Tenth Annual Report (1984)*. COM (85) 516 final, 4.10.85 Brussels

COMMISSION OF THE EC 1986a Single European Act. *Bulletin of the European Communities*, Supplement 2/86 Luxembourg, Office for Official Publications of the EC

COMMISSION OF THE EC 1986b *ERDF: Eleventh Annual Report (1985)*. COM (86) 545 final, 20.10.86, Brussels

COMMISSION OF THE EC 1987a European Regional Policy. *European File* 14/87. Luxembourg, Office for Official Publications of the EC

COMMISSION OF THE EC 1987b The Single Act – a new frontier for Europe. *Bulletin of the European Communities*, Supplement 1/87. Luxembourg, Office for Official Publications of the EC

COMMISSION OF THE EC 1987c Proposal for a Council Regulation on the tasks of the structural funds and their effectiveness and on the coordination of their activities between themselves and with the operations of the European Investment Bank and the other financial instruments. *Official Journal of the EC* C245, 12.9.87. Luxembourg, Office for Official Publications of the EC

COMMISSION OF THE EC 1987d *Internal and external adaption of firms in relation to employment*. COM (87) final 229, Brussels

COMMISSION OF THE EC 1987e *Third periodic report from the Commission on the social and economic situation and development of the regions of the Community*. COM (87) 230 final 21.5.87, Brussels

COMMISSION OF THE EC 1988a *The Economics of 1992*. European Economy No. 35. Luxembourg, Office for Official Publications of the EC

COMMISSION OF THE EC 1988b *Europe without Frontiers: Completing the internal market* CB-PP-88-AO1-EW-C. Luxembourg, Office for Official Publications of the EC

COMMISSION OF THE EC 1988c *Common standards for enterprises*. CB-PP-88-AO1-EW-C. Luxembourg, Office for Official Publications of the EC

COMMISSION OF THE EC 1988d *The single financial market*. CB-PP-88-CO3-EW-C. Luxembourg, Office for Official Publications of the EC

COMMISSION OF THE EC 1988e *European Economy: Creation of a European Financial Area*. Luxembourg, Office for Official Publications of the EC

COMMISSION OF THE EC 1988f The Social Policy of the European Community: looking ahead to 1992. *European File* 13/88. Luxembourg, Office for Official Publications of the EC

COMMISSION OF THE EC 1988g *Bulletin of the European Communities* No.7/8. Luxembourg, Office for Official Publications of the EC

COMMISSION OF THE EC 1988h The social aspects of the internal market. *Social Europe* 1, Supplement 7/88, D-G for Employment, Social Affairs and Education. Luxembourg, Office for Official Publications of the EC

COMMISSION OF THE EC 1988i La dimension sociale du marché intérieur. *Europe Sociale* Numéro spéciale. Luxembourg, Office for Official Publications of the EC

COMMISSION OF THE EC 1989a *Background Report*. ISEC/B25/89, 11.10.89, London

COMMISSION OF THE EC, 1989b *Background Report*. Speech by Mrs V. Papandreou, ISEC/B30/89, 11.12.89, London

COMMISSION OF THE EC 1989c *ERDF: Thirteenth Annual Report(1988)*. COM (88) 728 final, 10/1/89, Brussels

COMMISSION OF THE EC 1989d The European Community Budget. *European File* 11/89. Luxembourg, Office for Official Publications of the EC

COMMISSION OF THE EC 1990a *Community Charter of the Fundamental Social Rights of Workers*. Luxembourg, Office for Official Publications of the EC

COMMISSION OF THE EC 1990b The new structural policies of the European Community. *European File*. 7-8/90, Luxembourg, Office for the Official Publications of the EC

COMMISSION OF THE EC 1990c, Jacques Delors' introduction to the *Community Charter of the Fundamental Social Rights of Workers*. Luxembourg, Office for Official Publications of the EC

COMMISSION OF THE EC 1990d The Community Charter of Fundamental Social Rights for Workers. *European File*, 6/90. Luxembourg, Office for Official Publications of the EC

COMMISSION OF THE EC 1990e *Background Report*. ISEC/B25/90, 5.10.1990, London referring to Commission of the EC (1990) COM (90) 406 final, Brussels

COMMISSION OF THE EC 1990f *Europe Sociale* 1/90. Luxembourg, Office for Official Publications of EC

COMMISSION OF THE EC 1991a *Background Report*. ISEC/B15/91 28.5.91

COMMISSION OF THE EC 1991b *Background Report*. ISEC/B20 22.7.91, London

COMMISSION OF THE EC 1991c *Background Report*. ISEC/B33 18.2.91, London

CONFEDERATION OF BRITISH INDUSTRY 1988 *1992 – How it affects you*. London, Confederation of British Industry

CONSERVATIVE CENTRAL OFFICE 1989 *Leading Europe into the 1990s*. London, Conservative Central Office

CONSERVATIVE POLITICAL CENTRE 1989 *Europe: Onwards from Bruges*. By 'the no-turning back' group of Conservative MPs. London, Conservative Political Centre

CONTEMPORARY EUROPEAN AFFAIRS 1989 *1992 and after*. Oxford, Pergamon Press

COUNCIL 1975 Regulation (EEC) 724/75 creating a European Regional Development Fund (1975). *Official Journal of the European Communities* L 73, 21.3.75. Luxembourg, Office for Official Publications of the EC

COUNCIL 1979 Regulation (EEC) 214/79 amending Regulation (EEC) 724/75 establishing a European Regional Development Fund (1979). *Official Journal of the European Communities* L 35, 9.2.79. Luxembourg, Office for Official Publications of the EC

COUNCIL 1984 Regulation (EEC) 1787/84 on the European Regional Development Fund replacing Regulation (EEC)724/75 (1984). *Official Journal of the European Communities* L169, 28.6.84. Luxembourg, Office for Official Publications of the EC

COUNCIL OF THE EC 1986a *Speeches and Statements made on the occasion of the signing of the SEA*. BY-47-86-705-EW-C. Luxembourg, Office for Official Publications

COUNCIL OF THE EC 1986b *Single European Act*. Luxembourg, Office for Official Publications

CROXFORD G 1988 *The implementation of European Community regional policy: a study of the ERDF and the ESF in the UK*. Unpublished PhD thesis, Department of Geographical Sciences, Polytechnic South West, Plymouth

CROXFORD G, WISE M 1988 The European Social Fund: retrospect and prospect. *Regional Studies* 22 (1): 65–8

CURZON PRICE V 1988 *1992: Europe's last chance? From common market to single market*. London, The Institute for Economic Affairs

CUTLER T, HASLAM C, WILLIAMS J, WILLIAMS K 1989 *1992:The Struggle for Europe*. Oxford, Berg Publishers

DAHL R A 1956 *A Preface to Democratic Theory*. Chicago, University of Chicago Press

DAHRENDORF R 1989 *Whose Europe*. Sussex, Goron Pro-Print

DAHRENDORF R 1990 *Reflections on the Revolution in Europe*. London, Chatto and Windus

DALTROP A (1982) *Politics and the European Community*. London, Longman

DANKERT P, KOAJMAN A 1989 *Europe without frontiers*. The Netherlands, Van Gorcum

DELORS J 1988 *Europe 1992: the social dimension*. Address to the TUC Congress, Bournemouth 8 September 1988. Brussels, Commission of the EC

DELORS J 1989 *Report on economic and monetary union in the European Community* CB-36-89-401-EN-C. Luxembourg, Office for Official Publications

DELORS J 1990 Committee for the Study of Economic and Monetary Union *1990. Report on Economic and Monetary Union* (the so-called Delors Report produced at the request of the European Council; available from EC Commission)

DEPARTMENT OF TRANSPORT 1987 *A Guide to goods vehicle drivers' hours*. Department of Transport, GV262, London

DEWHURST J 1989 *Your Business in 1992*. London, Rosters

ECONOMIST 1988a Vrrrm for competition. *The Economist*, 13 February, London

ECONOMIST 1988b Plenty to declare. *The Economist*, 24 December, London

ECONOMIST 1989 Europe's internal market. Survey in *The Economist*, 8 July, London

ECONOMIST 1990a The tale of two parties. *The Economist*, 23 June, London

ECONOMIST 1990b Its cold in cloud-cuckoo-land. *The Economist*, 10 November, London

ECONOMIST 1990c The Commission's new kingdom. *The Economist*, 22 September, London

ECONOMIST 1990d Renault and the EC. *The Economist*, 26 July, London

ECONOMIST 1990e Changing tracks with Mr Major. *The Economist*, 22 September, London

ECONOMIST 1991a Never on a Sunday. *The Economist*, 19 October, London

ECONOMIST 1991b Workers of the EC (except Britain) unite. *The Economist*, 19 October: 80

ECONOMIST 1991c The deal is done. *The Economist*, 14 December, London

EL-AGRAA A M 1983 *Britain within the European Community. The way forward*. London, Macmillan

EMERSON M et. al. 1988 *The economics of 1992*. Oxford, Oxford University Press

ERNST & WHINNEY 1988 *The cost of non-Europe: Road transport of merchandise, Research on the cost of non-Europe*. Luxembourg, Office for Official Publications of the EC

EUROPE 2000 1989 Foreign direct investment in the UK. *Europe 2000*, Vol.1, No.4, pp.35–42

EUROPEAN COUNCIL 1988 *Communique Meeting of Heads of State and Governments, Hannover, June 1988*. Luxembourg, Office for Official Publications of the EC

EUROPEAN PARLIAMENT 1990a Report of the Committee on Social Affairs, Employment and the Working Environment on the ...action programme relating to the implementation of the Community Charter of fundamental social rights for workers. *Session Documents*, Series A, Document A 3-0175/90

EUROPEAN PARLIAMENT 1990b Debates of the European Parliament. *Official Journal of the EC* No 3-386, 12-16.2.90

EUROPEAN PARLIAMENT 1990c Debates of the European Parliament. *Official Journal of the EC* No 3-393, 10-14.9.90

EUROPEAN STUDY SERVICE 1989. EEC transport policy within the context of the single market. Rixensart, Belgium

EUROSTAT 1975–90 Annual editions of *Basic Statistics of the Community*. Statistical Office of the EC. Luxembourg, Office for Official Publications of the EC

EUROSTAT 1989 *Basic Statistics of the Community*. Statistical Office of the EC. Luxembourg, Office for Official Publications of the EC

EUROSTAT 1990a Rapid Reports, Regions, 2. Luxembourg, Office for Official Publications of the EC

EUROSTAT 1990b *Europe in Figures*. 1989/90 Edition, London, HMSO

FABIUS L 1984 Pour un espace européen scientifique, industriel et social. *Politique Etrangère* (49) 1 Paris

FEATHERSTONE K 1990 *European Internal Market policy*. Routledge, London

FINANCIAL TIMES 1989 1 January, London

FINANCIAL TIMES 1990 29 November, London

FRANKLIN M, WILKE M 1990 *Britain's future in Europe*. London, Pinter

GALBRAITH K 1967 *The new industrial state*. London, Hamish Hamilton

GEORGE S 1985 *Politics and policy in the European Community*. Oxford, Clarenden Press

GEROSKI P A 1988 *Completion and innovation, Research on the cost of non-Europe*. Vol.2. Luxembourg, Office for Official Publications of the EC

GEROSKI P A 1989 The choice between diversity and scale In *1992 myths and realities*. Chapter 2, London, London Business School

GIBB R A 1985 No-passport excursions to France; A case study of tension management. *Area*, Vol.17, No.2

GIBB R A, TREADGOLD A 1989 Completing the internal market: implications for the regions. *Area* 21 (1): 75–82

GLEED R 1989 *Deloitte's 1992 guide*. London, Butterworths

GUARDIAN WEEKLY 1991a 17 November

GUARDIAN WEEKLY 1991b 22 December

GUARDIAN WEEKLY 1992 16 February

GUIEU P, BONNET C 1987 Completion of the internal market and indirect taxation. *Journal of Common Market Studies*, Vol.25, No.3

HAALAND J I 1990 Assessing the effects of EC integration on EFTA countries: the position of Norway and Sweden. *Journal of Common Market Studies*, No.4

HAAS E B 1968 *The uniting of Europe*. 2nd edition, Stanford, Stanford Press

HEITGER B, STEHN J 1990 Japanese direct investment in the EC – response to the internal market. *Journal of Common Market Studies*, No.1, pp.1–15

HENDERSON D 1988 *1992: The external dimension*. Occasional paper No.35, New York, Group Thirty

HILL B E 1984 *The Common Agricultural Policy – Past, Present and Future*. London, Methuen

HMSO 1967 *Treaty setting up the European Economic Community*. London, HMSO

HMSO 1971 *The United Kingdom and the European Community*. Cmnd; 4715, London, HMSO

HOLLAND S 1976 *Capital versus the Regions*. London, Macmillan

HOLLAND S 1980 *Uncommon Market: Capital, Class and Power in the European Community*. London, Macmillan

HOUSE J W 1980 The frontier zone: A conceptual problem for policy makers. *International Political Science Review*, Vol.1, No.4

HOWE G 1988 1992 – The external dimension. *The Anglo-Japanese Journal*, October–December, Vol.2, No.3, pp.2–3

HOWE G 1990 Resignation speech to House of Commons, 13 November 1990. *Guardian Weekly* 143 (21) 25.11.90: p.6

IONESCU G 1972 *The new politics of European integration*. London, Macmillan

JENKINS C, SHERMAN B 1979 *The collapse of work*. London, Eyre Methuen

JOHNSTON R J 1982 *Geography and the State: An Essay in Political Geography*. London, Macmillan

JOHNSTON R J 1984 Marxist political economy, the state and political geography. *Progress in Human Geography*, 8, pp.473–92

JOHNSTON R J 1989 The state, political geography and geography. In: R Peet and N Thrift, (eds) *New Models in Geography: the Political-Economy Perspective*, London, Unwin Hyman

DE JONQUIERES G 1988 Mitsubishi plans big expansion in Europe. *Financial Times*, 14 August

KAHN R 1987 La nouvelle politique régionale des pays européens. *Problèmes Economiques* 2049, 18 novembre:17–24

KAISER K 1983 *The European Community: progress or decline*. London, Royal Institute of International Affairs

KAY J A 1989 Myths and realities. In: *1992 myths and realities*, Chapter 1, London, London Business School

KAY J A, SMITH S R 1989 The business implications of European fiscal harmonisation. In: *1992 myths and realities*, Chapter 3, London, London Business School

KEATING M, JONES B 1985 *Regions in the European Community*. Oxford, Clarendon Press

KEATING M, WATERS N 1985 Scotland in the European Community. In: Keating M, Jones B, (eds) *Regions in the European Community*. Oxford, Clarendon Press: pp.60–88

KINNOCK, N. 1988 *Speech by the Leader of the Labour Party to the Socialist Group of the European Parliament*. Glasgow, mimeo

KOLAKOWSKI L 1978 *Main Currents of Marxism; Vol.1 The Founders: Vol.2 The Golden Age; Vol.3 The Breakdown*. Oxford, Oxford University Press

LANGHAMMER R J 1990 Fuelling a new engine of growth or separating Europe from non-Europe? *Journal of Common Market Studies*, Vol.XXIX, No.2, 133–57

LAURSEN F 1990 The Community's policy towards EFTA: regime formation in the European Economic Space (EES). *Journal of Common Market Studies*, Vol. XXVIII, No.4, 303–27

LINDBERGH L 1963 *The political dynamics of European integration.* Oxford, Oxford University Press

LINDBERGH L, SCHEINGOLD S 1970 *Europe's would-be polity.* New Jersey, Englewood Cliffs

LIPIETZ A 1988 'L'Europe: dernier recours pour une relance mondiale. *Le Monde Diplomatique* May

LOCAL GOVERNMENT INTERNATIONAL BUREAU 1990a *European Information Service* 115, 5.11.90, referring to Commission of the EC, COM(90) 228 final, 13.6.90, Brussels

LOCAL GOVERNMENT INTERNATIONAL BUREAU 1990b *European Information Service* 113, 20.8.90

LOCAL GOVERNMENT INTERNATIONAL BUREAU 1990c *European Information Service* 114, 1.10.90

LODGE J 1989a The European Parliament – from assembly to co-legislature. In: Lodge J (ed) *The European Community and the Challenge of the Future.* London, Pinter Publishers

LODGE J 1989b Social Europe: fostering a People's Europe? In: Lodge J (ed.) *The European Community and the Challenge of the Future*, London, Pinter Publishers: pp.303–18

LUDLOW P 1982 *The making of the European Monetary System.* London, Butterworth

LUDVIGSEN ASSOCIATES 1988 *The EC 92 automobile sector, Research on the cost of non-Europe*, vol.11. Luxembourg, Office for Official Publications of the EC

MARTINS M R, MAWSON J 1983 The development of the 'Programme approach' in the Common Regional Policy. *Town Planning Review* 54 (1): 63–82

MATHIS J, MAZIER J 1979 *Niveau des coûts de production et performance extérieure, des grands pays industrialisés.* IRES, Paris

MAYNE R 1967 The role of Jean Monnet. *Government and Opposition* (special issue) 2–3, London

MEADOWS D 1972 *The limits to growth.* A report for the Club of Rome's project on the predicament of mankind. London, Postmac Associates

MENY Y 1985 French regions in the European Community. In: Keating M, Jones, B (eds) *Regions in the European Community.* Oxford, Clarendon Press: pp.191–203

MIKESELL R F 1967 Decisive factors in the flow of American direct investment to Europe. *Economia Internazionale*, Vol.20, pp.431–57

MILIBAND R 1973 *The State in Capitalist Society*. London, Quartet Books

MILIBAND R 1977 *Marxism and Politics*. Oxford, Oxford University Press

MINSHULL G N 1990 *The new Europe: Into the 1990s*. 4th edition, London, Hodder and Stoughton

MITRANY D 1933 *The progress of international government*. London, Allen and Unwin

MITRANY D 1966 *A Working Peace System*. London, Royal Institute of International Affairs

MITRANY D 1975 *The functional theory of politic*. Robertson, London

LE MONDE 1991 Europe: l'engrenage du marché unique. *Dossiers et Documents*. avril 1991 73–8

MONNET J 1962 A ferment of change *Journal of Common Market Studies* Vol. 1, pp.203–11

NERB G 1988 *The completion of the internal market: A survey of European industry's perception of the likely effects*. Research on the cost of non-Europe. Luxembourg, Office for Official Publications of the EC

NEUBERGER H 1989 *The economics of 1992*. Luxembourg, Socialist Group European Parliament

NUGENT N 1989 *The Government and Politics of the European Community*. London, Macmillan

O'CLEIREACAIN S 1990 Europe 1992 and gaps in the EC's common commercial policy. *Journal of Common Market Studies*, No.3, pp.201–17.

OECD 1991 *The international financial situation of central and eastern European countries*: In: Financial Market Trends, WO.48, OECD, Paris

OWEN R, DYNES M 1989 *The Times Guide to 1992*. London, Times Books

PADOA-SCHIOPPA T (ed) 1987 *Efficiency, Stability and Equity: A strategy for the evolution of the economic system of the European Community*. Oxford, Oxford University Press

PELKMANS J, WINTERS A 1988 *Europe's domestic market*. Chatham, House Papers No.43, London, Routledge

PERRY K 1984 *Britain and the European Community*. London, Methuen

PETERSEN J H 1991 Harmonization of Social Security in the EC revisited. *Journal of Common Market Studies* XXIX (4): 505–26

PINDER J 1991 *European Community: the building of a union*. Oxford, Oxford University Press

PORTER M 1990 'Europe's companies after 1992. In: *The Economist*, 9 June. London

PRATTEN C 1988 *A survey of the economies of scale, Research on the cost of non-Europe*. Vol.2 Luxembourg, Office for Official Publications of the EC

PRESTON C 1983 Additional to what? Does the UK government cheat on the European Regional Development Fund? *Politics* 3 (2), Oxford, Pergamon Press

RAUX J 1984 *Politique agricole commune et construction européenne*. Paris, Economica

REGNIER J 1977 The real meaning of Community. *Fisheries of the European Community*. Edinburgh, White Fish Authority

RIDER-IRIS ASSOCIATION 1989 *Conséquences socio-economiques de l'achèvement du marché intérieur pour les régions de tradition industrielle de la Communauté Européenne*. Louvain-la-Neuve, Université Catholique de Louvain, Belgium

ROCARD M 1988 *Financial Times* 24 October, London

ROCHE D 1988 *Europe 1992: what is it?* London, Morgan Stanley

SCHUMAN R 1950 *The Schuman Declaration* (reprinted in Europe: a Fresh Start. *European Documentation* 3/1990. Luxembourg, Office for Official Publications of the EC)

SCHWALBACK J 1988 *Economies of scale and intra-Community trade, Research on the cost of non-Europe*, Vol.2. Luxembourg, Office for Official Publications of the EC

SECRETARIAT D'ETAT AUPRES DU PREMIER MINISTRE, COMMISSARIAT DU PLAN 1983 *Quelle stratégie européenne pour la France dans les années 80s?* La Documentation Française, Paris

SHACKLETON M 1989 The Budget of the European Community. In: Lodge J (ed.) *The European Community and the Challenge of the Future*. London, Pinter Publishers: pp.129–47

DE SMIDT M 1966 Foreign industrial establishments located in the Netherlands, *Tijdschrift voor Economie*, No.1, Jan 1966, pp.1–19

SMITH A, VENABLES A 1988 *The costs of non-Europe: An assessment based on a formal model of imperfect competition and economies of scale, Research on the cost of non-Europe*, Vol.2. Luxembourg, Office for Official Publications of the EC

SMITH S 1988 *Indirect taxes and the internal market*. London, The Institute for Fiscal Studies

SWANN D 1983 *Competition and Industrial Policy in the European Community*. London, Methuen

TAYLOR P J 1985 *Political Geography: World Economy, Nation-State and Locality*. London, Longman

TAYLOR P J 1989 *A Brief Political Geography of States and Governments in the Twentieth Century*, Department of Geography, University of Newcastle upon Tyne, Newcastle upon Tyne

TEAGUE P 1989 *The European Community: the social dimension*. London, Kogan Page

THATCHER M 1988 *Britain and Europe*. Text of the Prime Minister's speech at Bruges on 20 September 1988, Conservative Political Centre, London

TOUCHE ROSS 1986 *Completing the internal market, a guide to 1992*. London, Touche Ross International

TRADES UNION CONGRESS 1988 *Europe 1992*. London, TUC

TREATIES 1987 *Treaties establishing the European Communities*. Luxembourg, Office for Official Publications of the EC

VANDAMME J 1984 Pour une nouvelle politique sociale en Europe. *Economica*, Paris

VENTURINI P 1989 *1992: The European Social Dimension*. Commission of the European Communities, Luxembourg, Office for Official Publications of the EC

VREDELING H 1987 *NATO independent European programme group, Report of a group of experts*. NATO, Brussels

WADLEY D 1986 *Restructuring the Regions*. OECD, Paris

WALLACE H, WALLACE W, WEBB C (eds) 1983 *Policy-making in the European Community*. London, Wiley

WALLACE W, HODGES M 1981 *Economic Divergence in the European Community*. London, Macmillan

WALLIS K F 1968 The EEC and the United States foreign investment: some empirical evidence re-examined. *Economic Journal*, Vol.78, pp.717–19

WELSH M 1987 *Labour market policy in the European Community: the British presidency of 1986.* Discussion Paper No.4, London, Royal Institute of International Affairs

WIJKMAN M 1990 Patterns of production and trade In: (ed). Wallace W. *The dynamics of European integration.* London, Royal Institute of International Affairs

WILLIAMS A M 1991 *The European Community: the contradictions of integration.* Oxford, Blackwell

WILLIS N 1989 *TUC Bulletin* 34, June 1989

WILSON J 1980 The Community's Regional Policy. *Local Government Studies* 6(4): 11–28

WISE M 1984 *The Common Fisheries Policy of the European Community.* London, Methuen

WISE M 1989 France and European unity. In: Aldrich R, Connell J (eds) *France in World Politics.* London, Routledge: pp.37–73

WISE M 1991 War, Peace and the European Community. In: Kliot N & Waterman S (eds) *The political geography of conflict and peace,* London, Belhaven Press: pp.110–25

WISE M, CHALKLEY B 1990 Unemployment: regional policy defeated? In: Pinder D (ed.) *Challenge and Change in Western Europe,* London, Belhaven Press: pp.179–94

WISE M, CROXFORD G 1988 The European Regional Development Fund: Community ideals and national realities. *Political Geography Quarterly* 7 (2): 161–82

WISTRICH E 1989 *After 1992: The United States of Europe.* London, Routledge

YANNOPOULOS G N 1990 Foreign direct investment and European integration. *Journal of Common Market Studies,* No.3, pp.235–59

Index